Art Center College of Design
Library
1700 Lida Street
Pasadena, Calif. 91103

the language of dynamic media

WORKS FROM THE DYNAMIC MEDIA INSTITUTE
AT THE MASSACHUSETTS COLLEGE OF ART

2000 – 2005

ART CENTER COLLEGE OF DESIGN

3 3220 00231 4115

the

language *n.*
—a system of elements combined according to the rules of a grammar for the purpose of communication

of

dynamic *adj.*
—relating to or caused by motion
—characterized by continuous change or progress
—an interactive system or process

media *n.*
—from "media of communication" referring to means of dissemination of information
—form through which something else is represented or transmitted
—materials used in a specific artistic technique

741.609744
L287
2005
c.2

the language of dynamic media

WORKS FROM THE DYNAMIC MEDIA INSTITUTE
AT THE MASSACHUSETTS COLLEGE OF ART

2000 – 2005

exhibition organized by the Dynamic Media Institute,
the graduate program in design

Patricia Doran Graduate Gallery,
Massachusetts College of Art in Boston

curated by Jan Kubasiewicz

ACKNOWLEDGMENTS

Both the exhibition and this catalog represent an effort of many individuals and institutions, whom the curator would like to thank for their support and help:

The Dynamic Media Institute former and current students and faculty for the opportunity of presenting their work to our academic and professional community.

Kate Nazemi and Lauren Bessen for their meticulous work on the catalog design and Mei-Fen Tsai for helping in the catalog production.

Elizabeth Lawrence, Krzysztof Bebenek, Joe Quackenbush and Brian Lucid—a crew of excellent editors for making these occasionally difficult texts comprehensible.

Leila Mitchell, Heather Shaw, and Sam Montague, the Dynamic Media Institute alumni for their time and expertise in organizing and producing the exhibition at the Patricia Doran Graduate Gallery.

George Creamer, Dean of Graduate Programs at MassArt for his continuous support of the Dynamic Media Institute and his unstinting commitment toward this exhibition and catalog.

Kay Sloan, MassArt President, Johanna Branson, Senior Vice-President, and Elizabeth Resnick, Chair of Communication Design Department for their help in this and other initiatives of the Dynamic Media Institute.

Tom Glennon of Hanson Printing for his assistance in producing the catalog.

We are pleased to present the works from the Dynamic Media Institute, the graduate program in design at the Massachusetts College of Art in Boston.

Of course, there is no need to access this catalog in a linear fashion. If you have never heard of us, the last section of this book *About DMI*, describes who we are and what we do, from the program's curriculum structure and course descriptions, to a list of faculty, advisors, critics and all DMI alumni and current students from 2000 on.

The visual index and the cover, map and organize the works according to section and year of project completion. If you are intrigued by an image on the cover or in the visual index, jump directly to the page indicated beside that image for a full description of the project.

The following four sections in this catalog elucidate projects that are included in the show: *Exhibited Work* section presents student projects through short articles, from four to twelve pages each; *Motion + Sound* represents student movies through series of sequential stills; *Collaborations* presents five examples of extracurricular projects which were developed as collaboration between DMI and outside partners; and *Thesis Abstracts* presents all MFA degree thesis projects organized by year and alphabetically within each year. The student work presented in this book clearly reflects the Dynamic Media Institute's curricular and pedagogical priority.

Faculty Perspectives includes four short essays by DMI professors, each referring to the language of dynamic media and their individual approaches to dynamic media design education.

— Jan Kubasiewicz
Coordinator of the MFA Program in Design, the Dynamic Media Institute

ate.

art.technology.experien

176

170

166

148

159

148

157

153

34

80

124

142

128

62

54

132

191

190

189

187

188

188

186

186

New

WHO WE ARE

xt is an abstraction phase. Fro
exploratory systems, patterns b
ich a characterization of the d
orked out. In later phases, the
that the abstractions are suffi
ably build a promised system v
rties. Finally, engineering know
handbooks and texts. Informat
at the end of its first explorat
rs in this book are mostly expl
w techniques and interesting s
these, we can abstract severa

qing
ADJ. PURE.

清

radical   phonetic

191

190

189

188

187

187

187

186

2000

2001

2002

2003

CONTENTS

faculty perspectives

motion literacy and the language of dynamic media

JAN KUBASIEWICZ

COMMUNICATION AND A "LANGUAGE"

Since the inception of the Basic Course at the Bauhaus, design education has been profoundly influenced by the concept of "visual language," which applies the metaphor of linguistic structure to teaching the fundamentals of visual form and expression. At the Dynamic Media Institute the concept of a "language," understood as a system of elements combined according to the rules of a grammar for the purpose of communication, provides both a method for studio experimentation and a viable platform for theoretical discussion.

The creative context of dynamic media incorporates the challenges of synthesizing multiple "dialects" and "codes" that have traditionally been segregated into distinct disciplines. Fluency in the language(s) of dynamic media seems synonymous with the ability to choose and employ the most appropriate media, channels, and vocabularies to effectively communicate through the integration of content and context. And effective communication is both the main focus and the litmus test in all theoretical and practical aspects of the design process at the Dynamic Media Institute.

INJECTING MOTION INTO DESIGN

With the growing accessibility of kinetic tools, motion is becoming integral to the discipline of communication design. Fostering motion literacy—the act of trying to understand how motion can be used to communicate more effectively—through the Dynamic Media Institute curriculum is essential.

Motion is a natural state of things, and of course, it has already been explored by various disciplines of science and art. But now designers must start regarding the communication design environment as dynamic rather than static. That means seeing design parameters not in terms of Platonic opposites (big/small, much/little, light/heavy, hard/soft) but rather as a taxonomy or a matrix of design variables. It is a process of *forming* rather than *form*—less either/or than if/then. Communicating effectively through motion

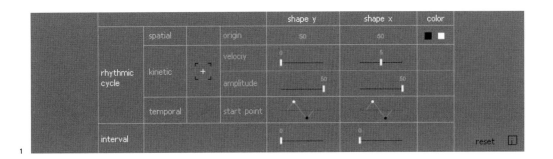

1

involves familiarity with the grammar of kinetic form, which is defined in both spatial and temporal parameters.

1. A control panel of design properties and motion parameters in one of Isabel Meirelles's interactive experiments.

This point of view is well represented in the thesis of Isabel Meirelles (MFA 2003), entitled *Dynamic Visual Formation: Theory and Practice* (page 80), which focuses on the most elemental constituents of the dynamic environment. Meirelles, in her rigorous, almost Wittgensteinian investigation, proposes "a 'system of dynamic visual formation' to investigate new complexities in the visual realm brought about by computational media." She examines, both theoretically and experimentally, the process of image transformation. The interactive on-screen tools Meirelles has developed let users adjust design and motion parameters in order to experience that transformation as "a variable spatio-temporal whole, a modifiable process changing in time. …in the course of becoming, of forming and trans-forming." [1]

Kinetic form has the potential to convey a range of notions and emotions across time, from a sensible gesture, through a dramatic tension, to a violent collision. Combining kinetic form with other "languages"—with words, imagery, and sound—multiplies designers' opportunities to create meaning.

MOTION AND CINEMATIC VOCABULARY

Like all aspects of communication design, communicating effectively via motion on a screen relies on mastering certain conventions and artistic techniques. The language of cinema provides many spectacular examples of meaning made through motion. Studying examples of traditional cinematic vocabulary, such as a cross-fade between two scenes (conveying a lapse of time), or a split screen (implying simultaneous action) is often a source of inspiration for motion designers. For in its hundred-year history, the cinematic vocabulary has evolved into a complex, universally understood system of communication, a system capable of translating a multi-sensory human experience into a kinetic sequence of audio-visual events, where motion serves to integrate of all other channels of communication.

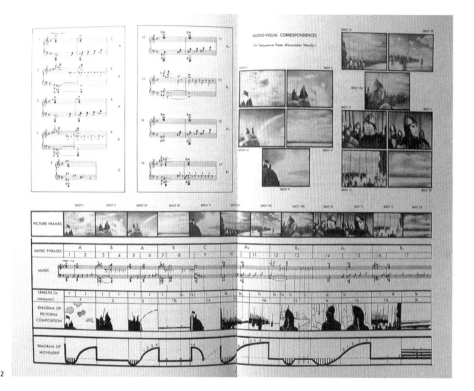

2

2. A post-production storyboard for the 1938 film "Alexander Nevsky" in: Sergei Eisentstein, "The Film Sense."

One of the most spectacular historical examples of the design process for a multimedia structure is a post-production storyboard for the 1938 film *Alexander Nevsky* by Sergei Eisentstein, a Russian director and one of the first theorists of the medium. That storyboard is a timeline in which visual representations of the film's various components are precisely synchronized into a sequence of "audio-visual correspondences"—that includes film shots, the musical score, a diagram of pictorial composition, and a diagram of camera movement. [2] Choreographed very precisely, in fact to a fraction of a musical measure, this "diagram of movement" attests to how essential on-screen motion is for the cinematographer, and to the necessity of meaningfully integrating it with all other elements of his vocabulary. This same challenge of integrating motion as a meaningful component of communication design serves as the focus for the great majority of experiments at the Dynamic Media Institute.

A graduate elective course, *Design for Motion and Sound,* was specifically created to intensify the study of time-based structures and compositions. Meaning is created through an exploration of image, sound, time, and motion in linear and non-linear narrative structures. The *Motion and Sound* section of this book presents work developed in response to a project entitled *Sound + Sight,* in which students were asked to explore the visual representation of sound, pacing and rhythm. (page 148)

The first step of the process was to mix or compose a sound sequence. That represented a major challenge for many students, since sonic design requires expertise far beyond the usual scope of visual designers.

The following step was to analyze this sound sequence and to identify various dimensions of contrast in time-based structure. That led to creating a visual map or a diagram of the sound sequence—an initial step in studying the basic correspondences of different vocabularies. Then they developed a visualization for their final deliverables—short movies.

The ultimate goal was to create a *cinematic* (visual/sonic/kinetic) experience by exploring rhythmic and synchronous as well as arrhythmic and asynchronous relationships between image, sound, and motion. [3]

MOTION, TIME AND NARRATIVE

As the mind perceives visual, sonic, and kinetic information over a period of time, it continuously organizes discrete units or messages into a story, however abstract that story might be. A story must have a beginning, middle, and end (after Aristotle), though (after Godard) they need not necessarily be told in that order. A designer's awareness of two distinct timelines—one for the story, another for the storytelling—is therefore essential.

The intersection of narrative and interactive media has become an important area of exploration at the Dynamic Media Institute. In her 2005 thesis, *Interactive (N.)arrative. An Alternative Approach,* Christine Pillsbury argues that "interaction and participation were always components of storytelling, but they are now moving from implicit to the explicit." Of course, examining the role of audience participation in narrative raises the question of authorship. "Why is [authorship] an issue for designers?" asks Pillsbury. Her answer extends the context of authorship to the domain of interactive design. "In addition to writing and visualizing a narrative, [authors/designers] must consider the dynamic systems of the procedural front and backend. The story, the user experience, and the procedural system are not mutually exclusive layers of a narrative, but the elements that must be balanced to create a greater whole."

Through multiple case studies (page 42), including *Market Garden—A Narrative Interface For Portfolio Management* and *Contact 911: A Proposal For An Interactive Cinema Documentary,* Pillsbury proposes a holistic approach to interactive narrative, in which "the conceptual process must consider three aspects in conjunction: the Story…, the System…, and the Experience….The successful interplay of these three equal parts will result in a viable… system that communicates authorial intent while allowing for meaningful, informed participation from a non-authoring user."

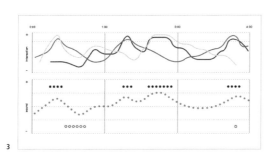

3

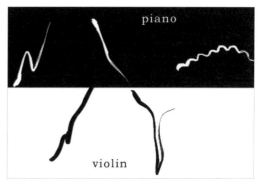

KINETIC BEHAVIOR OF DESIGN OBJECTS

Each and every on-screen object that designers use to communicate, be it image, typography, or diagram, has the potential to be animated. That potential—the concept of the kinetic "behavior" of an on-screen object—especially behavior triggered interactively by a user—is a central facet of motion literacy.

For the designer, the specific qualities and degree of motion, which will be perceived as the object's "kinetic behavior," must be precisely defined according to a matrix of specific parameters of transformation, mapped to specific variables of input. In other words, motion is expressed in terms of algorithmic thinking and computation.

Many examples of work developed at the Dynamic Media Institute successfully incorporate the concepts of computation through truly personal vocabularies of expression and highly creative design.

In his 2005 thesis *The Articulation of Visual Experiences through Algorithm,* Carlos Lunetta investigated "the relationship between code and visual language." Lunetta developed numerous case studies native to the computational medium, in which he "explored a range of topics including: musical intervals, generative and interactive form systems, interactive op art, database visualization, and the plastic components of time." (page 70) One of his case studies, *The Sound in Space,* drew its inspiration from the nineteenth-century scientific instrument known as a harmonograph (attributed to a Professor Blackburn

3. A visual map of the sound sequence—an initial step in studying the basic correspondences of different vocabularies. Evan Karatzas (left) and Karolina Novitska (right)

in 1844) that was used to represent sound intervals visually. Lunetta created a "harmono-graph" simulation in a new media context, where users can choose a musical interval and see it visually represented by a particular kinetic behavior. As a result "musical theory can be translated into pure visual information; octaves and other known intervals can be understood by their visible counterparts." That, according to Lunetta, is the core of computation: "the translation that converts certain [numerical] inputs to different outputs." [4]

4

4. Carlos Lunetta's "Near Dorian Experience", drew it's inspiration from the nineteenth-century scientific instrument known as a har-monograph (attributed to a Professor Blackburn in 1844) that was used to represent sound intervals visually.

5. In "Envisioning the Human Brain," Fenya Su employs interactive small multiples with opacity and scale sliders. That helps resolve the difficulty in observing incoming signals over multiple images obscured by repetitive brain structure in the background.

Evan Karatzas's 2005 thesis, entitled *Proximity Lab: Studies in Physical-computational Interface and Self-directed User Experience,* explores the concept of kinetic behavior on another level. It uses a human-scale physical interface, based on social behavior and inter-action between participants and the space they occupy.

The *Proximity Lab* installation is "an 8-foot by 16-foot walkable surface fitted with radio frequency ID (RFID) technology…enabling the system to track and record [the par-ticipants'] positions in real-time." It is "an experimental interface designed to visualize relationships between users and mediated spaces [that] directs attention to the intersection of physical and computational space." (page 94)

In his 2003 thesis *Interactive Media and the Poetic*, Mike Wiggins attempted to "illu-minate the core qualities of poetic messages delivered through interactive media." Many of the case studies Wiggins developed for his thesis, including *Acoustic Reflections* and *Inter-active Dialog: A Prototype of an Interactive Narrative,* brought him to a detailed investiga-tion of interactive media's capacity to communicate "the poetic experience." (page 34)

MOTION AND VISUALIZATION

The synthesis of motion and information graphics holds tremendous potential in learning environments. In many cases, dynamic diagrams, charts and timelines seem to be the only practical solutions for capturing the complexities inherent in large-scale information struc-tures. This topic is at the center of Fenya Su's 2003 thesis, entitled *Envisioning The Hu-man Brain: A Case Study for Dynamic Interactive Visualization in Human Brain Research.* This project was developed in collaboration with scientists from Massachusetts General Hospital in Boston. The thesis proposed a number of dynamic interactive visualizations to facilitate exploring and manipulating the complex information contained in large-scale and high-resolution spatiotemporal brain imaging data. [5] (page 128)

5

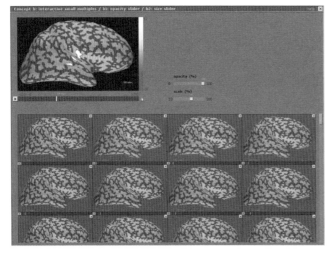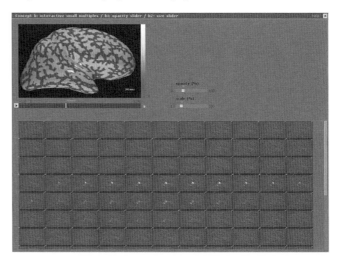

Interacting with complex data structures entails viewing dynamically linked information in different formats: text, image, audio, video, etc. Such multiple representation of information benefits the user tremendously but creates a challenge for the interface designer. Effective interaction design rewards the user with a sense of walking a unique personal path from data to knowledge, according to one's own expertise, preferences, special needs and individual pace. This path is a product of the user's actions and reactions—a kind of stimulus-response loop. It may involve a great deal of complexity and multiple layers of motion: an animated diagram, a timeline explaining an event, or a short movie telling a personal story. It involves the motion of interaction itself: moving a cursor, clicking and dragging, selecting and scrolling through windows. It also promotes a transformation in a broader social sense, through the learning experience that takes a person from one point to another on the difficult path to knowledge.

In this process, designers of dynamic media act as choreographers who arrange a user's learning experience. Motion is inseparable from learning—indeed from any human experience. The verb "to experience" implies motion since it implies a duration of time. Motion, in all its complexity is part of the temporal dimension of everyday life; it plays much the same role in communication design.

Awareness of time as a fundamental element of design lies at the center of motion literacy. This includes awareness of the "plasticity" of time, of the designer's ability to manipulate how time is represented and perceived using motion and sequentiality. Intertwined with motion, time becomes the most important structural element of communication design, an organizing principle to which all other elements must relate. Accordingly, the perception and representation of time through motion constitutes perhaps the ultimate task of all design.

Fostering motion literacy as an approach to design is the Dynamic Media Institute's curricular and pedagogical priority. The works from 2000–2005 presented in this book clearly reflect this approach.

Jan Kubasiewicz is a Professor at the Massachusetts College of Art

writing and the language of dynamic media

JOE QUACKENBUSH

One of the challenges of understanding dynamic media is to understand the language of dynamic media. In constant flux, the field is a melting pot of multiple disparate disciplines each with its own formal, conceptual, and symbolic language.

As in so many cases related to the digital world, the language one speaks is rooted in one's analog experience. Designers tend to define new media in terms of composition, color, and visual elements. Programmers tend to define new media in terms of computation, algorithm, and modularity. Filmmakers tend to define new media in terms of non-linearity, time, and sequence. Information architects tend to define new media in terms of organization, relationships, and user experience. No one set of terms adequately describes dynamic media, yet using all the terms is unwieldy.

Graduate students face a double jeopardy: how to understand the language of the field at large and how to understand the language of their own work.

In addition to project-based studio work and extensive contextual research, graduate students in the DMI program at the Massachusetts College of Art pursue their thesis study of dynamic media through a disciplined writing program.

Why write? Writing requires both intellectual rigor and careful reflection that influences enormously how and what students think about their work. Writing can unearth connections, expose weaknesses, reveal strengths, confirm suspicions, and inspire brilliance. Ideally, writing can fuse thinking to making, enrich design work, and create authentic knowledge. Writing is the visible expression of language.

WRITING IN THE DYNAMIC MEDIA INSTITUTE PROGRAM

Students begin an intensive writing program, running parallel to studio courses, in the first semester of their final year that culminates in the second semester with a substantial written thesis document.

Early on, process is emphasized, style is ignored. The point is to use writing as a tool to develop a conceptual framework for their thesis work.

Weekly writing assignments, rooted in their ongoing thesis work, demand that students reflect deeply upon their dynamic media projects. One important example is a project called *Common Threads*. Students are asked to develop a comprehensive list of thesis-related projects—however tenuous they may seem—completed before and during graduate school. Students are then asked to analyze what the common threads are between the projects. What issues keep appearing in their work? What words do they use to describe their work? What are the formal or conceptual relationships between projects? What issues are surprising?

Assignments are paired with readings from: *The New Yorker*, Jorge Luis Borges, Paul Auster, Steve Martin, Jeffrey Steingarten, and William Gibson. The readings are selected as much for subject matter as they are for being models of clarity, style, and narrative structure. On the surface, Bill Buford's essay in the September 6, 2004 issue of *The New Yorker*, "In the Kitchen: The Pasta Station," has little to do with new media. But the protagonist's quest to appreciate, understand, and prepare the perfect pasta has much to offer the graduate student struggling with the process of developing and understanding their own dynamic media work.

Gradually, assignments grow in complexity, adding synthesis and exposition to the practice of reflection. Students must clarify, develop, and sustain a persuasive argument. Expectations shift from writing as a tool to writing as expression, as the primary way of articulating their thesis study. Armed with new insight, students often rework key aspects of their projects after writing. Writing becomes a catalyst for thoughtful reflection, critical analysis, and design refinement.

By the end of this first semester, students have completed a considerable body of written work and made writing an inseparable part of their design process. More importantly, through writing, students begin to define the language of their thesis study.

Early in the second semester, students work to strengthen their arguments, hone their style, develop their point-of-view, and find their voice. Writing assignments are now customized. One student may be asked to further clarify a particular theoretical point while another may be asked to simplify the scope of a specific section.

Students complete a rough draft of their entire thesis document by mid-semester. Required sections include a thesis abstract, introduction, contextual research, project analysis, conclusion, and bibliography. The rough draft forces students to meld their writing into a coherent and sustained argument.

Students are strongly encouraged to shape their thesis document with a narrative structure that reflects the spirit of their work.

For example, Heather Shaw (MFA 2003), weaves personal memories of India into her document, *A Journey Through India: Designing the Interactive Documentary,* creating a meta-narrative while reflecting both her subject matter and her final project. (page 54)

In her thesis document, *Animation, Motion, and Education,* Julia Griffey (MFA 2005) fashions a chronological narrative structure that reveals the process of her thesis development from her first inchoate ideas about physical movement to her final museum installation *The Barn Owl Project,* a perfect symbiosis of animation, motion, and education. (page 120)

Students, working with an editorial advisor, revise and resubmit their drafts as necessary while working on the presentation of their document. Given DMI's roots in visual communication, students are expected to craft a visually compelling document that expresses the nature of the subject. For example, in his thesis, *Interactive Media and the Poetic: An Exploration Into the Elements of Interactive Media,* Mike Wiggins' use of visual sequence, repetition, juxtaposition, and collage both exemplify and reinforce his discussion of interactive semiotics. (page 34)

Completed thesis documents are delivered on the day of final oral presentations. More often than not, the presentations are a testament to the value of writing. Students, having found the native language of their own work, speak with clarity, passion, and authority.

TRANSCODING THOUGHT

In *The Language of New Media,* Lev Manovich's persuasive attempt to directly confront the language problem, he proposes five principles of new media or "general tendencies of a culture undergoing computerization:" numerical representation, modularity, automation, variability, and transcoding. Of these, transcoding, yields the greatest cultural influence.

"In new media lingo, to 'transcode' something is to translate it into another format," states Manovich. "The computerization of culture gradually accomplishes similar transcoding in relation to all cultural categories and concepts. That is, cultural categories and concepts are substituted, on the level of meaning and/or language, by new ones that derive from the computer's ontology, epistemology, and pragmatics."

To write is to translate thought into visible language. Inchoate ideas, concepts, and hunches are substituted by precise statements of clarity, intent, and purpose. The graduate student articulates, on the level of meaning, a new language, one native to their own experience. The raw materials of research, work, and reflection are transcoded gradually through writing into a document that is at once a record of work, a unique personal expression, and a refined contribution to the evolving language of dynamic media.

Joe Quackenbush is an Assistant Professor at the Massachusetts College of Art

the shaping of things to come: education and the elements of (dynamic) media

BRIAN LUCID

Starting the day one of our primitive ancestors recorded his or her experiences upon a cave wall, our methods of communication have advanced towards more effectively conveying the rich range of human experience within the limitations of our technology. Writing, the photographic image, cinema—each stands as a discrete stepping-stone in our ever-growing desire to extend, make permanent and share our fleeting sensory experiences.

Of course, new forms of communication do not suddenly appear in mature and coherent form. Prompted by technological innovation, each must be slowly drawn out from the synthesis of the dominant media that came before. As Marshall McLuhan observed, every "new" medium not only builds upon, but is essentially made up of, the wide variety of media that precede it.

The "birth" of a new medium is, in practice, a slow process of revelation. The true form of a new medium—the ways in which it encapsulates and represents experience; the effect and manipulation it has upon content; the possibilities it brings for expression; how it places itself within society and culture; and how it differentiates itself from media that have come before—reveals itself slowly as the perceptions of both authors and audiences move further away from the standards and expectations of previous media.

At the Dynamic media Institute, we have the distinction of producing work in a time of such "revelation." The projects represented within this catalog and its accompanying exhibition are the products of creative thought, applied research, and judicious authorship undertaken to question, define, present, and humanize the emerging medium of dynamic media.

As graduate students and faculty at the Dynamic Media Institute, we are serving as active researchers in the *incunabula* years of dynamic media. Like filmmakers in the first three decades of the twentieth century, we are challenged with the role of helping define a new medium. It is our task to engage dynamic media in the communication of knowledge and, through our developing literacy, push the content and form of the medium so it is interesting and viable to audiences.

Our success in drawing out and shaping this new medium lies in continuing to identify the unique properties that separate dynamic media from the media of the past and reflecting upon how those new properties affect the elements of media with which we have more historical familiarity. In order to facilitate constructive research and new design knowledge, one is required to have a familiarity with the formats, structures, and expectations derived from earlier communication technologies.

The emergence of the digital—the transformation of both abstract and tangible knowledge into numerical representation—has meant that the traditional products of the visual, aural, and textual are described and manipulated in the same way. Structured by the procedural nature of machines that process, transform and transmit this raw data, we are presented with a platform of communication that is not only encyclopedic in the way it encapsulates the media of the past, but challenges us by reconfiguring and re-contextualizing content in dynamic response to its audience.

While the Dynamic Media Institute was born as an outgrowth of a visually-focused undergraduate and graduate program in communication design, the nature of dynamic media has demanded that our curriculum and philosophy be expanded to include theories, products, and processes that lie outside the traditional boundaries of design education.

Authors of dynamic media must consider the implications of communication within the synthesis of visual, aural, temporal, haptic and kinesthetic elements. Touching upon issues disparate as human factors, usability, systems theory, logic, computation, learning theory, narrative, and authorship, the first-year of the DMI curriculum is devoted to developing the intellectual foundation and creative processes necessary to mix such diverse elements into systems that are rule-based and responsive.

While the entire DMI program of study focuses upon communication issues that arise in the light of dynamic media, one course specifically focuses on developing awareness to the wide range of media encapsulated within dynamic media. The goal of *Elements of Media*, a studio-based elective course that emphasizes imagemaking and the manipulation of sound and video, is the development of sensitivity to the properties of different media while considering how dynamic media affects and is affected by them.

Observations made within this introductory course of study are done with the expectation that they will lead to more complex explorations within thesis development. For example, Heather Shaw (MFA 2003) took her explorations into editing with persuasive voice and allowed them to grow into a thesis that considers the roles and challenges of documentary authorship within dynamic media. (page 54) The sonic documentation of a subway station by Leila Lee Mitchell (MFA 2003) developed into a thesis contemplating issues of sound within public and private spaces. Keiko Mori's (MFA 2005) projects in time-based storytelling led to interface studies in which time and motion were emphasized, making them more emotive and clear. (page 151)

Elements of Media seeks to extend research, thinking, and making into three connected areas of study: an investigation into human sensory reception, the consideration of how different technologies and media extend and address those senses, and—most importantly —developing fluency in the many "language" structures that have naturally evolved to effectively convey meaningful statements though each selected media channel.

As the mechanics of communication will forever be held in check by the immutable laws of perception, it is natural to begin study with an examination into the full range of human sensory reception within the designed environment. Sensitivity to these principles facilitates perception and user understanding, enhances the depth and quality of interaction and experience, and helps define the physical limits of communication.

The second area of study explores the media and technologies that are employed to augment and extend the natural senses previously explored. The goal here is to understand the roles that different media fill in the communicative landscape, develop sensitivity in the appropriate use of media types, and become comfortable selecting appropriate forms for the creation of specific experiences or interactions. It also involves becoming more aware of the role each of those media play within contemporary culture and communication.

The investigation into this second area of study also functions as a "tool-gathering" period where researchers can develop skills necessary to create creative work within diverse media including—but not limited to—tools for the static and dynamic composition of text and image; the capture and editing of audio and video; and the elements of computer programming, algorithmic thinking and computational form.

The third area of study proposes developing literacy in the syntactical structures that make these different media technologies function in an expressive way. This includes studying how image and sound are encoded and decoded to convey abstract concepts; observing how the juxtaposition of such elements convey complex statements; and considering how elements such as time, interaction and user participation re-contextualize such statements.

For example, in one assignment, students use montage editing to compare two opposing points of view, gradually leading the audience to the revelation of their own personal point of view. Initially, communication is attempted via image alone. Sound is added later coupled with reflection upon how it affects the original reading of the composition. Throughout the assignment, communication with clarity and intent is the goal.

The task of developing this type of literacy lies in the awakening of knowledge that is implicit and embodied. Living in a post-industrialized culture, we are all expert consumers of a wide variety of media; we have little difficulty decoding complex sign and symbol relationships when placed before us. The process, however, is often unconscious and we often feel at a loss when we attempt to put those same forces into service for our own communicative ends. To become fluent in the languages of such media is to transform that implicit knowledge into an external vocabulary that can be used to communicate with intent. This transformation takes place through the making of, reflection upon, and discussion about repeated attempts to communicate with intent through each selected medium.

The integration of these areas of study within the *Elements of Media* curriculum aims to develop a better facility within the construction of multi-sensory messages, build sensitivity to the roles different media play in defining experiences, and raise awareness to the contributions and modifications each media makes to the overall meaning. This knowledge serves as a foundation upon which continued exploratory research into dynamic media can begin.

The process of coaxing an emergent medium into final form is essentially the metamorphosis of an archival technology into a functional and expressive method of communication. It is a transformation that has occurred throughout history within the development of every medium engaged in human communication. Through being sensitive to the materialities and properties of earlier media forms—and being attentive to how new media affect and are affected by them—we place ourselves in a fitting position to push aside the mantle of formats, structures, and expectations derived from earlier communication formats. This allows us to push this medium forward toward its unique strengths.

Brian Lucid is an Assistant Professor at the Massachusetts College of Art

teaching design as experience

GUNTA KAZA

I feel resistant toward writing this article. Why? Am I afraid of exposure and judgement ("Will I sound smart enough? What if it's boring…")? Or is my distracted state due to some selfish impulse to withhold information? Just as importantly, how do these internal responses shape and inform the work in front of me? If I pay attention to these shadowy processes lurking just beneath the surface, and then if I take the time to clarify and respond to them with creative awareness, my work will become infused with an interest and a humanness that not only strengthens the quality of output intended for others, but teaches me something valuable about myself, as well. The creative process continuously mines the unknown. We create something out of 'nothing'—and 'nothing' is not really nothing, it's just initially hidden from our conscious awareness. The classes I teach at DMI, *Design as Experience I & II,* confront anxieties toward these unknowns and, through a spirit of play, encourage students to not only tolerate these anxieties but to use them as catalysts for creative thinking and problem solving.

Each week students are presented with an object, or a word, phrase or place that they are asked to "respond" to by the following week. The objects or words, however simple, might be initially confusing to the student, as they often relate to me personally–parts of projects I've been exploring, popsicle sticks my kids like to stick between the TV and VCR, hair balls from my dogs…they're certainly not the typical corporate design specs they are familiar with. Students are challenged to make personal sense of this odd request. What ensues is the struggle of making meaning out of seemingly nothing important. There are no preconceptions. They must ask of themselves: "How do I represent this? How do I put this into context?"

Rapid prototyping and designing intuitively are encouraged—no overworking or over-intellectualizing allowed! Also, the responses are to be drawn from personal content and observations. Because I often reveal some vulnerability through the assigned object, students may feel safer revealing something about themselves. Do the students think I'm a wacko? Have I lost my rocker? Probably, but in a spirit of exploration, of play, a sense of safety develops and we learn.

One of the rules that is agreed upon in the first class is to keep all of the class experiences within the classroom. In other words, what is exposed within the group experience becomes just that—a group experience—discussed, analyzed and interpreted within the group, not privately among a few select members. This helps to reinforce a safer learning environment.

An example: I brought with me an old book of Shakespeare and asked students to take from the book what they wished and 'activate' this in combination with the phrase, "My life is an open book." (I was feeling particularly exposed that day, so this phrase had meaning for me.) Carlos responded the following week: "My response was to let the energy *flow* through the book and scatter it, in two parallel actions. One became a book dough, was chopped and baked into a book cake; the other was burned and ashes were thrown into the air and documented. Two images represent the book after the action. In both cases, the main characteristics of the book—it's words—can be seen. The typography survived." His conclusion was that life is not an open book, that while the context and presentation changes, life's complexities, entangle the type. Twisted, mutated, distorted parts are lost and unreadable, inaccessible. My response was to ask what kind of a reaction he expected from his presentation. He'd given me an answer to my riddle, instead of creating a dialogue. Was he concerned only with the making of these objects? Why did we feel removed from the experience? Another student, Lynn, had created a book jacket. Her presentation was literally a "jacket" made of the pages within the book. It was meant to be worn, but we observed that, although presented on a coat hanger, the jacket looked too delicate and frail to be physically worn. The class questioned whether or not it needed to be interacted with. Her carefully considered meaning, which addressed a longing to live in a culture she recognized and whose customs she was familiar with (she is from South Africa), had stimulated the making of her response.

Another project began with a visit to the Christian Science Church in Boston. Obviously, the religious aspect was not a significant component; rather, the architecture of "place" was what I encouraged students to experience. The first stop was the reflecting pool designed by I.M. Pei and Partners; the second was the avenue of trees, also designed by Pei; the third, the Hall of Ideas, containing an interactive installation designed by David Small and sculptor Howard Ben Tré. My request was to create a response in relation to an experience of "place," whether of one place or all three.

Kate had combined her experience of all three into one project of a relationship between the natural and synthetic environments. Initially she created a mobile which combined curved, string-like material with sharp and angular wires. The class response indicating a lack of viewer participation encouraged her to try again. She then created a wire hand-cranked structure, which, when cranked, plays soft musical notes—a fusion of her first project with sound elements. I asked students to write questions or words in response to Kate's presentation. *Whimsy* and *whimsical* were the most common words that surfaced. The next week, I asked students to write about the experience of seeing, making, interpreting, and integrating. Kate spoke of a resistance to writing, to verbalizing and making sense of these visceral experiences. I asked her why she had to make sense of it? Could she just "babble?" (Babbling is what I do when I don't have the right words with which to say something.) As a final project I asked students to respond to the word *tropos* (a Greek word that means "to draw out, to bring out from within.") Kate's direction combined the initial mobile and crank, with the concepts of *whimsical* (the freedom to babble), and *tropos*. Her final presentation included three soft-sculpted heads, that, when interacted with (you have to pull something out from them), squeak and mumble. She spoke of the difficulty in retrieving internal experiences and translating them into sensible external messages. These "heads" presented this experience in a whimsical and humorous way.

Stephen had presented a montage of images of the natural world in combination with seeds for the first part of the same assignment and a question was raised as to what the viewer's response should be. Was it a montage for observation, or was there anything the viewer should do with the seeds? Having been inspired by this question, Stephen brought in a beautifully wrapped paper container. He carefully and slowly carried the package around the room and invited all of us to take something from within. Each of us was given a gift—an apple. He spoke of a gift verifying the existence of another. Similar to the way that I.M. Pei's reflecting pool and avenue of trees was a gift for us, Stephen's gifts were an indication of temporality and permanence as we consumed the apple.

Finding criteria for evaluation—a way to discuss each project—is challenging. "No aspect of human life, be it music, medicine or technology, can be adequately discussed if we are always restricted to a scientific mode of discourse. If we wish to discuss a human activity, there are times…when there is more insight to be gained from knowing what something feels like—knowing what its existential meaning is—than from knowing how it works and measuring it," writes Arnold Pacey in his book *Meaning in Technology*. Since there is no right or wrong, no objectively measurable good or bad, how do we evaluate the responses? I may ask students to write a question of each other's projects in response to what they make, before we discuss them. Sometimes, the questions posed in class about each response lead to further investigations. Ideally, each class builds upon the next in relation to a larger concern or interest that each student may be developing.

It is no easy task to teach by this method. Each class, begins with the same unknown for me: "What if I don't know how to respond to a particular student's project? What then?" I have to listen and pay attention to each moment, and be aware of what my own internal responses alert me to. The teaching method is very improvisational. There are times when a student displays their response on the table and no one has anything to say. Can we ask a question? What is it? What does it do? Can you hang it? Can you throw it? When we begin to question, we come to understand what the intention is. In turn, observations of our interactions with the object are fresh and allows the students to understand what this class is all about: a synthesis between what students make and how what they make affects the other. If what the student has made invites no response, we have to ask, "why not?" As a result students begin to transform their visceral experiences into compelling, tangible interactions.

The *Random House Dictionary* states: "Experience implies being affected by what one meets with (pleasant or unpleasant), so that to a greater or lesser degree one suffers change." Additionally, in the classroom we define experience based upon limitations —isolating emotion and distilling meaning. Universal meanings derive from personal beginnings. Ben Shahn writes, "In being average to all things, [generalities] are particular to none...but let us say that the universal is that unique thing which affirms the unique quality in all things...a de Chirico figure, lonely in a lonely street haunted by shadows; its loneliness speaks to all human loneliness." The personal experiences students feel, interpret, and bring to synthesis as creation become a part of a collective awareness.

Slowly, we observe what is of importance to each student. Personal mythologies emerge when new forms and meanings are discovered in relation to familiar themes. These mythologies teach us something about ourselves and the world in which we live. What results is a reflexive communication between the maker and the work, which invites the audience to partake in the conversation. Projects are presented as needs surface in discussions with students. Improvisational relationships between myself, the students and their projects allow for investigations that promote interactive exchanges and emotional maturation.

This class within the DMI poses a laboratory of study that examines and explores human interaction, adaptability, growth and transformation. In the practice of developing visual responses that have acquired meaning from 'nothing' we are training our non-verbal skills to integrate with the still small voice inside each of us; to become more familiar with utilizing multiple senses; to become involved and concerned with the 'other;' to create experiences which result from intimate, personal responses transformed into universal truths; and to bring our humanness to the forefront of our creations. Motivation for this vision is spurred by the changeability of our everyday experiences. Personal, cultural and social experiences lead the way to a new form of examining who we are and who we are becoming. The dynamism of this invitation becomes too seductive to ignore.

Gunta Kaza is an Associate Professor at the Massachusetts College of Art

exhibited work

9 notes

LAUREN BESSEN

Class of 2006

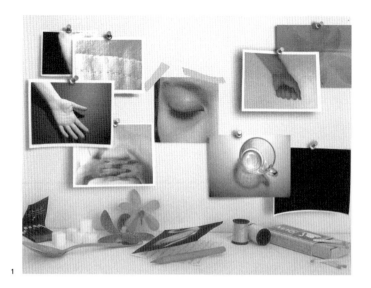

1

The visual metaphor is a basic principle of effective interface design. Meaning, in a GUI, arises from the representation of a real world concept in a digital world. Familiar objects mimic their real-world analogues, yet often extend their purpose with "unreal" capabilities. This is true of the desktop GUI. Its world of folders, briefcases, address books, trashcans, and other office implements is not quite the same as its real-life version. At the same time, it is so commonplace that we barely notice it. A metaphor less familiar to users, however, has the potential to let the interface itself create meaning. The complex relationship between representation and real-life object in this virtual environment holds potential for narrative.

9 Notes is an experimental interface that examines and extends the concept of a visual metaphor as interface. Nine cool-hued pictures, attached by thumbtacks, cover a wall while a scattering of objects—matches, a spoon, sugar cubes, orchid blossoms—lines a narrow shelf. Drawing influence from classical still lifes, informal scrapbooks and the "desktop" GUI, the space is unfamiliar and ambiguous, but obviously personal. Object functionality both mimics the real world and creates unreal experiences. Users can drag and rearrange the note cards by pressing and moving the thumbtacks. Clicking on and dragging an object, meanwhile, creates a translucent facsimile of that object. Dragging and dropping these "copies" onto the pictures will trigger the playback of brief motion-graphics pieces inside the framed image, the static pictures becoming unreal windows onto moving content. Multiple notes can be triggered at once, and the note cards can be spatially rearranged

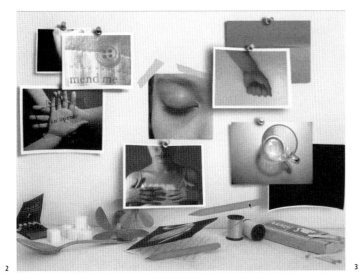

2

3

while the videos play. Each object, however, will trigger only one specific picture, and it is up to the user to determine which goes with which.

Beyond the visual metaphor, *9 Notes* is a collection of mini-narratives that all touch upon themes of intimacy. Using meticulously hand-rendered typography and evocative imagery, each short video concludes with a brief poetic message. The author, subject, and recipient of these graphic odes and meditations remain hidden, and the user is unimpeded to explore and seek out the messages in each "note."

This freedom is similar to a conventional desktop or other GUI, but the conceptual purpose of the piece is mysterious. It is a visual playground for us to examine and mine for experience, a puzzle that invites the user to discover its logic. Like a puzzle, too, *9 Notes* comes to a resolution: the "notes"—once the user has learned how to trigger them—do not loop endlessly but rather conclude with a static image, brilliant and warm-toned. In this aspect, the piece follows the arc of a traditional narrative. However, spectatorship here requires active participation—narrative does not proceed without the user's curiosity. Intrigue arises from the enigmatic nature of the space.

1. The default interface prior to user interaction.
2. An instance of clicking and dragging an object.
3. The interface after several movies have been triggered.

4

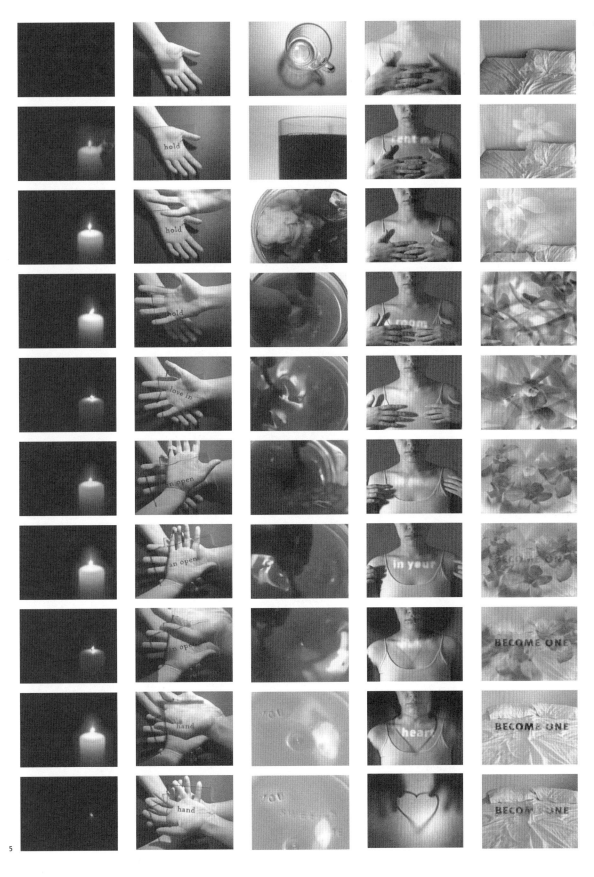

5

qualities of the poetic experience

MIKE WIGGINS

Class of 2003

This paper attempts to illuminate core qualities of poetic messages delivered through interactive media. Mediums have unique 'vocabularies' used to communicate. For example, photography utilizes camera angle, film grain, and focal length. This vocabulary can be used to communicate both poetically and informationally. Poetically, a photographer may use a low camera angle to give the viewer a sense of awe, wonder, or fear. Informationally, he may use a particular camera angle in order to reveal a specific attribute of the subject matter.

Within interactive media the complexity has increased due to a convergence of the vocabularies of previous mediums into this new interactive environment. We are currently dealing with a host of old elements compounded by an entire new set. Contextual issues also contribute to this complexity. Taking the vocabulary of film out of the theater and placing it within interactive media fundamentally changes its communicative properties. For example, the vocabulary of sound is a common element to both the cinema and the stage, but the use of silence communicates differently within both of these mediums. Silence within the cinema is a dramatic tool that can be used to punctuate a moment, but silence within a play is interpreted very differently. As common vocabulary moves to the interactive environment it must be utilized with sensitivity and thoughfulness.

This investigation operates on the premise that an interactive experience is fundamentally the same as any 'human' experience. Therefore, human experience will often be used to illuminate and exemplify the qualities of a poetic interactive experience.

DEFINING THE POETIC

Throughout this investigation, 'poetic' refers to the ability of language—verbal and non-verbal—to communicate concepts or ideas that live specifically in the mind, like fear or joy, as opposed to informational language that focuses on objects and their relationships to physical space. The following statement refers to works of art specifically, but is an appropriate definition of 'poetic' within this context.

"The understanding that the artistic sign establishes among people does not pertain to things, even when they are represented in the work, but to a certain attitude toward things, a certain attitude on the part of man toward the entire reality that surrounds him, not only to that reality which is directly represented in the given case."
(Semiotics of Art, 237)

The poetic does not refer to physical objects even when that is what is depicted. It refers rather to the reader's attitude towards his "entire reality that surrounds him." It first makes an internal reference, pointing within the reader, affecting his individual attitude and outlook. It then points outward in regards to how the reader sees his world around him.

Another element that sets poetic communication apart from informational language is its relationship to contextual over external references.

"Thus, in poetry, as against informational language, there is a reversal in the hierarchy of relations: in the latter attention is focused above all on the relation, important from the practical point of view, between reference and reality, whereas for the former it is the relationship between the reference and the context incorporating it that stands to the fore."
(Semiotics of Art, 157)

Jan Mukarovsky uses the phrase "it's turning dark" as an example (Semiotics of Art, 155). If interpreted informationally, the phrase is understood on the basis of its relationship to physical reality. Is the light abating? If, on the other hand, the phrase is interpreted poetically, the emphasis would be placed on context. What texts surround the phrase that point to the intended interpretation? It could be referring to a character's circumstances or life situation, but it depends heavily on context. This does not mean that informational language does not rely on context, but that poetic communication depends on it to a greater degree.

POETIC IN OTHER MEDIUMS

Lev Manovich, in *The Language of New Media*, said, "As theorized by Vertov, film can overcome its indexical nature through

  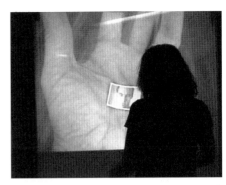

montage, by presenting a viewer with objects that never existed in reality." (149) Here Manovich points out that early film was primarily concerned with informational communication, or communication about physical objects. I believe every medium in its early stages communicates primarily about physical objects rather than abstract concepts. For example, early film was indexical in nature and the focus of the message was on the objects referenced, whereas contemporary film references objects that are often secondary to the message. A scene of a woman chopping tomatoes is not about the objects involved, but rather some other message entirely, like setting a mood of tension or danger. Interactive media seems to be in this early stage.

The concept of montage is key to communicating the poetic in the medium of film. By placing two concrete objects next to one another a director can create a third conceptual message. Sergei Eisenstein, in the book *Film Sense*, presents a scene of a women in a black veil and dress standing next to a grave.

"The woman...is a representation, the mourning robe she is wearing is a representation—that is, both are objectively representable. But "a widow," arising from a juxtaposition of the two representations, is objectively unrepresentable—a new idea, a new conception, a new image."

Graphic designers speak poetically when they give visual form to the core values of corporate institutions. For example, it's appropriate for a bank to communicate the concepts of strength and stability through the visual form of their branding. These concepts exist only in the mind but the vocabulary of graphic design, if used with sensitivity, can communicate these concepts with great success.

Eisenstein continues on to suggest that the concept of montage can also be found in other mediums of communication. For example, ideograms in the Japanese and Chinese language often combine two concrete objects to indicate the conceptual. Within the realm of poetry, a Haiku poem presents the concrete in an effort to point to the transcendental. If this concept exists within multiple mediums it seems natural to apply it to interactivity as well.

We have discussed utilizing visual mediums to communicate concepts that have no visual form, but interactivity is more than a visual medium. It has the potential to utilize all senses, which is why many refer to this medium in terms of 'experience'. This provides the basis of looking to human experience as an educational foundation within the interactive medium.

DEFINING THE POETIC EXPERIENCE

The focus of this investigation is not on all experience, but rather the poetic experience. Experience always has the potential to communicate on two levels, the literal and the poetic. Generally, turning on a faucet would be interpreted as a literal experience. A person acts, the object reacts, and the experience is concluded before

ART CENTER COLLEGE OF DESIGN LIBRARY

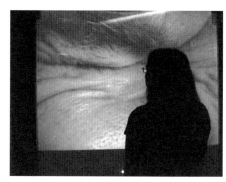

reaching the poetic. In contrast, hiking through the Grand Canyon can be interpreted as poetic, meaning the experience goes beyond itself. An individual literally experiences the hiking boots, blisters and sore knees, but he also experiences something that points beyond his immediate environment to the way he perceives his entire world. He may begin to see his life as small and insignificant which could lead to a sense of peace or unity with nature. Watching a sunset or standing on the edge of the sea may also be interpreted in this manner. So again, what becomes important is context, the context of the individual involved in the experience. An individual's interpretation of a sunset depends heavily on his state of mind or life situation.

Through the use of interactive media we now have the power to represent experience as never before. The intention of my work is not immersion or simulation of physical experience in a virtual environment along the lines of IMAX films or Star Trek's Holodeck. Rather, my intention is to use this medium in a way that is informed and inspired by experience. What follows is a collection of qualities and processes that I have explored in an effort to produce this second level of interpretation. In short, it is the result of my efforts to utilize interactive media to communicate the poetic.

QUALITIES OF THE POETIC EXPERIENCE

The following concepts do not exhaust the qualities of the poetic experience, but rather represent a few core concepts that I have attempted to explore within my work.

Identity (Control, Participation and Observation)

Within any given experience a person will identify himself as the one in control, a participant, or a mere observer. I propose that within a poetic experience a person identifies himself with all three. For example, while riding a skateboard I control the fact that I am on the board, my general direction, and my final destination. In regards to physics, I participate in an exchange of actions with the board; I move, the board changes directions, I respond. I am also participating in the environment and with other people. They look at me, sensing I am in their space, and I react the same to them. I avoid hitting them and they pause for me. And finally, I observe the environment around me, enjoying the breeze, taking in my surroundings (e.g. sky, homes, buildings, cars, etc.).

Control

The intent of the *Acoustic Reflections* installation is to allow the user to participate in all three levels of identity. His own actions control very specific images on the screen; by yelling at a certain volume he gets a standard reaction from the screen. The user quickly understands that if he makes no sound he will be left with a static image, but if he makes a sound the image will respond. It is important to be conscious of how much control is given to the user. It is tempting to give him total control, but this does not reflect the common poetic experience.

Within my *Interactive Dialogue* piece the user is given limited control to either go forward in three directions or backward. He cannot simply jump forward, nor does he have any understanding of what is in front of him. The user cannot skip over content, he must choose one direction or another, and must always deal with the content that confronts him. This is unlike most web sites where the user is given an overall structure and can place himself wherever he chooses.

In many ways this piece simulates human experience in that we can choose our direction, but once we do, we are confronted with the consequences. And like life, once the content is given it cannot be taken back. Sure, in my piece you can choose to go back, but knowledge has already been gained; a piece of the puzzle has been revealed. Hitting the back button doesn't make you forget.

Participation

Within my *Acoustic Reflections* work, the user is engaged in participation as well as control. For example, when the user claps or yells in order to open my hand and reveal the photograph, he is limited by his own capacity to clap or yell. As the hand closes the user may yell again to re-open it, or possibly modulate his voice to open and close it in a rhythm. The user acts and reacts depending on what he sees. The subtlety of the movement and the sensitivity to sound brings the user into an exchange. The images respond to him but he also responds to the images.

Observation

Participation and control are based on observation. Consequently, the user's actions are directly related to his observations. He may become interested in the way my hand moves at a certain point, or how my eyelashes bend as I close my eye.

Why is it important to the poetic experience that all three identities are engaged? How do they contribute to someone looking beyond this experience to how they see themselves? If an experience is too heavily weighted within one identity, control for example, the user has no room for reflection. While turning on a faucet the user has total control of the experience from start to finish, yet lacks the opportunity to reflect. If the experience is mainly participatory it may be too consuming to ever see beyond it. It may demand too much of the user's mental or physical capacity. If an experience weighs heavily on observation, it runs the risk of becoming boring, which is probably why it takes a dramatic experience, like an extraordinary sunset, to be both poetic and weighted toward observation. But even in that situation the person is often in control of his location (e.g. beach, mountain-top, etc.). I believe life in general is weighted toward control and participation but lacking in observation. This explains why the poetic experience often occurs when observation plays a heightened role (e.g. hiking, going to the beach, watching a sunset, etc.).

Intimacy

One definition of intimacy is "a private and personal utterance or action." (encarta.com)

Why is intimacy important to the poetic experience? On some level, for an experience to become poetic it must become personal and internal, it must point inward. Returning to the Grand Canyon example, internally the experience may promote feelings of insignificance or a unity with nature. But these thoughts in turn point outward as to how the individual perceives his reality.

The images of my hand opening and closing, revealing and hiding, reflect an intimacy. It is a metaphor for revealing or giving, which are intimate actions that point inward. All of the actions within my *Acoustic Reflections* work reflect the concept of opening and closing or revealing and concealing (e.g. opening and closing my hand, eyes, mouth...).

Also, the user's actions point back to him. By manipulating objects with his voice, he uses something very personal to him, something used in other personal interactions. Our voices are employed in language, communication, and expression. It is interesting that we use abstract noises to express our thoughts and emotions, like "ahhhhh" (i.e. "I understand") or "um" (i.e. "I'm trying to decide what to say"), or signs of frustration like grunting or screaming. These are the actions used most often within my work.

Ambiguity

In what way are poetic experiences ambiguous, or what role does ambiguity play in a poetic experience? I am referring to the way a person must contribute in order to reach the poetic level. A poetic experience is not laid bare but rather incomplete, and can only be completed by the participant. This explains why poetic experiences rarely say the same thing to two people, nor does the same experience affect a person the same way twice. This goes back to the importance of context. If a person experiences something for a second time his mental context has undoubtedly changed. His life circumstances, emotional state, and mindset have all changed based on the original experience. This is illustrated when reading the same book for a second time. The reader will often notice new things or be struck by different events. It is the reader who has changed, not the text.

Ambiguity permeates media, from the simplest cartoon to the most complex works of art. Paul Rand often referred to it within design. The other day I was watching a Tweety Bird cartoon with my eighteen-month old daughter. Tweety had been kidnapped by two thugs; at one point an old stout woman in a housedress poked her head in and barked orders at the two thugs. She was obviously the boss. The old lady's face was never shown, it was always cropped off the top of the screen, leaving her face to the imagination of the viewer. It provided room to participate; the mystery or ambiguity gave each viewer something unique: authorship. I was able to create my own identity for this woman.

When I ride a skateboard I fill in each part of the story as I go. I have authored much of it; my destination, the streets I take, my speed. But much of it is spontaneous. Each movement is a response to the unknown. How much I shift my weight in order to turn is determined by how fast I am going, whether there is a stone in the road, what the texture of the road is like....

Within *Acoustic Reflections* much is left for the viewer to fill in. One aspect I continue to work on is giving the user enough elements to point him in the right direction while not giving away too much. The user is presented with a closed hand and no prompt as

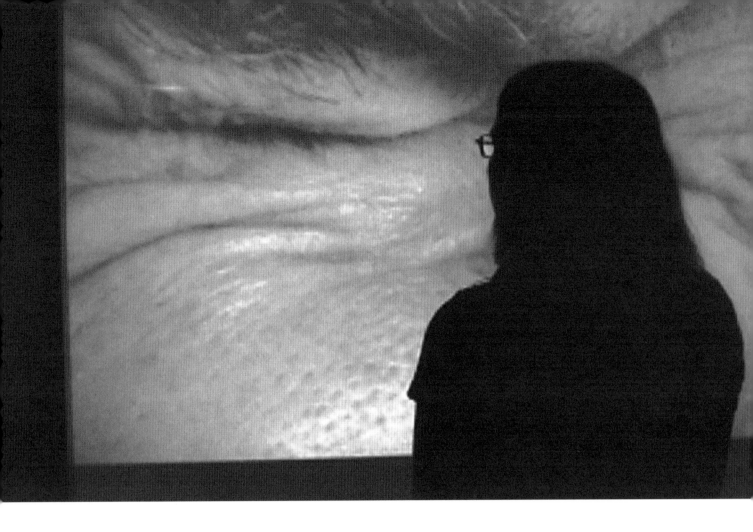

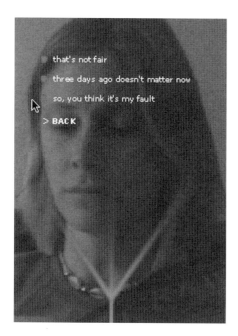

to what is expected of him. It is anticipated that the user will make some kind of noise and notice the reaction from the screen. This should lead to more exploration from the user in regards to making noise and getting a response. After the user understands the rules of the game, the screen will change to an image of my face with my eyes closed. Again, an interaction between noise and response will take place. The piece continues in this manner through a series of images finishing with an extreme close-up of my eye. The user is given no information about where the piece is going or what it means; it is left completely to the viewer. While ambiguity is a definite strength of my project, the project still relies heavily on other qualities to create a poetic experience.

Multiple meanings and references represent another aspect of ambiguity. For example, a poet uses a word that has multiple meanings, but does not reveal which is intended. Within my *Acoustic Reflections* piece the word "loading" appears on top of the images for a moment when they first appear. Two out of four times it appears on top of my face. This is a representation that may have multiple interpretations. Most obviously the word signifies an activity of the computer; it is busy processing data and is an explanation of its apparent inactivity. But its placement on top of a head (often representative of knowledge or thought) mingles two concepts. The combination could signify the process of learning, cognition or enlightenment. This ambiguity of meaning, or oscillation of signifying and signified, is again helpful in pointing the user outside the experience.

Memory

Within experience we have different forms and uses of memory. Short term memory tells us what we have just done and what we should do next (i.e. we have turned on the faucet and now need to wash our hands). Acquired and cultural memory informs and contextualizes experience (i.e. American sense of independence based on revolutionary beginnings).

Short Term Memory

Within my Acoustic Reflections work the user is carried from one set of images to the next, repeating the same kind of interaction. It is expected that the user will remember what he has just seen and done, and that it will inform his current experience. When the user is manipulating the eye, my hope is that he will remember the hand and the mouth and the actions he just performed. This is important from a practical standpoint, but also from a conceptual perspective as it relates to the progression of images.

Acquired Memory

Memory reveals connections, especially within the poetic experience. We carry within ourselves acquired information, our memories. Within any experience, especially those that point inward, connections are made with previously acquired information. Our memories live in the present but point to the past. While watching a sunset we may be reminded of friends we have seen other sunsets with, or it could connect us metaphorically with someone who has passed away. Experience can be iconic in that its structure points to other experiences with similar structures. The difficulty of climbing to the top of a mountain is often connected with experiences like succeeding at work or winning in sports (i.e. difficulty followed by a reward).

Long-term memory within my work is used as a means of connection. I am hoping that people remember what it is like to hold something in their hands, or to open their hands. Connecting what they see with what they have previously experienced may begin a cycle of reaching beyond this moment. If they begin to look outside of this experience, or rather inside of themselves for connections, a poetic experience is possible. The simple and common motions on the screen are intended to connect with the user's everyday experience, but the scale and mode of interaction are intended to reveal them in a new way.

Cultural Memory

Like any society, we have a collective memory, rich with cultural influences, ideas, thoughts and experiences. When we walk through the Grand Canyon, we experience something that millions of others have also experienced. We experience it both alone and collectively. These common experiences often speed communication. I had no idea how dependent language was on cultural memory until I lived in England for a time. I found that as soon as I engaged a Brit in conversation beyond the introductory I had trouble understanding. We both constantly referred to elements from our different cultural memories. I was unaware how often I used figures of speech or referred to events, movies or stories that were common to my culture, but not to another. It was a great lesson on how culture affects our worldview.

Currently, the structure of my *Acoustic Reflections* work is fairly monotonous, moving from one image to the next, placing equal emphasis on each section. The progression emphasizes the experience rather than the narrative, reminiscent of a walk through a forest or a stroll in the park. If the structure were more like a traditional narrative, with a beginning, middle and end, the experience would be self-contained, pointing only to itself rather than striving to reach beyond. Therefore, this monotonous and steady structure leaves room for the mind to wander.

CONCLUSION

The importance of this discussion rests in the fact that the longevity and significance of the medium depends heavily on its ability to contribute to the important texts of humanity. To steal from Brian Lucid's earlier essay, how do we coax this emergent medium towards its final form? This is a complex and difficult issue, which leaves me continually grateful to the Dynamic Media Institute's depth of thinking and facility to explore such relevant questions.

ANOTATED BIBLIOGRAPHY

Sergei Eisenstein, *Film Form, Essays in Film Theory* (Harcourt, Brace and Company, 1949)
A series of 12 essays, written between the years of 1928 to 1945, by the renowned Russian filmmaker and theoretician Sergei Eisenstein. It explores the aesthetics of film, pulling examples from literature, language, music and other mediums.

R.L. Gregory, *The Intelligent Eye* (McGraw-Hill, 1970)
The text explores many aspects of human perception and is filled with many examples and activities for the reader. Gregory suggests that symbolic language is changing they way our brain functions and our use of logic and problem-solving is slowly divorcing us from these natural functions.

Lev Manovich, *The Language of New Media* (MIT Press, 2001)
This book places new media within a historical context and illustrates how the conventions of previous media have come forward to influence the new. He uses concepts from film theory, art history, literary theory and computer science to illuminate the current landscape of new media. Particular importance is placed on the role of cinema and the theories surrounding it.

Ladislav Matejka and Irwin R. Titunik, *Semiotics of Art* (MIT Press, 1976)
A series of 21 essays dealing with the concepts of semiotics and how they apply to the arts, in particular drama, poetry, fiction and the visual arts. All essays were contributed by the Prague School, an influential institution in European linguistics.

interactive (n.)arrative: an alternative approach

CHRISTINE PILLSBURY

Class of 2005

Interaction and participation were always components of storytelling, but they are now moving from implicit to the explicit. A participatory audience is branching out from the cognitive to the tactile, and authorship itself is being reconsidered.

Why is this an issue for designers? Authorship is becoming more like the process of design. Authors are well accustomed to designing the structure of their narratives. But now, in addition to writing and visualizing a narrative, they must consider the dynamic systems of the procedural front and backend. The Story, the user experience, and the procedural system are not mutually exclusive layers of a narrative, but the elements that must be balanced to create a greater whole.

1. ON AUTHORSHIP

Understanding authorship is key to understanding how interactivity will change the way we create and experience narratives in the future. An author has a point of view. She constructs a scenario to express that point of view. The reader is confronted by it and forms a personal connection based on her own subjectivity and life experiences.

The value of hypertext for collaboration is easy to see. Yet, Interactive Narration is but one possible form of Interactive Narrative. Do most people spend their time writing books or reading them? Would everyone prefer to imagine all forms of entertainment and cultural enrichment—conceived only from the limits of their own experience?

To observe and to explore implies that there is something that already exists. So it is false to contend that true Interactive Narrative requires a user to write the story. A user can meaningfully modify a narrative without adding content to it. Mark Meadow, the author of *Pause and Effect,* states: "Interaction operates on something. It's a form of dealing with pre-existing material. It's modification, not generation."

The difference between an author and a participatory audience is not the quality or quantity of contribution. Rather it is the impact of that contribution. Quality and quantity are extremely important issues, but they speak to the experiential aspects of narrative, not what creates narrative. By analyzing the impact of contribution we can begin to define user roles in interactive environments. [1]

Ask three painters to paint a horse; the result would be three different subjects. Picasso would paint Time. Warhol would paint Culture. And Pollock would paint Emotion. Subjectivity—the key to great narrative. The author's intent sparks the foundation of observation—no matter how many tangents may evolve. Therefore, if the text (in the broadest sense) cannot exist without the observer (from the critic to the user), then, the observer cannot exist without the author.

2. ON NARRATIVE

A narrative consists of three layers—the Plot, the Story, and the Discourse. [2]

The Plot

The underlining blueprint—thousands of years of human nature have developed patterns of psychology and sociology. There are only so many plots, about 20 or less.

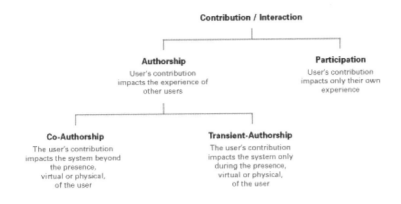

Forbidden Love: the lovers ignore social convention and pursue their hearts, usually leading to disastrous results.

The Story

Refers to the actual chronology of real time events in spatial temporal context—it can only exist in the abstract. It is the implied reality that we can summarize when finished experiencing the Discourse.

The real time events of Homer's Odyssey happen over the course of almost two decades, versus the week to read the book.

The Discourse

The presentation layer of a Story that is manipulated by:

1. The reordering and restructuring of the Story's real time events into a unique interpretive chronology.
2. The subjective representation of those events. This is why the same Story can have many narratives associated with it.

Rosencrantz and Guildenstern Are Dead by Tom Stoppard versus Shakespeare's *Hamlet.*

2.1. Structural Aspects of Narrative

The word narrative has many definitions, ranging from the overly simplified to the outrageously complex. In general, the word is used in three ways:

1. As an adjective: "The painting has a narrative quality."
2. As a verb: "He narrates the history lesson for the students.
3. As a noun: "The narrative of God is present in many cultures."

If one is to refer to narrative as a noun, an actual thing, one must be able to formulate the structural aspects that cause it to be in existence. The author of any given narrative will tell you that a story is not successful without the 5 Ws: the Who, What, When, Where, and most importantly the Why. The 5 Ws are the functional and aesthetical driving forces that make a narrative more than a stream of consciousness. Their presence is what creates a whole greater than the sum of its parts.

Narrative (n.)

A sequence of events occurring in a specific place and time, experienced, caused, and or recounted by one or more agents, representing a continuant subject and constitute a whole, communicated by one or more narrators to one or more narratees.

2.2. Story As Database

To think of a Story as a database one must think of the content of a Story as a collection of related object-oriented pieces. Each object must be describable in an algorithmic sense—metadata. This metadata is how the software will mediate the presentation of content based on user interaction. Some examples of metadata possibilities are scene, character point of view, topic, duration, legibility, functionality, etc. To create a (N.)arrative, all possible combinations of the separate Story objects must work together to create a continuant whole; a beginning, middle, and end. This creates cause and effect relationships between the separate story-objects on a micro and macro level that communicate the authorial intent and drive the narrative forward.

The mere implication of control will

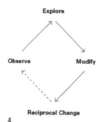

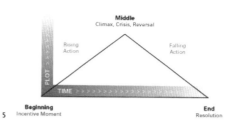

3

4

5

entice a user to interact. However, if everything is controllable by the user, it becomes impossible to create a continuant subject. The opportunity to interact with a narrative should be conceptually related to the Story and the results of that interaction should manifest a unique Discourse. Therefore, in an Interactive (N.)arrative system certain aspects must be mandated while others are variable.

For example, if the Story is a murder mystery and the author has put the user in a position to stop that murder then one could strategize the following:

- At least two endings; the murder takes place, the murder is prevented
- Duration of the narrative is fixed—creating a sense of urgency within the user
- The murderer character is a fixed identity
- The victim character is variable

Alternatively, one could strategize:
- The end is fixed, the murder takes place
- Duration of the narrative is variable
- The murderer character is variable
- The victim character is fixed

In the first example, the author's strategy for user participation can be surmised as giving the user power over the destiny of the potential victim. In the second example, the user is given the power over the destiny of the potential murderer.

The variable aspects of the narrative must be conceptually relevant to and exemplify the themes of the Story. The authorial intent of a narrative is to communicate a specific Who, What, When, Where, and most importantly Why. The reader's goal is to form a personal understanding of those 5 Ws. This implicit discourse between the reader and the Story should be what informs the explicit influence the reader provides.

Deciding the metaphysical location of the user will determine their functional role within a narrative. There are three possible metaphysical positions of a user: The Voyeur, First Person, and the Subject. In the first example, the user must be placed within the narrative as a First person character. In the second, the user could be placed in either the voyeur, First person, or subject position. In the first example the author could decide

that the user is the murderer, in the second example the user could be the victim.

2.3. Cause and Effect

Change happens over time, setting the pace of a narrative with the ultimate goal of transformation. For an author to communicate a Why, a narrative must present a change via cause and effect utilizing any or all of the 5Ws. [3]

One can see from the model above, a change must contain a beginning, a middle, and an end state. Or put another way, a narrative must constitute a whole in order for a reader to be able to form an opinion of the 5Ws about a particular narrative.

The specifics of the 5Ws must exist on the macro and micro levels of a narrative to create a "continuant whole". On the macro level we can refer to it as the Story. On the micro level it is the unique particulars of Who, What, Why, When, and Where that manifest a Discourse.

So, if these particulars on a micro level do not pertain to the macro level themes of a narrative, then why do they matter? Conversely, if these particulars don't exist on

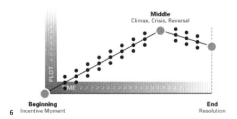

6 **Beginning**
Incentive Moment

Middle
Climax, Crisis, Reversal

End
Resolution

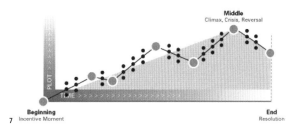

7 **Beginning**
Incentive Moment

Middle
Climax, Crisis, Reversal

End
Resolution

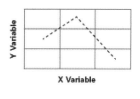

8

the macro level how will all the details on the micro level ever combine to constitute a whole greater than the sum of its parts. In short, narrative, the noun, is a very specific entity with a functional structure and a qualitative purpose that cannot be ignored. That purpose is authorial intent.

3. ON INTERACTIVITY

Every narrative is already interactive in the implicit sense. It is the reader's act of decoding the codified subject from the author. Each reader is an individual with his or her own identity, intellect, cultural background, life experience, opinions, and motivations. These things will bias their decoding process. Of course, this is not the type of interaction that is intended by the term Interactive Narrative where explicit interactivity—a user's detectable and actionable behavior within a system—is key.

There are various ideas about how much control to give the user yet, two things must be true: First, the user must be able to influence the narrative in such a way that its Discourse would otherwise not

exist without that user's explicit involvement. Second, the user must be in a position to make informed interactions. Arbitrary choice will not sustain conceptually relevant interaction.

Still, it is not enough for a system to mirror a user's actions. Reciprocal change is needed to create a truly interactive system. As the user modifies the system, the system should be learning about the user's behavior. In turn, the system should use that knowledge to influence the user's path within the Discourse, thereby influencing the user's perception of the narrative. The system must take this learned knowledge about the user and modify the Discourse in a manner that is thematically and functionally related to the Story. This mutable Discourse is an integral part of the narrative pace and will drive explicit interaction from the user. [4]

4. ON SYSTEMS

Though it is currently the most popular iteration of what an interactive narrative is, the multi-branching plot approach is problematic. Upon first glance, this methodol-

ogy seems to describe hierarchy, but when applied to the narrative form can only describe entropy. Progression is not analogous to transformation. These types of narratives are nothing new. They are no improvement of the choose your own adventure books. Instead of turning pages, a reader gets to click on links. Furthermore, there is no opportunity in this type of system for reciprocal change.

The narrative must have a balance between fixed and variable scenes in order to communicate authorial intent and allow for meaningful participation. Without this balance there is no pace, the result is narrative chaos. At least one of each of the following is needed. The Beginning, or Incentive moment—set's the premise of the Story and the user's role. The End, or Resolution, is the author's exit strategy. And the Middle, or transformative moment—which conceptually relates the beginning point to the end point.

So what is the balance between authorial intent and meaningful user participation? The German literary critic Gustav Freytag proposed a method of analyzing the rise and

9

9. "Interactive (N.)arrative"
A dynamic Discourse created
from a mutable sequence of
events occurring in a variable
place and time, experienced,
caused, and or recounted by
one or more variable agents,
representing a continuant
subject and constitute a whole,
communicated by one or more
variable narrators to one or
more participatory narratees.

fall of action within a narrative derived from Aristotle's concept of unity of action that came to be known as Freytag's Triangle. [5]

One can modify the diagram to make it more descriptive of a specific narrative. Doing so allows an author to strategize the macro level pace and plot points, while allowing for complex variability in between.

First, the end point should not be at the same plot level as the beginning point. This erroneously implies that no significant transformation has occurred other than the passing of time. A higher end point denotes a transformation resulting in a more positive end state than the beginning state. On the other hand, a lower point would denote a transformation resulting in a more negative state than the beginning state.

Secondly, the apex of the triangle that describes the Middle will not always fall directly in the center. By moving that point's placement to the left or the right, the diagram can begin to describe the pace of the Discourse over time. [6]

The modified Freytag diagram can be useful when planning Interactive (N.)arrative structures. Set plot points

combined with variability in the rising and falling action can produce multiple experiences of the same macro level constants.

The more complex a narrative grows, the more this pattern can replicate. If we look at a basic three-act play, this pattern will replicate three times, once for each act. It's amazing how a small amount of structure can support such a wide range of variability without turning into chaos.

But what can these black dots represent? The answer is any aspects of the Discourse: Events, Setting, Focalization, Duration, Representation, Sequence, etc...let your imagination run free, just make sure the choices are somehow relevant the Story. [7]

To achieve meaningful participation within a structured system an author must employ the use of small multiples. A small multiple is a singular algorithmic set of possibilities. A 3x3 grid can produce 27 possible experiences of three events. Yet, the author only has to write three events from three different points of view. [8]

The combination of many small multiple sets will create an unpredictable amount of possibilities. To construct a small multiple, the author must assign 2 variables: the X axis and the Y axis. These variables are any aspects of the Discourse, such as character, event, presentation medium, etc. This controlled randomness enables meaningful variation in the Discourse while still enabling an author to write in a constructive fashion.

5. ON EXPERIENCE

It is not enough for a user to interact by only clicking on a link. That has all the conceptual significance of turning a page. Textual links need to be procedural in nature. For example a link could time out, or appear, or draw attention to itself, all based on tracked user behavior.

The more visual Interactive Narrative systems become the more opportunity an author has to create the potential of a procedural Discourse. The user interface must be conceptually relevant to the narrative and allow for meaningful participation within the system. Systems of typography, color, shape, audio, spatial and temporal design become the procedural manifestations of user behavior. A cinematic vo-

cabulary can serve as a language for interactivity. A close up may mean that it is an opportunity to "jump" into that characters point of view. Or a wide panoramic shot may entice the user to investigate variable paths of a narrative.

Narrative immersion is increased by the transparency of technology. A physical environment of an installation can place the user in a metaphorical scene of the narrative. Every object in a room can become an interface. Using everyday objects rather than a mouse increases the user's ability to form a personal connection to a story via their sense of touch. The more senses that are engaged, the more a suspension of disbelief occurs.

Whether designing for the traditional computer screen or a large-scale installation the author must consider every detail of the experience; no decision should be arbitrary. Linking and non-linearity are old news. It is time to consider the procedural aspects of narrative visualization and presentation.

6. CONCLUSION. A HOLISTIC APPROACH

A holistic approach is needed to create Interactive (N.)arratives. The conceptual process must consider three aspects in conjunction: the Story (Database), the System (Software), and the Experience (Interface). The successful interplay of these three equal parts will result in a viable Interactive (N.)arrative system; a system that communicates authorial intent while allowing for meaningful, informed participation from a non-authoring user resulting in a dynamic and unique Discourse. The three aspects of Interactive (N.)arrative are cyclical; supporting, exploiting, and informing each other. If one link is weak, then the whole chain breaks. [9]

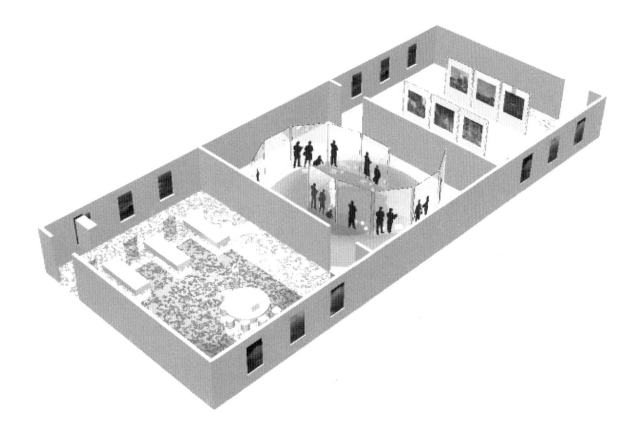

1

contact 911: a proposal for an interactive cinema documentary

This is a documentary that archives the personal accounts of 911 survivors from the World Trade Center in NYC. This narrative is focused on the minute and personal details of the survivor's experiences right before, during, and immediately after the attacks—not the disaster itself.

The installation is comprised of three rooms representing the beginning, middle, and end of the user's interaction with the narrative. The first room sets the user's emotional state by presenting large-scale photographs of the World Trade Center before the attacks. Since many people have never visited the WTC, this is an opportunity to witness the grandeur and the site's architecture within the context of bustling daily life it supported.

The second room is the heart of the narrative. A map of lower Manhattan is painted on the floor with a gradated bull's eye in the center of the room representing

ground zero. Radiating from the center of the room are two curvature sets of screen stations. Each set consists of five screens, or pods. Each pod will consist of three possible characters.

The users physical path through the main installation corresponds to the chronology of the narrative—the moments just before the planes hit, then the period between the crash and the building's collapse, then finally the chaotic hours that followed. The characters in the corresponding stations recount their experiences during these time intervals.

To activate the characters at each station the user picks up an object on the floor before the screen. The order and content of their dialog is dependant on which objects the user picks up, and in what order. This is a kaleidoscopic narrative with the virtual characters are speaking directly to the user. Now the user is placed within the narrative context as 1st person. This in itself creates a sense of immersion.

These objects, donated personal items from documented survivors, conceptually represent debris. Users form an emotional

and intellectual connection to the narrative via their own sense of touch.

INSTALLATION AS SYSTEM

Space as context

Create a space that is relevant to the subject of the narrative; put the user in a metaphorical location.

Space as narrative pace

Create a relationship between the user's movement in a space and the progression of the narrative.

Scale

The virtual characters are human scale. The user is psychologically in the company of characters, rather than just observing them.

Touch as immersion

Capitalize on a user's sense of touch to form a meaning connection to the narrative. The user is able to pick up an actual object from the narrative itself—a bridge between the virtual and physical worlds.

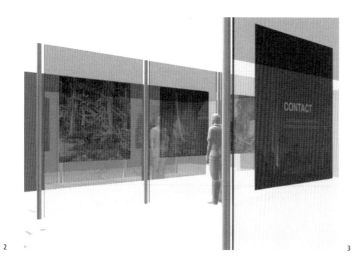

2

3

1. Installation model.

2 – 5. Each pod consists of 3 characters. There are a total of 3 Acts in the narrative: Before, During, and After. Each Act contains at least 3 scenes/3 sets of dialog.

5. The final room represents conclusion. Users take time to absorb their experience, speak with other users, and express their personal reactions at community computers.

6. "Dialog Matrix"
Possible combinations between characters A, B, and C as the story progresses.

4

5

	Act 1			Act 2			Act 3		
	Scene 1	Scene 2	Scene 3	Scene 1	Scene 2	Scene 3	Scene 1	Scene 2	Scene 3
A	A	A	A	A	A	A	A	A	A
A,B	A,B	A,B	A,B	A,B	A,B	A,B	A,B	A,B	A,B
A,C	A,C	A,C	A,C	A,C	A,C	A,C	A,C	A,C	A,C
B	B	B	B	B	B	B	B	B	B
B,C	B,C	B,C	B,C	B,C	B,C	B,C	B,C	B,C	B,C
C	C	C	C	C	C	C	C	C	C
A,B,C	A,B,C	A,B,C	A,B,C	A,B,C	A,B,C	A,B,C	A,B,C	A,B,C	A,B,C

6

hydroponica: an analogy for interactive narrative systems

The user enters the circular meditation chamber and is directed to sit by the only light illuminating from the screen highlighting the pillow seat before the interface. Before her is a rear projected blue grid of circles behind an empty vase. The only sound is the flow of water beneath the vase beckoning her to use the resting ladle. As the vase is filled, a digital plant flourishes upon the grid. Quickly growing with every pour, slowly dying with every pause. As the digital plant form interacts with its background music plays; beautiful in the rise and fall of the plant's life cycle.

Hydroponica is not a traditional screen based experience—the user is simply immersed and interacting freely in their environment—no wires, no suits, no mouse. The second point is the mechanism of input. Pouring water into a vase is not only an intuitive action, but is directly conceptu-

ally relevant to the systems output—a living plant. Hydroponica points to a future of creating situational context for a narrative.

Open switches running up the spine of the vase are closed when the conductive water allows electricity to flow. A simple piece of software running on a Basic Stamp converts the switches to numbers and feeds the data to a virtual Java Server running on the MAC G4 OSX. Macromedia Flash interfaces with the Java Server by opening an XML socket. Flash keeps track of whether the water level is rising or falling by simply comparing the current number to the previous one.

Each randomly generated bloom coming into contact with a circle triggers a random single note from a complete octave. By limiting the note database to a single octave I know that the dynamic composition will always work together, thus demonstrating the potential of a controlled random algorithm.

The resulting audio and visual representation is highly dynamic due to the varying layers of small controlled random multiples working together as a composed whole.

A delicate juxtaposition of control and chaos within a digital composition allows a participatory audience a unique experience with the object, while still maintaining my authorial intent.

The algorithm strategy for the project starts with the idea that an unpredictable and vast amount of randomness can be generated via the culmination of smaller semi-predictable units embedded within each other—small multiples.

Breakdown of the linear construction of a stem:

- Length = A random number between 1-250
- Curvature Angle = A random number between 1-3
- Curvature Length= Length divided by a random number between 1-4
- Bend Direction (L or R) = A random number between 1-2
- Bloom frequency = A random number between 1-300

A random number between 1 and 2 is hardly dynamic. A random number between 1

and 300 is not that impressive either, in a computational sense. But when these small units are combined, or wrapped up into each other the product is exponential variability. This is an important point allowing for the ability to author or compose a composition that is highly dynamic without total chaos. One of the greatest challenges currently in authoring Interactive Narratives is that the system cannot become so complex that the author cannot write all the threads of the story. This method of controlling randomness using small multiples is a strategy for dealing with the authorial process within unpredictable systems.

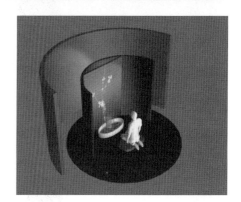

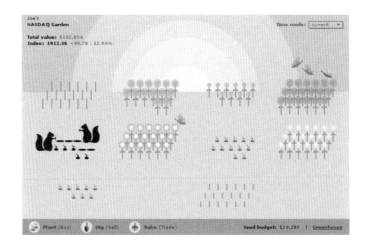

market garden: a narrative interface for portfolio management

The *Market Garden* is a dynamic visual interface for the average-joe stock trader. By using the "storyphor" of a garden—plant growth, death, pollination, bright sky, cloudy sky, the functions of plant (buy), dig (sell), and rake (trade)—a user can digest the complex information of a stock portfolio without losing the necessary detailed information.

The sky serves as the macro-level scene or stage for the action; it represents the NASDAQ average. As that average becomes higher the sky is bright and sunny, correspondingly as the average drops the sky becomes gray and cloudy.

The stock beds work in a similar fashion with the exception that the data comparison happens between the purchase price and the current value of the stock.

The purchase price is represented as a seed. The stages of the stock's profit correspond to the growth steps of the flow-

erbed—from stem to bloom to butterflies. Equally, the stock's loss matches up with the death cycle—from dead seed to hole in the ground to hungry squirrels. The tasks that one would perform are conceptually integrated into the scene—to buy is to plant, to sell is to dig up the bed, and to trade one stock to another is to rake by dragging and dropping. When a user rolls over a particular bed an info card designed to look like a plant ID spike offers the most needed detail information with the option to click for more specifics. The Greenhouse would be the administration page where a user could manage the details of their inventory or portfolio.

Though this system has a narrative quality, it is not an Interactive Narrative. An underlying plot (the life cycle of a garden) is not enough, even if one can argue that it constitutes a whole. A cliché cannot invoke an intellectual and emotional discourse between the reader and the text in a deeply meaningful and personal manner.

The individual characters (the plant beds/stock beds) have almost nothing to do with each other except for the fact that

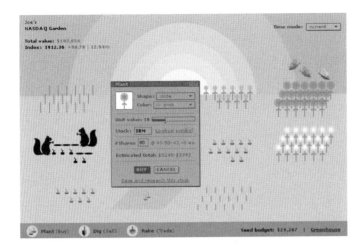
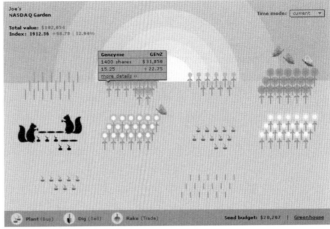

they are all flowers or stocks in a state of flux. Personification is absent and therefore transformation is not possible. There is no protagonist or antagonist and therefore there is no series of cause and effect relationships uniting the separate characters together.

The middle must be the apex or climatic point in a narrative, not the temporal eventuality between a random beginning and end. The *MarketGarden's* movement through time is entropic not transformative. Finally, this system, from an algorithmic point of view, is a successful application of small multiples but they haven't been applied to the qualitative aspects of a narrative—they merely represent disparate units of numerical data. The flowers are nothing more than a stylization of a traditional chart over time.

a journey through india: designing the interactive documentary

HEATHER SHAW

Class of 2003

Certain experiences in life inspire us to try new things leading us towards a path of uncertainties. The introduction to my documentary mentions my first experience in India: stepping off the plane, the smells, sights, a complete sensory overload from being dropped in an unfamiliar place. It was this journey that inspired me to apply to graduate school. Although I had been pondering it for some time, the trip sealed it, and when I returned home I applied to MassArt. What inspired me to return to school brought me full circle; now my case study has become the focus of that journey.

When I originally arrived at MassArt I had grand plans of traveling back to India to build an interactive documentary, comparing the life of a girl in India to the life of a girl in America. This project was far too ambitious to undertake, as I had barely scratched the surface in my research at that point. Fortunately I waited, researched, and realized that this effort would have ended in futility. I would have ended up shooting the content and trying to retro-fit it to an interface later.

However, the concept of developing an interactive documentary about India was still compelling. I couldn't think of a better case study to take advantage of an interactive environment. I had resources at my fingertips and a wealth of information; I had already done my "research" about India two years prior when I lived and worked there for three months. My instincts regarded India as the perfect case study to create a "synaethesic" experience. Furthermore, I didn't have any video content. This was strangely liberating as it forced me to be more resourceful with my approach. New ideas in the approach to interactive documentary began to flow.

A JOURNEY THROUGH INDIA

After much research into film theory, semiotics, documentary, and interactive narrative, *A Journey Through India* became the focus of my thesis topic. At this point in my experience I came to some clear decisions before designing my thesis case study:
- I am the author of this piece
- It will have a single point of view

- the journey is finite
- the journey has a critical path

Conceptual Development

Some of my initial brainstorming included a desire to create a total experience for someone, beyond video, beyond photographs, beyond my own stories. I wanted there to be enough room for discovery; without creating a scavenger hunt for information. I knew that I wanted to include artifacts from the trip as part of my documentary, but whether they were tangible or in the digital domain was undecided. I liked the concept of having things emerge from the shadows when rolled over, but had no basis for this approach yet. How could the richness of such an experience be represented visually and interactively?

I wanted my interface to behave like India. Moderately confusing. We expect timelines and maps from seeing previous online documentaries—practical information about a topic. However, India is anything but practical. Time is meaningless, and you can't count on anything happening

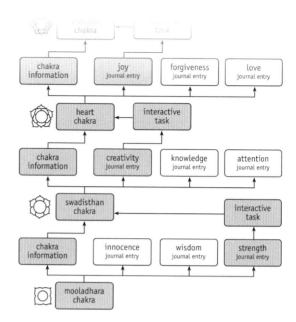

1

2

when it is supposed to. I wanted to eliminate the aspect of time as a part of mapping the journey; however I didn't want to create a situation that forces the viewer to grope through darkness and confusion. More like a sense of surprise around every corner—perhaps some unknowns, but through these unknowns come discovery of new things.

I chose the concept of metamorphosis—there are two kinds, the physical (external) and the internal. There were some physical changes during my trip: I colored my hair, and pierced my nose. However, it is the internal metamorphosis that I found most compelling to try and communicate via interactivity. The internal metamorphosis is not so easily captured via video (which is good, seeing as I didn't have any to work with) and I wanted to convey an experience that cannot so easily be represented via photography; such as memories, learning, and personal reflection.

Content Architecture

After choosing this as my concept I needed to develop an approach for guiding the viewer through the content. My first thoughts to use a timeline, map, or chart were all practical means for approaching this topic, however, none of these things fit my desire to have the interface behave like India. In order to map out the journey, it needed to have a more subtle approach. Something that transcended time, place and space. This thinking lead me towards developing the critical path based on the subtle system. Eastern cultures have long understood the body's physical and mental connection via the body's seven chakras. They are represented throughout the nervous system as bundles of nerves and are believed to govern the overall health of the body and mind. Each of the chakras have aspects related to them that exist in the self, such as innocence, creativity, and joy. I couldn't have chosen better words for describing this journey. Using the seven chakras as my basis for navigation was the best metaphor for guiding my viewer through the journey; and my hope was that the viewer would experience the internal metamorphosis for themselves by learning about the seven chakras. How do I subtly invite someone to experience my journey via the seven as-

pects? How do I use it creatively as a basis for navigation?

Eastern cultures believe that enlightenment is achieved via a vertical path, starting at the base of the spine and moving through the chakras in an upward direction. I based my site architecture on this concept; thus the reason why the documentary has a critical path, and why the interface slowly guides the user forward. This concept needed some explanation, as many viewers may be unfamiliar with the chakras and their symbolic meaning. Knowing this, I needed to incorporate an additional element to the documentary: the explanation about the chakras. There also needed to be a point of view. In addition, how could I make the interface "behave" like India? Based on all these challenges, *A Journey Through India* became a 3-tiered concept:

1. The story (or "video" components) is based on journal entries.
2. The viewer needed to learn about the chakras.
3. There needed to be the element of "experiencing" each chakra's aspects (ie. joy, creativity, etc.)

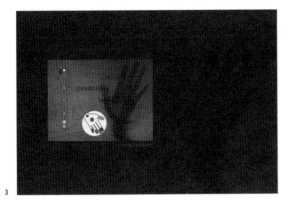

3

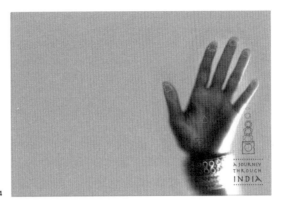

4

1. Chakra chart
2. Site Architecture for "A Journey through India"
3. Animated introduction explaining the chakras
4. Digital hand holding the charkas; the chakras location on the hands corresponds to their location on the spinal column.
5. Chakra "introduces" itself by its main aspect.
6. On rollover, the chakra reveals a more "tangible" aspect of itself.

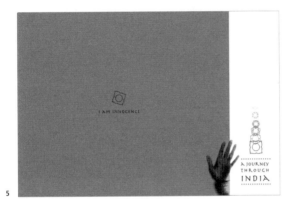

5

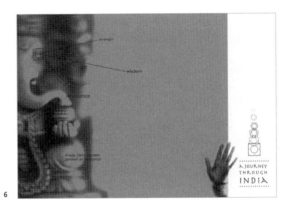

6

Journal Entries

The journal entries were critical in the "telling" of my experiences in India. Basing the story content on journal entries works well because each entry is a small story unto itself. I didn't have to worry about their sequence, nor did I have to "thread" together an elaborate plot in an effort towards creating a coherent narrative. This supports the fact that from the very beginning I was disinterested in writing multi-threaded narratives and gaming-like plot structures. The journals allow me to tell a series of stories, that when viewed under the umbrella of the interface, provides the viewer with the overall tone and personality of my experience. These are told in first person, with voiceover and accompanying footage.

Chakra Information

It is imperative that the viewer is made aware of the significance of the chakras and their relationship to the interface, as it is not a metaphor that will be easily recognized by most. Moreover, the chakra is the "key" to moving forward in the interface.

Once the viewer has navigated into a section about a chakra, they are then guided onto the next section. (This will be explained visually in "Interface Design.")

Experiencing the Aspects

Originally called "interactive tasks" this part of the interface allows the viewer: to rollover and change artwork on walls, move through a symphonic landscape, and essentially, experience the aspects of the chakras. The goal is to present aspects such as creativity, joy or enlightenment in the interactive environment. How does one experience "creativity?" Or "silent joy?" These sections invite the viewer to "experience" these aspects; and this is the moment of integration between the physical journey (photos, journal entries, objects) versus the metaphysical journey (the charkas and spirituality).

Interface Design

The interface needed to be clean and simple, while pushing the design as far away from interface conventions as possible. My

goal was to achieve a balance between the slick commercialism of a professionally designed website versus the clumsiness of a prototype. Moreover, I didn't want the interface to merely be based on clicking in viewing; I wanted to give the viewer the option of more experiences, and deciding when and where these concepts would be presented.

First, I needed to introduce the chakras and give a brief overview of what they are. A one-minute introductory animation drops the viewer immediately into one of my journal entries, and briefly explains the chakras and the aspects. This gives the viewer enough information to know what the symbols represent and their metaphor for the navigation. [3]

Second, the interface then opens up with the navigation. The chakras reside on the spinal column, but they also correspond to locations on the hands and feet. I choose to use the hands to "hold" the chakras because it further abstracted the concept (rather than using a full-body chakra chart). Moreover, India is full of handicrafts; many of the objects in the

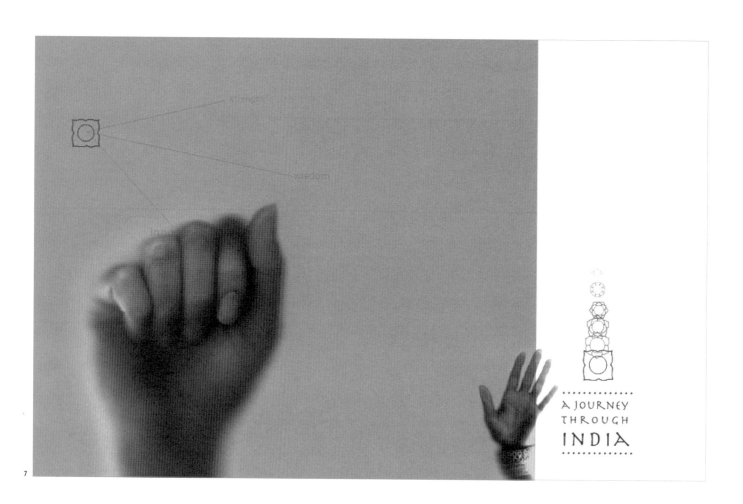

A JOURNEY
THROUGH
INDIA

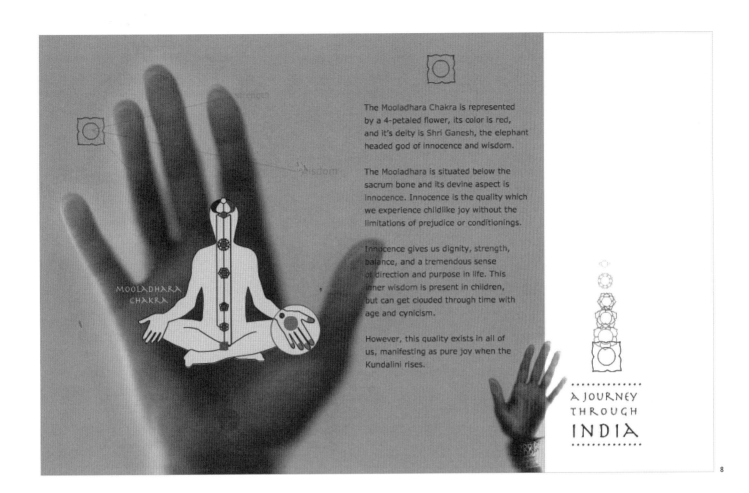

The Mooladhara Chakra is represented by a 4-petaled flower, its color is red, and it's deity is Shri Ganesh, the elephant headed god of innocence and wisdom.

The Mooladhara is situated below the sacrum bone and its devine aspect is innocence. Innocence is the quality which we experience childlike joy without the limitations of prejudice or conditionings.

Innocence gives us dignity, strength, balance, and a tremendous sense of direction and purpose in life. This inner wisdom is present in children, but can get clouded through time with age and cynicism.

However, this quality exists in all of us, manifesting as pure joy when the Kundalini rises.

MOOLADHARA
CHAKRA

A JOURNEY
THROUGH
INDIA

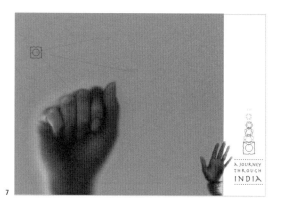

7

8

7,8. Before and after shots of viewer rolling into the hand; the longer the viewer stays on the hand, the more information they receive about that chakra.

9,10. Additional screens for different charkas.

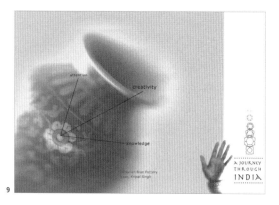

9

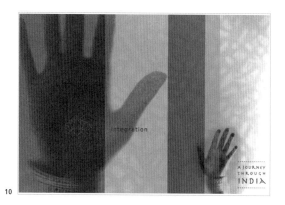

10

interface design are hand-made items, everything you touch in India has that aspect of being hand-made. I also thought it was interesting that we use our hands to navigate the interface, so in essence that also combines the aspect of the physical hand to the hand in the digital domain.

Or is it the metaphysical domain? This is up for interpretation.

When the viewer first arrives at the homepage, only one chakra is in color and is "active." (the mooladhara) The longer the viewer interacts with the interface, more chakras will become "illuminated." It's a step-by-step process, whereby the viewer needs to view each chakra in specific order as determined by the site architecture.

When the viewer rolls over the chakras, they spin in a clockwise motion. This behavior supports the concept that chakra translated means "wheel" (stated during the introduction) and it is believed that when the chakras are clear they spin in a clockwise motion. Though this detail may not be easily recognizable to the viewer, these behaviors instil characteristics of

eastern thought even on the most subtle level. Once the viewer clicks a chakra on the hand, the chakra then "introduces" its main aspect via animation, and moves to another part of the screen, while its aspects grow out from its center. [5, 6]

At this point in the interface the viewer now has four distinct choices: to click on one of the three aspects to view journal entries (one will have an "experience" attached to it) or to click on the chakra itself. When rolled-over, the aspects reveal a small "clip" of their journal entry. Again, these clips have the appearance of emerging from the shadows, a slight hesitation towards giving too much information too quickly. When the viewer rolls-over the chakra, the chakra reveals a more "tangible" object that relates to its main aspect. These rollovers tie into my initial concept of having the interface slowly "reveal" things. [4]

If the viewer clicks on an aspect, they will then be met with a video. This video could potentially link to an "experience" section afterwards. This is dependent on the aspect and ease of translation to inter-

activity. If the viewer clicks on the chakra, a hand will emerge. When the viewer rolls over the hand, it opens, revealing specific information about the chakra. The longer the viewer hovers over the hand, the more information the viewers receive. This area clearly defines's the chakra's location on the body and its relationship to the hand (reaffirming the navigation's purpose) and provides contextual information. The text grows from the bottom, moving in an upward direction, again subtly reaffirming that the path is always upwards.

Once the viewer is complete with learning about a chakra, s/he can click on the smaller hand to get back to the main navigation. The viewer can always click on the smaller hand to get back to the main navigation, but it is only after s/he have visited the information about the chakra that the interface will "illuminate" the next chakra on the hand. All the chakras follow a similar pattern, but obviously with different journal entries, unique interactive experiences, and each has information specific to the chakra.

CONCLUSION

Summary

This research introduces *A Journey Through India*, a new approach to the interactive documentary. This work explores new ways of delivering documentary for interactive environments, by presenting the journey via both physical and metaphysical concepts. *A Journey Through India* allows the viewer to access content via three ways: journal entries, contextual information about the chakras, and a way to connect the physical journey with the spiritual journey via interactive explorations.

Contribution

A Journey Through India approaches interactive documentary from the point of view of the designer as author. Each interactive documentary must be handled on a case-by-case basis, as the design and behaviors of the interface should be driven by content. This body of work refutes an "all-in-one" formula for approaching interactive documentary, and supports the need for distinct authorship.

This work proposes that the viewer does not need to "change the story" to necessarily create an interactive or immersive narrative; that the content itself and the delivery of that content is key towards creating narrative immersion. Documentary content is driven specifically by the author's ability to present a concept and/or idea, and it is the author's responsibility towards the "telling" of that story. Documentaries are created with specific intent and that intent should always remain in the hands of the author, not the viewer, and be clearly defined by the interactive experience.

A Journey Through India approaches narrative content in small "chunks" versus developing a larger, more fluid narrative. This allows to viewer to experience the breadth and depth of information being presented; such as the interface behaviors, and more specific contextual information, rather than focusing on a distinct story path and fluidity. It is through creative use of interactivity, such as intertwining the behaviors of the interface with the content itself, that makes the documentary all the more immersive.

The narrative for *A Journey Through India* is based on discreet journal entries, allowing for more flexibility in my interface design. The narrative is only part of the journey; eliminating the need for a fluid narrative allowed me to focus on interface behaviors and explore deeper concepts in interactivity; such as "experience creativity." My research in semiotics supports the fact that it is the underlying units that make up the whole. Structuralists believe that humankind uses "structuring principal to understand cultural phenomena."[1] I feel this approach provides the viewer the overall tone and immersion of my experience, without having to build a multi-threaded narrative structure.

Lastly, the beauty of the interactive documentary lies within its attention to detail. The chakras' spinning in a clockwise direction when rolled over, the artifacts slowly emerging from the background, the hand opening to reveal information—these details are all about the author's overall intimacy with the content and intent when presenting the information. All these elements add to the richness of the experience and packaging of the content.

Future Developments

I feel that having video content for the journal entries would strengthen the overall quality of *A Journey Through India*. Although not having video content was liberating at first, now that I have a better understanding towards this approach the production value of the piece would benefit greatly by having better quality journal entries with professional editing and writing. The designer as author does not eliminate the need for collaboration with field professionals, such as a camera crew and writers/editors.

Furthermore, there has been some interest from a yoga group in Boston towards developing this interface as a presentation tool for holistic health fairs and conferences. Although *A Journey Through India* is specifically a documentary and not a teaching tool, the interface has a unique and understated approach towards explaining abstract concepts in eastern thought to a broader audience, and allows for viewers to "experience" such concepts as the chakras'

aspects for themselves. I will need to work in conjunction with a developer to iron out technical details with the interface. However, this may be my ticket back to India to get some "real" footage.

Closing Remarks

A friend of mine described India in such a way that "you have to let India happen to you." My hope is that the same is true for this documentary. It requires patience while the chakra introduces itself, and things take time to reveal themselves. It behaves like India. There are two kinds of time; real time, and "Indian time" (add 3 hours to "real time") India is not a place to be mapped out with practicality and precision; it is a place to wander, experience, to lose yourself and find yourself at the same time. It is a world of gray areas. This interface is not about presenting information pertaining to a trip concisely and efficiently, but rather to express that information—the sights, sounds, the synaethesia I sought to create.

1. Dr. Mary Klages, *Structuralism and Saussure*, 2001 p48. www.colorado.edu/English2012Klages/saussure.html

experience of place: an investigation of digital soundscape

LEILA MITCHELL

Class of 2003

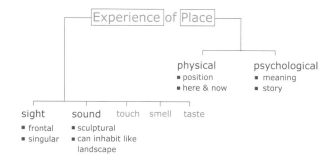

1

1. Experience involves our body through a multi-sense process. Place is described through both physical and psychological qualities.

2. Through listening, sound perceptions are linked to spatial perceptions.

3. Qualities of an experience attaches meaning to a place and through cognition allows us to orient ourselves and connect with our environment.

"The spaces through which we go daily are provided for by locations, their nature is grounded in things of the type of buildings. If we pay heed to these relations between locations and spaces, between spaces and space, we get a clue to help us in thinking of the relation of man and space."

— Martin Heidegger

EXPERIENCE, PLACE, AND PERCEPTION

I do not consider myself a visual designer, but rather a spatial or environment designer. As such I have approached this thesis through the eye of an architect. I believe architecture is, and has always been, concerned with man and his relationship with space. Once we build in space we create a container, transforming space to a space. Because we embody architecture, there is an inherent personal relationship between our physical body and this space. We become aware of the specific characteristics of this space by means of a multi-sense experience, and the boundary between ourselves and the space is softened. We acknowledge the space's attributes and identify with it as a place. The definition of place answers the question "Where am I?" The physical qualities of the form are a tangible position, the here and now. The psychological qualities explain the story of the place: "What happens here?" [1]

Historically, representations of architectural spaces have materialized using mostly visual media. These have developed into accepted, practical forms such as the plan, section, and perspective. However, these only consider the space two-dimensionally, utilizing only a singular sense. Looking at these representations does not approach anywhere near the three dimensional, multi-sense experience of architecture. The viewer is left to draw only from his personal experiences to reconstruct the form. While sight is frontal in nature, sound is sculptural with dimensions, texture, and density. The perception of a sound is determined through listening modes: causal reduced, semantic, and referential. (Sonnenschein, David. *Sound Design: The Expressive Power of Music, Voice and Sound Effects in Cinema*) A physical space and psychological space is perceived from these modes. Using a bell tolling for example, the causal mode understands that there is a metallic object making this sound. The reduced mode describes the sound as slow in speed with a long reverb. The semantic mode attaches the meaning of "death" and the referential mode links the act of mourning. [2]

Much like the experience of walking through architecture, sound is like entering a landscape with all your body instead of with just your eyes. When we listen to the sound, we perceive both physical and psychological qualities of that landscape. Once we qualify this space, we can link it to a meaning of place. When we comprehend where we are, we draw connections to a larger group or event. As such, architecture acts as a link between man and his environment and man and his community. Therefore, the

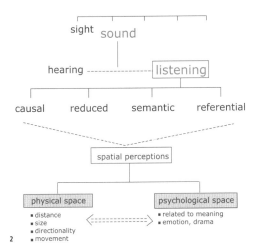

2

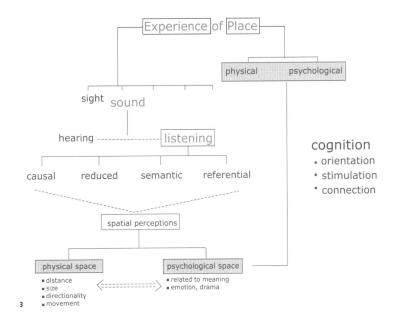

3

addition of sound as a second element, can significantly enhance the representation of the experience of a place. [3]

APPLICATION: THE VIRTUAL CITY

At the start of this case study, I was very interested in creating a project that allowed the visitor to explore a space they did not currently embody. A significant space would allow the visitor to attach meaning onto this place through a personal connection. The spatial content and context are represented metaphorically with dynamic visuals and sounds. In order to create an appropriate vocabulary of sound and visuals, a collaborative team of visual, sound, and spatial designers is needed. The success of such a virtual space would take the visitor beyond the two-dimensional screen, suggesting a three dimensional, multi-modal experience in which the visitor can identify. Not simply as voyeur—but voyager.

The city has been represented many ways as visual interface. Space and information may be organized similar to an urban design where there are meeting halls, shopping centers, schools, and personal "rooms." However, the experience of the city is lost when only an exact visual representation is applied. The Place, which encompasses physical and psychological spatial relationships, is absent. With creatively designed visual and sound associations, the visitor can fully explore such digitally presented spaces. This leads to successful navigation, uninhibited movement, discovery of narratives, and builds a sense of community within this virtual realm.

The main case study centered on Charlestown, Massachusetts, a small town just outside of Boston with distinctive and definable spaces. Residential areas have a lower traffic volume and more children's vocals. The religious district has a distinct pattern of bells every hour with long reverb. The Town Center is bustling and chaotic. The interactivity of this city as interface is prime for adding a sonic component to visuals for referencing the physical and narrative characteristics of each area.

The Virtual City: Phase I

Phase I concentrated on a schematic study and visual representations of the spaces. I walked the physical paths of the actual spaces and divided them into distinct sections. The user would need to look at these as a whole before choosing to enter into a specific area. An aerial view of Charlestown seemed a logical beginning as a visual. The spaces were rendered as three-dimensional illustrations and together with interactive functions and variety of audio behaviors, the user establishes an understanding of the quality of each area. Each neighborhood had a distinct sonic rhythm, which was heard on a rollover as it was visually highlighted. If pressed, small movie clips, scrolling text, and stills will act as signposts to specific points in the area. At the same time, another sonic element, distinctive of that space, enters as another audio layer. For example, a rollover of the Navy Yard area plays a slow, mellow tune. As the user presses that area, a video of The Constitution navy ship, scrolling text, and a ship's bell became part of the description. [4]

4

5

6

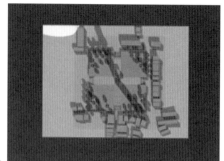

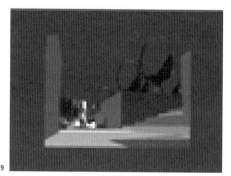

7

8

9

In narrowing down the details for study, a specific progression to the Bunker Hill Monument was rendered. The specific path flies the viewer into the Monument section. Meta sounds, which are sounds non-descriptive of the space, but gives the user additional information such as motion, are added for the transition between spaces. The visitor moves through the small residential streets and up the hill to the Bunker Hill Monument—a prominent landmark of Charlestown. Looking down a quiet street, a seductive dark video plays while a lonely sax fills the sound space. The visitor continues up onto the Monument park and up into the monument, ending with a view down where they once were. [5 – 11]

The Virtual City: Phase II

Due to my lack of music and sound design skills, the sonic qualities in Phase I suffered. It was essential to consult with sound designers in Phase II and add their expertise to the project team. I was fortunate enough to have the opportunity to work with Neil Leonard at Berklee College of Music as a Teaching Assistant in his Interactive Multimedia class. The first project of the semester was making an interactive sound mixer using Macromedia Flash sound technology. I was able to familiarize myself with the five students and assess their musical and technical strengths. I introduced the *Virtual City* project as a group project, a first for most of them. We invited Chris Hegstrom of Stormfront Studios and a Berklee alumni, to give a talk about his experience working as a sound designer on video games such as *The Lord of the Rings*. He was given an

overview of the project and during an early project meeting, was a positive spark to get the team rolling.

I presented our situation as a simulation of a condition they will most likely encounter in the professional field as Music Synthesis majors.

"The *Virtual City* is an interface for a kiosk that sits in an exhibit at the top of the Hancock building in downtown Boston. Through this interactive kiosk, visitors may explore Charlestown and hopefully be encouraged to go there physically. A prototype will be developed to show potential buyers."

The Phase I prototype was presented, a schedule was set and an outline sketch of the project specs were given. Students were encouraged to voice critique as their involvement influenced the project direction. Collaboration with other team members was followed through weekly critiques, group meetings, and a project website. The project team consisted of 1. a project manager: introduces project scope, oversees direction and production of entire project, 2. visual designer: creates initial sketches and continues to develop visual imagery, 3. sound director: oversees the sound design team, 4. sound designers: develop music and sound effects and 5. programmer: implements technical requirements during production

The team followed a skeleton structure that borrowed from cinematic and game design techniques, as well as Phase I. Each section of Charlestown is like a world in game design and can be referred to as a "Field." Each Level is like a scene in a movie.

The visitor will interactively choose the Field and Level through mouse roll-overs and clicks. With this tool (the mouse or

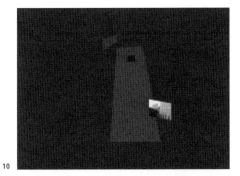

10

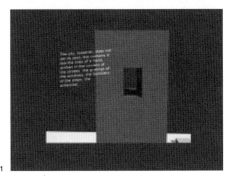

11

Field 2: Navy Yard

Field Sound	slow rhythm, reflective, low pitch, calming	
Level 1	loud muffled voices, historical navy, slow wind, large area, reverb	
Level 2	deep boat horns, metal poles , clinking rhythm, chaotic dialogue, center of Navy Yard , pan around, barracks close by.	
Level 3	On Constitution, tour guide telling specific story, wooden creaks, lapping water, hollow sounds of beneath ship.	

12

4. On a press of the Navy Yard section, the highlight area is darkened, scrolling text, video, and audio is changed.

5–11. The progression from the initial aerial view of the interface, into the Bunker Hill Monument area, and ultimately in the Monument allows the user to explore different aspects of the space through visual and sonic representation of this place.

12. The Navy Yard Field and Level descriptions given to the sound design team as a skeleton structure in which to build soundscapes.

13. Soundmap of Town Center. Prominent elements are denseness, major traffic and pedestrian noise, contained central area with narrow roads.

14. Diagram of sound sequence for two different fields, the Navy Yard and Town Center. Music composition began the sequence at the top level and changes mostly to sound effects at the bottom level when a visitor is inside a building or on a ship.

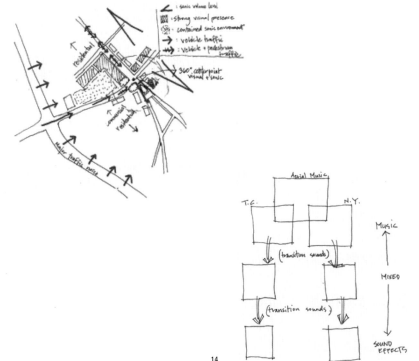

13

14

 15

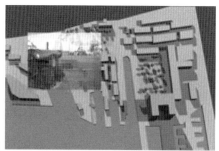 16

 17

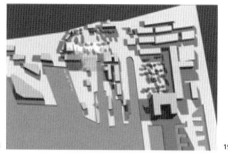 18

 19

 20

 21

 22

 23

 24

 25

 26

 27

 28

 29

30

31

32

33

15–33. Screen shots through the Navy Yard Field and its three levels.

15. On a rollover aerial music volume is lowered while snare drums are highlighted.

16–20. Fly through transition begins with meta-sounds, Navy Yard music and images of the space.

21. Transition from illustration to photographic image informs visitor that he has entered Level 1.

22. Transition sound layer stops and Level 1 music loop begins with the Navy Yard rhythm. Options available on Level 1 include video and voiceovers telling stories about the space.

26. Pathway to progress is clicked and transition to Level 2 begins again as a 3-dimensional fly-through. Level 1 music loop stops and familiar transitional sound begins again.

30. Illustration becomes photo again, on entrance of Level 2.

31. Level 2 audio loop begins, a mixture of the Navy Yard score and sound effects. This level adds a panoramic interaction together with the video voiceover options.

32. Pathway leads into Level 3.

33. Level 3 audio loop begins, a mostly sound effects (creaking of ship, sea-gulls, water lapping) with slight rhythm. Same interaction options available.

touch screen) the visitor can probe into each Field or Level by hearing the soundscape and seeing visuals, before committing with a click. Once the visitor has entered into a Field and onto Level 1, the sounds and visuals are more focused toward that Field. Clicking on different objects within Level 1 will move the visitor deeper and into Level 2, while the sounds become more specific.

Initial drafts of Field and Level descriptions were summarized for the sound designers to visualize the aural landscape. Four fields were chosen with three levels in each. Each level gets deeper into that field, and places the user at a closer relationship to her surroundings. The four distinct neighborhoods were Town Center, Navy Yard [6], Residential, and Residential 2.

Neil Leonard, the sound director, prepared an initial spec outline for sound composition and application.

1. Intro music should provide a dramatic transition to the new location. This music uses a full orchestral palette and is not primarily sample loop based.
2. Background music should set the dramatic tone. It can be sample loop based provided that it stands alone in aesthetic terms.
3. Aspects of musical components to be decided were
– Duration
– Instrumentation
– Tonalit—key, scales, progression
– Melody—vertical melody (outlines harmony), horizonal melody (does not outline harmony and is colored by harmonic change)
– Tempo—metronome setting(s), accel., ritard, a-tempo, more than one simultaneous tempo
– Meter—singular, multi, a-metric
– Dynamics
4. Aspects of sound effect components to be decided were
– Number of sounds
– Duration of each clip
– Instruments and software used
– Dramatic effect of each sound
– Original sound sources

The Virtual City: Phase III

Once the project scope was established the team was able to develop and clarify the visual and sonic structure. The visual designer brought in reworked drafts, while the sound designers began to do field studies of the space and launch a composition direction. Within two weeks we recognized our short time schedule and chose to reduce the prototype options.

The new plan concentrated efforts on two distinct fields for the prototype with three active levels. Teams of two worked on each section, while the fifth designer was responsible for the overall aerial and meta-sounds. This needed to be done at the start, as the other fields were derivatives of these initial compositions. The two distinct fields chosen were the Navy Yard and the Town Center. More specific sound maps were produced for these areas. [13]

The third and final phase of the prototype, allows the visitor to move through two neighborhoods of Charlestown with the sonic sequence flowing from an overall music composition to specific

34

35

36

37

38

39

40

41

42

34–42. Various screen shots from the Town Center Field.

34. Initial Town Center Field entrance.

35. Transitional fly-through with meta-sound to Level 1.

36. Level 1 is at street level with composed Town Center music.

38. Transitional to Level 2.

40. Level 2 is in the middle of the town square with pan- oramic and video interaction. Audio is a mixture of music and sound effects such as car engines, people talking, horns.

41. Level 3 is inside the Bank building.

42. Level 3 stops within a hallway. Audio is mostly sound effects of inside space, foot- steps on wooden floor, people talking, doors closing.

sound effects. Meta-sounds were also created for clicks, rollovers, and transitions between levels. The sound element design process was closely linked to the visuals in order for the production to run smoothly. For instance, the length of the transitional sound exactly matches the visual fly-thru from level 1 to level 2.

An overall musical composition was developed that in our (project team's) artistic view represented Charlestown. (We also discussed the audience for this piece and decided to gear the music toward young adults, persuading them to visit Charlestown). Although developed by two different groups, the Navy Yard's music was not that dissimilar to the Town Center's because both derived their qualities from the overall aerial composition. As a visitor travels into a field to the first level, the transition is linear and does not allow the visitor to interactive with these in-betweens. Instead, the visuals and sound carry the visitor through a three-dimensional rendering of the space. The first level is apparently reached when the illustrated 3-D space is transformed into a photographic representation of space and the transitional meta-sound is no longer on the audio layer. While on the first level, an audio loop is played, composed mainly of a musical score specific to that field. Interactively, there are additional information opportunities such as voiceover stories from previous visitors, video, and a path to the next level. This same process continues through the next two layers, allowing the visuals and sound to become more specific. The soundscape in the second level is a mix of the scored music and sound effects, while the last level of the sequence is mostly sound effects with an underlying element left over from the original field music. The visuals on the second level add panoramic interactivity and the third level ends within a building or on a ship. It is difficult to discuss sound through text or just the static visual layers. The prototype is understood through interaction, however, screen shots of the Navy yard progression and a few Town Center views are shown.

CONCLUSION

A number of architects have brought their theory and practice into the virtual realm, resulting in substantial experiments in building within this space. There have not been many who have approached their design through both a visual and aural language. A collaborative approach with a triad made of spatial, visual, and sound designers can be quite influential in the field of interactive multimedia. Each should have equal say in the project and its direction. Currently, these types of projects usually flesh out most of the visuals and then have the sound designers create music after conceptual and pre-production phases are over. A project manger, or architect, should oversee the direction of the project and have the ability to comprehend aesthetics and technology behind the visual and sonic aspects.

An approach to experience design should include sound as a distinct descriptor of place both physically and psychologically. While there have been interactive projects using multimodes for a fuller experience, the methods for sound selection are varied. I propose to initiate a method that explores the sound object and its parameters within the intended environment. This is similar to R. Murray Schafer's approach of investigating and implementing soundscapes.

My hope is that the initial development of these experiments and discussion may provide encouragement and motivation for those interested in continuing the journey. Don't simply continue to pass through spaces, but stop every now and then and reflect on your own experiences of place. Take note of the visual and sonic characteristics that describe both the physical nature of the place and the story of that place.

the articulation of visual experiences through algorithm

CARLOS LUNETTA

Class of 2005

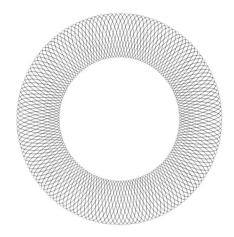

"Every work of art is the child of its age...Each period of culture produces an art of its own which can never be repeated."

— Wassily Kandinsky

New media design, as the name says, is really new. While cinema, another young form of expression, was created more than a hundred years ago, computers have been around as a medium for only a decade. The fast bloom of this newborn communication channel has caught designers in a landslide; there was a sudden, huge demand for visual and interactive solutions using the new dimensions opened by technology. Motion, form, color, sound and interaction were available to the designer, being intermediated by user-friendly software packages.

The computer became the tool and object of design; a new relationship between designer and machine was born. The territory of this relationship is one of the beacons of my thesis work—designers in the past were never really intimate with the conceptual framework of computing. The core computing process was always a mystery reserved for scientists and engineers. This lack of technical intimacy created an invisible wall and a relation of dependency with canned features offered by commercial software solutions.

The Articulation of Visual Experiences through Algorithm proposes an initial climb on the invisible wall. The true creative freedom with the computational medium can be achieved only when the designer knows the medium, is intimate with its concepts and aware of its framework. The true challenge of the new media designer is to absorb new types of knowledge, and at the same time retain his identity as a visual communicator.

The initial move toward the computational knowledge is to understand the conceptual ideas that rule a machine. Computation is about change; the personal computer is a highly evolved calculator, performing billions of arithmetical and logical operations per second. The processor works by getting certain inputs, performing calculations and outputting them—data is constantly being chopped to small instructions, calculated and rebuilt.

Let's use a keyboard, for example: The physical keystroke is converted to a binary signal. That signal is processed and converted to a visual output—the graphical representation of the key—that is displayed on screen. The core of this computational process is the translation that converts certain inputs to different outputs.

The creative use of computation takes advantage of the nature of data processing in favor of design. There are situations where traditional design meets the limits of human labor; a computer can address a greater scale extremes than can human hands in artistic creation, dealing with the extremely large, the extremely small, the incredibly precise, so on and so forth. There are also ideas that cannot be easily drawn or represented statically; motion and interaction may be part of the initial concept of a design project. These ideas require the employment of new media capabilities that exist through computation.

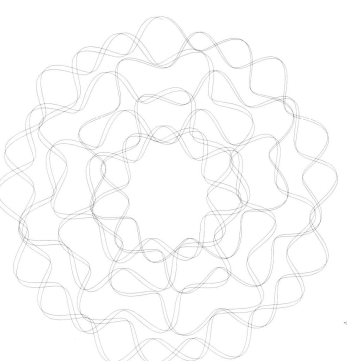

Some of the core computational concepts are:
– Transformation: as stated above, the main concept of computation is to transform data.
– Repetition: a processing instruction can repeat itself eternally, as long as its physical part works. An element can repeat itself over time or over space—the replication is lossless.
– Randomness: true randomness comes from nature, in events like radioactive decay. Computer systems feature pseudo-random numbers, a formula that produces no repetition, smooth numeric distribution, and more important: the lack of predictability.
– Precision: computer processing elements can be extremely exact and precise when necessary.
– Predictability: once a set of rules is created, the code behaves accordingly. Just like the physical world is attached to the laws of physics, a program can be attached to a set of unbreakable laws that will be always obeyed.
– Discretion: program elements can be discrete; events can be triggered by any kind of input rather than linear time. This is the key of interaction.
– Complexity: computation can achieve and display unbearable amounts of visual or logical information.
– Simplicity: the opposite of complexity; the ability to complete a task with a clear, austere and minimal output.
– Remembrance: the ability to store data, and recall it later, with no logical capping of time or quantity—the only limit is physical.

These concepts are implemented in a computer code as formulas, or sets of instructions, known as algorithms.

The algorithm is a tool for expression; like the photographer uses a camera, the designer can build and use his own algorithms. The case studies developed for the thesis exploration are ideas transformed into visual stimuli using algorithms; they each tackle different issues within the realm of visual expression, and can be categorized as *sound in space, form systems* and *patterns of time*.

SOUND IN SPACE

The *Sound in Space* case study was based on a nineteenth-century device called a "harmonographer." The analog equipment consisted of three pendulums: Two pendulums would oscillate a pen into the x and y position, while the third one would oscillate a sheet of paper. When in action, geometric shapes would be drawn according to the pendulums' movement. Aside from building intricate visual patterns, the harmonographer could be used to visually represent sound intervals, with each pendulum oscillation match a sound frequency, the sheet of paper rotation simulate the passage of time. Different frequencies on each pendulum resulted into different drawings, faithful visual representations of sound pitch interactions.

My work was to create a harmonograph simulation in a new media context, where users play around with different frequencies, generating different visuals. Musical theory can be translated into pure visual information; octaves and other known intervals can be understood by their visible counterparts. Apart from the musical experiment, the virtual harmonograph produces trance-inducing shapes and motion, interesting for those who do not relate to sound theory.

The *Near Dorian Experience* video is a practical application of the harmonographer experiment. A musical piece was written based on interval visualizations—the score was composed according to the most appealing visual combinations. The different instruments are represented as layers on the screen, and with visuals and music synchronized the geometric structure of music can be clearly perceived.

FORM SYSTEMS

A "form system" is defined as an expression form centered on structure and on the rules of element interaction inside this structure. Instead of creating a composition, the designer creates a support for infinite compositions.

The *Roto-Champ* sketch was developed as a part of the form system explorations; it recreates Marcel Duchamp's *Roto-Relief* series, in which rotating painted record discs, create various visual impressions. Duchamp's work fits an idea of an analogical form system idea. The structure consisted of a rotation device, and various painted discs that were alternated. The user experience varied according to rotation speed, positioning, and disc placement, the variables of the structure. The new media version of roto-relief plays with perspective and different rotation ratios of a fixed set of shapes, distributed according to the classic geometric Golden Ratio. The user can explore different points of view of the rotation, creating interesting optical illusions.

Also related to the form system ideas is the *Flow* sketch; an interactive version of Bridget Riley's *Cataract 3*, an op art painting. Riley explored the relationships between nature and vision, and how the dynamic forms of nature could be represented in their essence. It is the sketch intent to translate the organic, natural feeling of *Cataract* by taking advantage of the computational medium; fluid interactive motion is used, reinforcing the natural aspect and connecting it to the audience.

PATTERNS OF TIME

Today time is usually represented as a line; a common way to represent facts in history is to build a straight line whose segments represent time periods, and add historical events to certain points in that line. *The Patterns of Time* case study explores the possibility of representing time through the three dimensions of space. It explores the possibility of visualizing cyclical patterns—the rhythm in which events repeat themselves, like a day comes after another day, a month comes after another month, so on so forth. These cycles in time are not a closed circle—events don't start again after they finish, but they rather succeed—a different month starts after a month ends. The opened aspect of a circular pattern is represented by a coil that features a repeating period along a progressive path. Since events in time can be considered to have a diverse scales (larger time events contain shorter time events, like a year that contains twelve months) the coils are recursive. A coil contains others that that in turn contain others, in an infinite progression. The case study is software development of this concept—a concept difficult to represent through traditional means, but elegantly achieved through algorithm. The levels of time recursion can be explored through different points of view and different time line compressions. The user is able to tweak diverse parameters in different moments, like position, number or alignment. In addition to the time theory, the sketch produces appealing geometric visuals, creating an aesthetic experience in itself.

The universe of visual concepts represented through computation is immense, and these case studies are only droplets in it. Once a harmonious relationship is established between designer and computational media, visual ideas gain freedom to move in any direction. Creativity is borderless.

For More Information

To learn more about *The Articulation of Visual Experience Through Algorithm* visit http://www.lunetta.com.br/avea/

dynamic visual formation

ISABEL MEIRELLES

Class of 2003

"Art does not reproduce the visible but makes visible."

— Paul Klee, *The Thinking Eye*

It is common sense that every new visual environment, every new medium, requires a different approach to the creation of visual elements. The forces at play are different for each case and thus demand new ways of conceiving in the visual realm. What is new in the creative process of image-making in computational media? Does visual language—and the basic elements as traditionally taught—suffice for the creation of visual forms in interactive media? And if not, what would the basic elements be? What and how to teach visual language both for and in a dynamic environment?

1. VISUAL LANGUAGE

Point, line and plane (and volume for 3-D environments) are considered the basic elements of visual language—and of Geometry—and have been discussed in most books on visual language since the Bauhaus courses in the '20s. However, the distinction between point, line and plane is no longer necessary or even valid in a dynamic environment, where the spatial structure is a process which changes in time. In other words, each point, line and plane is now one of many states of a "dynamic visual formation."

Traditionally, a visual element is described by seven basic attributes: shape, scale, orientation, position, tone, color and texture. In the static visual world the seven attributes suffice for the creation of spatial structures and even the indication or inducement of spatial and temporal relations. However, in a dynamic environment the attributes as such are not enough. The dimension of time must be incorporated in such a way that space and time are no longer isolated.

2. DYNAMIC MEDIA

Computational media are of a different nature and require a different approach to the creation of visual elements. Essential to the creation of visual elements in the computer environment is previous knowledge of certain fundamentals:

- "traditional" visual language used in the creation of static spatial structures;
- "temporal" visual language used in the creation of spatio-temporal structures (such as in films);
- perception of visual forms whether static or temporal.

But these fundamentals are not enough There is a need for new modes of visual sensitivity and conceptualization, as well as new modes of perception and creation of visual forms.

With the objective of examining theoretically and experimentally the creative process of image-making in the computer environment, a "system of dynamic visual formation" is proposed. The main argument is that images are no longer fixed, unique and eternal. Rather, what is created in computational media is a variable spatio-temporal module.

The principle governing the proposed system is that the paradigm of the creative process of image-making has changed. As explained in this thesis, this shift has its origin in the 1920s. Four interconnected concepts are central to this change:

- spatial and temporal relationships within works of art;
- transformable qualities of works of art;

1. Diagrammatic representation of two scale rhythms with different values for Tone origin: o1 = 100% and o2 = 50%. The values for all other attributes (scale, shape, etc.) are the same.

2. Diagrammatic representation of three scale rhythms showing the four values for Starting Point defined in the system.

3. Diagrammatic representation of two scale rhythms with different values for Velocity: v1/v2

4. Diagrammatic representation of two scale rhythms with different values for Amplitude. a1 and a2 determine minimum values; a1* and a2* maximum values.

5. Diagrammatic representation of three scale rhythms with different values for Reference Point.

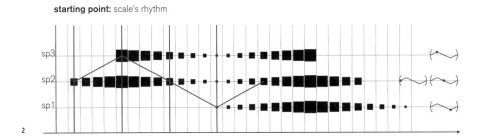

origin for attribute of tone: scale rhythm

1

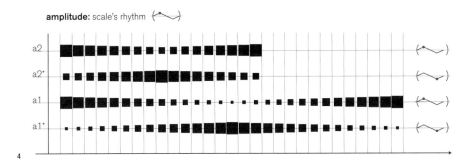

starting point: scale's rhythm

2

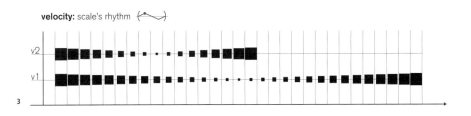

velocity: scale's rhythm

3

– participation of the viewer;
– relationships with other arts and with scientific fields of knowledge.

Also taken into account are the five principles of new media language proposed by Manovich: numerical representation, modularity, automation, variability, and cultural transcoding. (Manovich, 2001)

It is relevant to point out that, since this is new territory, there was a need to create new vocabulary that would name and describe the proposed system and its constituents.

amplitude: scale's rhythm

4

3. THE SYSTEM OF DYNAMIC VISUAL FORMATION

In order to explain the proposed system it is first necessary to consider the difference between "visual form" and "visual formation."

A visual form is a stable spatial structure. It is a time-independent spatial whole. Because there is no change with time, it is described only by spatial parameters.

Visual formation engages the spatiality of visual form with a temporal dimension. It is time-dependent in that it changes in

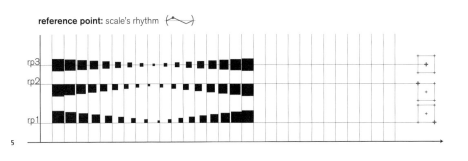

reference point: scale's rhythm

5

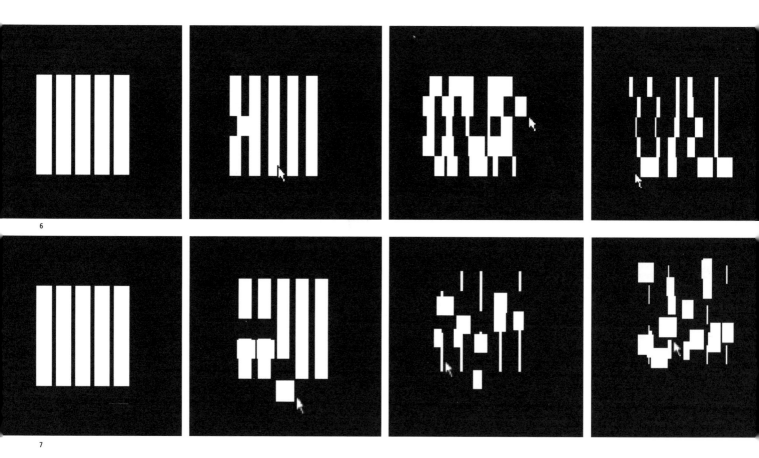

6

7

time, such that later parts are dependent on earlier ones in the continuous process of formation. Its dimensions of time and space cannot be isolated.

What is proposed is a "dynamic visual formation." The term "dynamic" indicates the possibility of modifying the process already changing in time. In this sense, it is not a fixed process. Rather it is a dynamic, an ever changing spatio-temporal whole: it is always in the course of becoming, of forming and trans-forming.

The fundamentals of the system of dynamic visual formation comprise the study of two processes:

1. the system of "inter-actions": the exchange of spatial and temporal information by two agents—an "active subject" and a programmed system.
2. the dynamic visual formation: the properties of visual attributes and the basic element of "rhythmic unit."

3.1. System of Inter-actions

A person (e.g. artist, designer, programmer), or a group of people, develops a program that circumscribes the possibilities for inter-actions by means of which visual formations can emerge. The program—which constitutes the system of inter-actions—defines a set of rules organized into three categories:

1. Rules of Formation—the content: define what information is given a priori and what information to exchange in the creative process.
2. Rules of Action—the methods: define how information is exchanged, including the active mechanisms, where they are active, and how to activate them.
3. Rules of Influence—the quantities: define how much information is exchanged.

3.2. Dynamic Visual Formation

The process of "dynamic visual formation" is described by two interdependent components. First are the most elemental constituents in the process of dynamic visual formation: the properties of visual attributes of the basic element. And the second is the basic element: the variable spatio-temporal module called "rhythmic unit".

3.2.1. The Properties of Visual Attributes

The properties of visual attributes constitute the information being exchanged in the system of inter-actions, in other words, what creates the basic element (rhythmic unit).

What is proposed is a set of properties for each of the seven basic attributes (shape, scale, orientation, position, tone, color and texture). Properties are variables that function as independent data settings. It is by means of inter-actions that data values are set. Data values are numerical. Properties are subjected to the rules of usage.

Properties are grouped in three separate but interdependent categories:

- *spatial:* property describing the spatial qualities of attributes. origin: defines the spatial quality at zero point in time of the cycle of an attribute. [1]
- *temporal:* properties defining the temporal qualities of attributes. starting point: defines the moment in time for the cycle to initiate. [2]
- *duration:* describes the period of time for the completion of the cycle.
- *kinetic:* properties defining the spatio-temporal dependent qualities of attri-

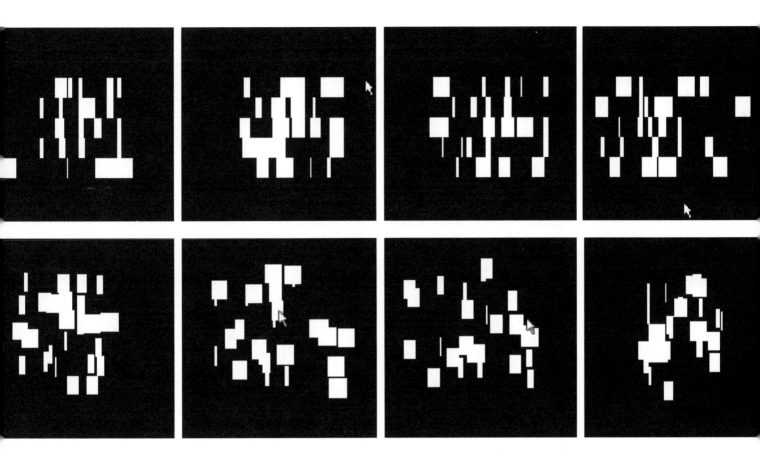

butes. velocity: defines the rate (speed and direction) of the process of change of an attribute. [3]

- *amplitude:* defines the extent of the process of change of an attribute. [4]
- *reference point:* defines the point in the spatial structure in relation to which the motion refers to. [5]

Although we are dealing with the same attributes as traditionally in visual language, now that they have properties within the spatial and temporal dimensions, each attribute creates a "rhythm" which defines the role it plays in the basic element.

Since the system attempts to search and, at the same time, to explore the most elemental constituents of dynamic visual formation, the "loop" is used as its organizing principle. In this sense, the attribute's rhythm is a loop, a compound of a cycle and an interval. The cycle is a periodic recurrence of the relationship among all properties of the three categories of the attribute. And the interval is the period of time between the recurrence of the attribute's cycle.

3.2.2. The Basic Element: Rhythmic Unit

What is proposed as the basic element is a "rhythmic unit." The rhythmic unit is a variable spatio-temporal module. As described earlier, it is created and recreated by means of a system of inter-actions.

The rhythmic unit is characterized by a rhythm (as a "loop") which is the visual formation process. The rhythm is a compound of:

- *rhythmic cycle:* a whole made of the relationship among all attributes' rhythms.
- *interval:* the period of time between the recurrence of the rhythmic cycle.

The rhythm of the rhythmic unit is complex. Unlike a static visual element, inner and outer qualities of a dynamic visual formation are created in a dual system of relationships. The first is the internal relationship among all properties of each attribute, the attribute's rhythm. The second relational system, similar to within a static form, is the relation among the attributes of shape, scale, orientation, position, tone, color and texture. This second system of relationships

is now more complex since each attribute already has internal relationships.

4. EXPERIMENTS

Can the elemental constituents of the proposed system allow for the creation of dynamic visual formations in computational media? Can complexity be created out of the exchange of the most elemental spatial and temporal information? How does the creation and re-creation of dynamic visual formations happen in practice?

6. Sequence of images captured of the experiment dve2.3.3.2 showing the process of inter-actions.

7. Sequence of images captured of the experiment dve2.3.3.2 showing the process of inter-actions.

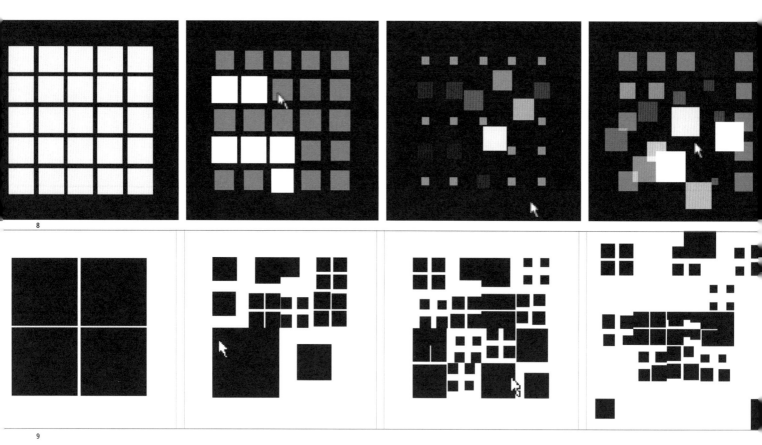

8

9

A series of experiments was created as exploratory environments of the system of dynamic visual formation in the context of rhythmic visual patterns. The experiments are constrained by a rigorous use of the most elemental formal and algorithmical parameters. Spatial qualities are those of elemental 2-D geometric forms, in the same way that the algorithms used in the exchange of information are the most basic ones. No colors other than black and white are used. The binary system of positive-negative or negative-positive is explored. The same rigor was applied for the choice of input and output, which again, are the most elemental ones: the mouse and the monitor screen.

All rhythmic patterns are modular and serial structures: a rhythmic unit is used as a variable spatio-temporal module that is repeated and organized in a rigid regular grid. All experiments are serial in two respects. One is the way in which units are organized in the structure of the pattern. And the other is the creation of serial rhythmic patterns in the process of inter-actions, when the oneness of units and

regularity of the patterns are disrupted and obliterated by qualitative and serial variants and trans-formations. [6, 7]

One of the central issues explored in the experiments is the perception of motion vis-a-vis the conception of dynamic visual formation, more specifically in relation to the perception and creation of rhythmic visual patterns.

The perception of motion is dependent on a system of references where the distinction between "thing" and "framework" is essential. Koffka (1935) explains that in a totally homogenous field a moving point would not be perceived in motion due to lack of frameworks of reference. The influence of object and field factors plays a major role in the perceptual (aka phenomenal) experience of motion as well as of time. [8]

Because "dynamic visual formations" are processes changing in time which are modified by means of inter-actions, so are the relationships among them. Both are time-dependent occurrences. The relationships among rhythmic units create spatial and temporal tensions which are influenced by two interdependent factors.

One influential factor is the nature of visual formations: the role of the attributes' properties in forming and trans-forming rhythms. And the other is the system of references: the distinction between "object" and "framework." In rhythmic visual patterns—as can be seen in the experiments—the system of references is plural. In these cases, a rhythmic unit is relative not only to the space where it happens (field) but to the other concurrent rhythmic units, also working as frames of references. [9]

5. CONCLUSIONS

A "system of dynamic visual formation" was proposed with the objective of examining theoretically and experimentally the creative process of image-making in the computer environment. Ultimately, the investigation searched for the most elemental constituents of dynamic visual formation.

The central question to the entire research was whether the proposed system —the basic element and its properties— suffice for the creation of visual formations in computational media. In other words, if

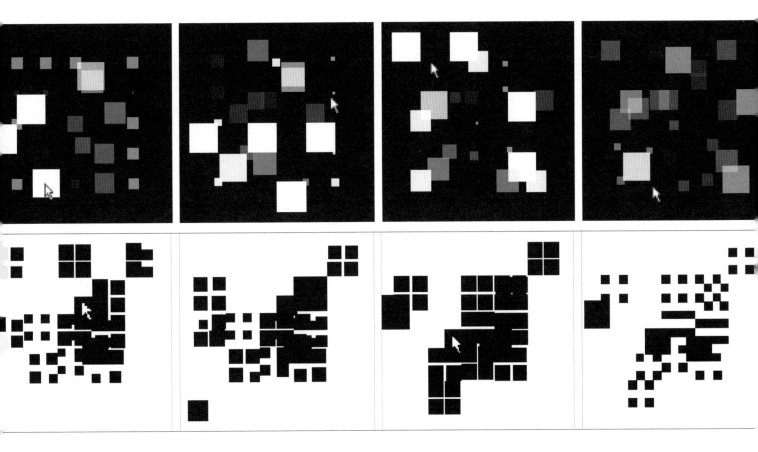

the conceptual framework sustaining the system would address and allow for any imaginable visual output. Even though this might seem ambitious, I believe there is a need for such a quest if we are willing to teach how to create visual forms for and in the computer environment.

I don't think I have answered the question yet. There is a need for further exploration and experimentation with the system in order to determine what is essential and what needs to be incorporated. In this respect, the series of experiments are still incipient and so far explore only rhythmic visual patterns.

On the other hand, it is possible to argue that experimentation with the system already suggests a few essential points towards a theory of dynamic visual formation:

1. The creative process of image-making in computational media is not an individual's isolated activity. Rather, it is a collaborative and participatory endeavor, where at least three agents are necessary: the creator of the program (who defines the system of inter-actions); an active subject and a programmed system (whose inter-actions create dynamic visual formations).

2. In the computer environment a visual element is a variable spatio-temporal module always in the course of becoming, of forming and trans-forming.

3. The most elemental formal and algorithmical parameters create complex and even unpredictable rhythmic visual patterns. The exchange of basic spatial and temporal information in the process of visual formation produces spatio-temporal complexity.

4. Two interdependent factors play a major role in the perception and the creation of rhythmic patterns: the nature of a dynamic visual formation's rhythm, and the system of references.

ACKNOWLEDGEMENTS

This is a reduced version of an article originally published in *Visible Language* #39.2 (July 2005). Text and images (1-7) reprinted with permission of *Visible Language*.

I would like to thank my thesis advisors Jan Kubasiewicz and Krzysztof Lenk to whom I am indebted for their invaluable support and inspiration.

REFERENCES

Klee, P. 1969. *The Thinking Eye: the Notebooks of Paul Klee,* J. Spiller (ed), London: Lund Humphries, New York : G. Wittenborn.
Koffka, K. 1935. *Principles of Gestalt Psychology.* New York, N.Y.: Harcourt Brace and Co.
Manovich, Lev. 2001. *The Language of New Media.* Cambridge, Mass.: MIT Press.

8. Sequence of images captured of the experiment dve2.3.2.1 showing the process of inter-actions.
9. Sequence of images captured of the experiment dve2.3.1.2 showing the process of inter-actions.

bodymachine
and jellyfish

CAROLIN HORN

Class of 2007

bodymachine

The human body travels from place to place, yet it is also a place in itself—even a multitude of spaces. Within the place of the body, each subspace, or body part, is defined mainly by that part's function. For example, the eyes are located up high, to ensure a good view. [1] But what would a body look like whose parts were arranged according to *other* criteria?

Taking an information-design approach, I developed a prototype that lets the user interactively rearrange a human body. Each arrangement leads to a new, strange looking figure: a creature. The project is about making another view of the human body possible, by changing boring values—like the weight of certain body parts—into something interesting and accessible.

REARRANGEMENTS

Rearrangement by Weight

There are currently two arrangements available. One possibility is to rearrange the human body by the weight of each body part. During the transformation, the body parts change their original location and move up or down depending on how heavy or light they are. The horizontal location of a body part indicates its weight in relation to the others'. In this way the muscles, the heaviest part, are at the bottom, and the eyes, the lightest body part, are on top. [2]

Rearrangement by Perception

The second arrangement is configured according to how frequently each body part is used to perceive the outside world. During this transformation, the body parts, which are connected to certain senses, change their size depending on how much they are used in relation to each other. In this way the eyes, representative for the visual sense, become bigger because they are used 87% in perception. The mouth, representative for the taste sense, becomes smaller because it is only used 1% of the time. [3]

DURING TRANSFORMATION

The course from one arrangement to another is structured. In this way the heaviest body part moves to its new location first, the lightest one last. Consequently, although you might not know what will happen next, you begin receiving information during the process of restructuring itself.

The transformation from one to another arrangement can be achieved automatically or manually. Through the automatic mode, the user becomes an observer of the event. By choosing manual control the user can use a slider to go through the transformation, and therefore has control over time. [4]

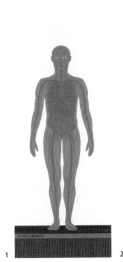

1

2

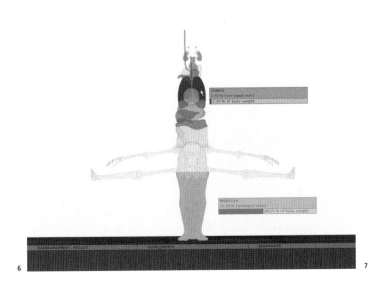

3

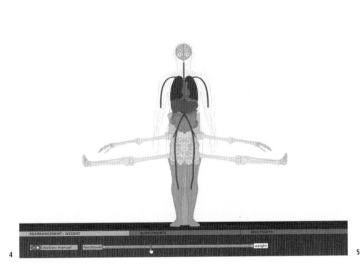

4

5

6

7

AFTER TRANSFORMATION

Exact numbers

After each transformation, the user has the option of viewing the exact numbers of the rearrangement by rolling over certain body parts. You can choose if and how information will be shown; for example, if it is in textual and/or audio form. [5]

In the textual form, bars supplementary visualize percent specifications. Additionally the information of a certain body part can be held and dragged, and in so doing gives the possibility for direct comparison. [6]

Manipulation of numbers

All statistic numbers used are based on averaged data. The user has the opportunity to manipulate these numbers and consequently the chance to change the figure depending on his or her wishes. For example in the rearrangement by perception, you can lessen the percents of visual perception. [7]

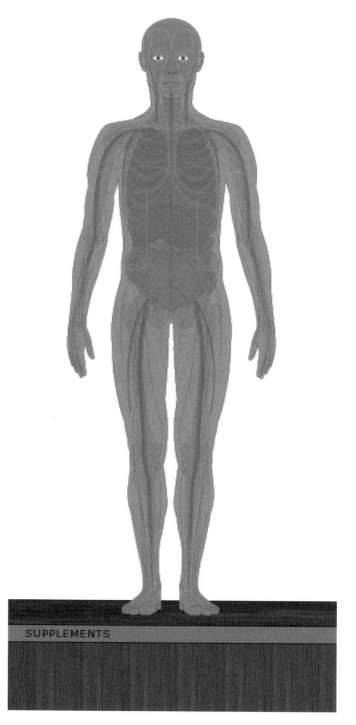

1 – 2

SUPPLEMENTS

BODYPARTS

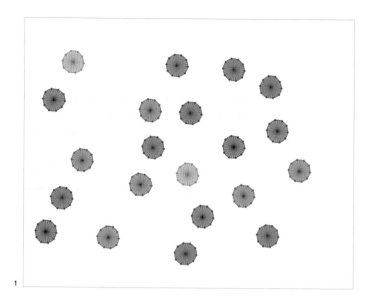

1

jellyfish

Jellyfish visualizes an encyclopedia of the arts. The project should be seen as an experiment, which deals with a dynamic interface. The purpose was to remove a static, conventional design and to achieve a playful interface. The application is developed in Processing and uses an HTML-database to update content.

JELLYFISHES AND THEIR BEHAVIOR IN GROUPS

The encyclopedia of the arts consists of six big families of jellyfishes representative of six main categories. [1] These are: visual arts, design arts, performing arts, literature, film and music. Each of these families is comprised of several family members—the subcategories. One jellyfish represents one family member. In this way the family "design arts" is composed of the jellyfishes architecture, furniture, interior, fashion, graphic design, and interactive design.

Besides a color-coding of the different families, the behavior of a jellyfish indicates the affiliation to its relatives. All jellyfishes can freely swim around during the running application. [2] By touching one, the relatives (the jellyfishes of the same main category) swim next to this jellyfish. The rest, the jellyfishes of the other families, move away from the chosen one. For example, by rolling over "furniture," all jellyfishes of the category "design arts" swim to it, whereas the others try to move away.

Small nametags inform about the type of jellyfish by rollover. In the same moment the names of the relatives are also displayed.

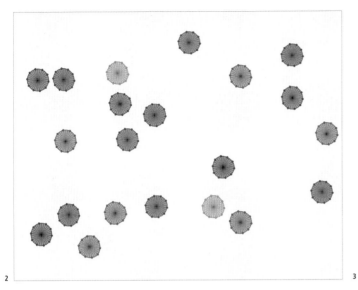

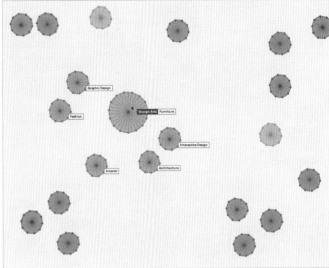

The search for a certain jellyfish is fast and easy through its color-coding, behavior and lettering. [3]

STRUCTURE OF A JELLYFISH

The structure of the single jellyfish is simple.

At the margin of a jellyfish the artists who have worked in this certain subcategory are represented as dots. By rolling over a dot the name and picture of a certain artist will be shown. In this way you can find, for example, artists like Michael Thonet and Charles Eames inside the jellyfish "furniture." [4, 5]

Clicking on a dot selects a certain artist. Thereby three things are triggered at once. First, a second circle grows out of the jellyfish. The margin of this circle is where the artist's works are located, which are represented as dots. After selecting the artist Michael Thonet, for example, you can find there his famous chairs. In addition a text field appears, containing information about the artist.

Finally, a connection to another artist becomes visible, which means that another jellyfish opens itself, showing a second artist. For example, by choosing Michael Thonet the jellyfish "architecture" opens and shows Le Corbusier. Through the dot on the connection line between both jellyfishes you can get information about the kind of this link. [6]

The artist's works are shown on the second circle. By rolling over a dot the name and picture of a certain artwork will be shown. In this way you can find *Chair No. 14* by Michael Thonet. [7]

By the same principle as choosing an artist, you can investigate a certain artwork, too. This time two things happen at once. [8]

A text field containing information about the work and a connection to another artwork appear. In the same way as before, you can discover information about this link. For example, you can find out that Toulouse Lautrec pictured *Chair No. 14* in the painting *Moulin Rouge*. [9]

LEVELS OF INFORMATION

There are different depths of information about the artists and their work. You have the possibility to scale up jellyfishes. Besides just bigger pictures, this offers a broader selection of artists (the number of dots on the jellyfish will be increased). Likewise the accompanying information text becomes more comprehensive.

The text field contains sound information, which offers a more detailed description. By rolling over bywords, indicated by bold type, you can listen to it. [10, 11]

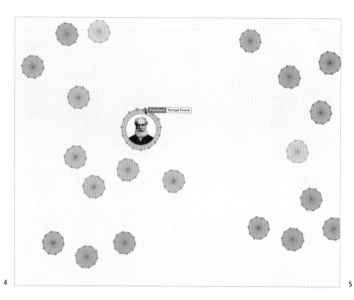

4

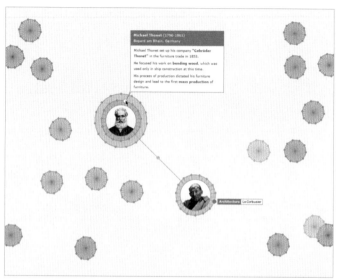

5

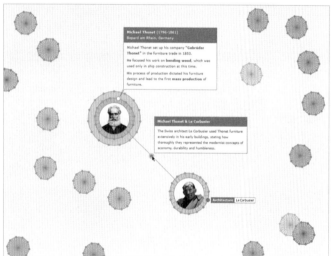

6

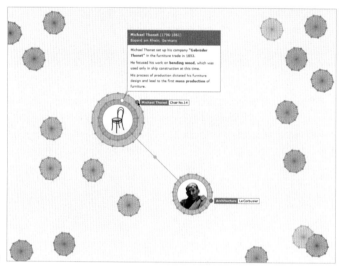

7

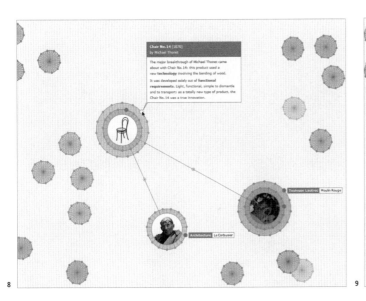

8

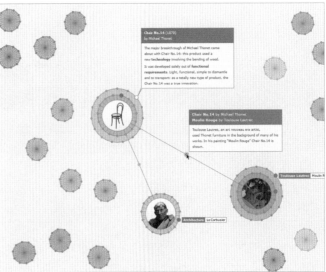

9

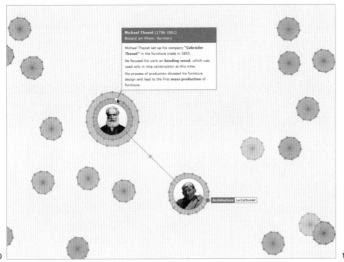

10

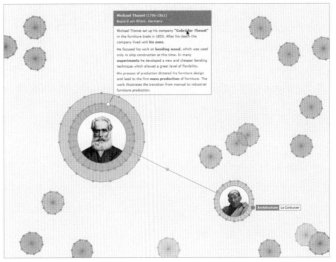

11

proximity lab

EVAN KARATZAS

Class of 2005

1

"The task of the designer is not to create a better button, but to determine if buttons are required in the first place."

— Florian Brody, *The Medium is the Memory*

OVERVIEW

Proximity Lab is a participatory installation and experimental interface platform designed to visualize relationships between users and mediated spaces. The system is self-referential, directing attention to the intersections of physical and computational interaction.

The platform is an 8-foot by 16-foot walkable surface fitted with radio frequency ID (RFID) technology. Participants wear shoes fitted with RFID tags, enabling the system to track and record their positions in real-time. Images projected directly onto the floor are accompanied by stereo sound as a continuous response to the actions and interactions of participants.

Proximity Lab has the unique ability to discern the individual identities of

participants regardless of how or where they move. Conceived as an experimental physical interface system, it allows architects with diverse intentions and aesthetic goals to create repeatable experiments in physical interaction.

INVESTIGATION

The study seeks to stimulate inquiry on the concepts of physical proximity, social interaction and computational mediation. Semi-facilitated experiences involving algorithmic logic, system observation of behavior, and dynamic role assignment are offered to participants for contemplation and discussion.

The central case study involves participatory installation where physical location brokers interaction between users and system. The investigation gives priority to the following issues:

– *natural interface*—utilize natural abilities of user as foundation for core user-system interface favored over introduction of additional interface layers
– *visibility of interface*—minimized to

reduce experience to essential content
– *disclosure of system rules*—minimized to exploit widest range of user responses
– *pluralistic interaction*—exploit ability for users to observe and respond to other participants (interacting with system and each other) to create new opportunities for discovery and re-appropriation
– *human scale*—exploit to elevate immersive qualities of experience both in terms of interaction and perception

PROGRAM MODULES

Two program modules have been developed for *Proximity Lab*—Social Circles and Loop Holes. Both programs are available to participants by way of an iconic menu representing the visual and kinetic forms for each program. Users step on one of the forms to begin the program, which runs at a fixed duration of three minutes.

Social Circles

Social Circles deals with the visualization of social activity and physical proximity. Small shapes bustling with movement

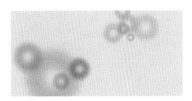

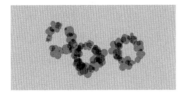

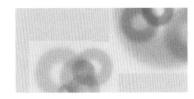

1. Participants interacting with "Proximity Lab."

2. Visual studies for "Social Circles."

3. Visual studies for "Social Circles" to explore concept of occassional color reveals to show distribution of colors.

4. Early visual studies for "Loop Holes," initially envisioned as smoke rings.

2   3   4

surround users and follow them as they navigate the platform. The molecules orbit around participants and react kinetically when users approach one another.

Molecules are color-coded to distinguish individual users. Molecules can be exchanged. As the session progresses, molecules mix and the distribution of colors reveals the unique interactions of the group.

Loop Holes

Loop Holes is a sound instrument that reconfigures itself based on user interaction. Sound spots are represented as simple shapes that reveal kinetic and sound properties when activated. Chance sound performance and composition coexist.

Each of the eight spots represents a note in a fixed scale. Each time the spots reconfigure the timbre and distortion of the sound set changes. At first, the notes are undistorted with short attack and sustain. As the loops progress, sustain gets longer, creating overlap and chordal opportunities. Frequency modulation also adds to the variation.

First configured in a simple and organized manner, the sound spots gradually

separate into scattered arrangements. Are these configurations random or based on the behaviors of participant? The progression and location of sound spots is based on interaction with the system. The user who interact with the system the least are targeted by the system. Sound spots reposition themselves around this users, perhaps encouraging more active users to approach less active users.

SPECIFICATIONS

An 8-foot by 16-foot by 7-inch walkable platform sits at the center of the *Proximity Lab* system. Combined with a set of five RFID-tagged slippers, the platform represents the sole input for the system. System outputs consist of a ceiling-mounted video projector pointed down onto the platform and amplified speakers positioned at opposite ends of the platform.

The platform is fitted with a collection of 1-foot square antenna loops which sit directly below the floor surface. These antenna loops are wired into a set of four RFID readers connected to a PC by way of

USB connection. A continuous data stream delivered from the readers is parsed to:

- qualify the presence of tags based on signal strength at preset frequency ranges
- convert the serial locations of qualifying signal values into the x and y coordinates to locate users on the platform

The program logic involves the specific rules that govern the mediated experience. It quantifies interaction between users and the system. It defines what visual and auditory events occur as well as the conditions that trigger them.

Electronics

The electronics for *Proximity Lab* consists of four RFID readers developed by TagSense Inc. Each reader is designed to accommodate four platform units or 32 individual antenna loops. The antenna loops attach to the reader via mini connectors. The male connector is soldered directly to the wire leads on the platform unit, the female connector is soldered directly to the reader board.

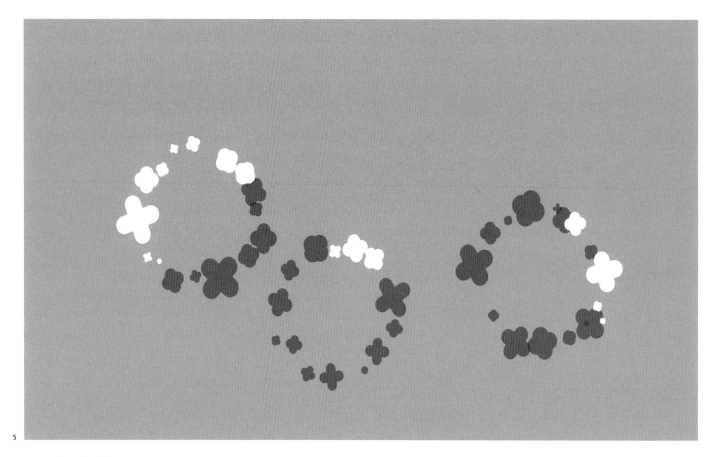

5

Each reader has its own power supply and sends data to the host computer independently via serial USB adapters which attach directly to the reader board.

Firmware residing on the reader handles all RFID functions. This code allows the reader to calibrate baseline signal strength by polling the connected antennas and comparing it to a reference signal generated by the board. It also handles the signal processing functions that allow the reader to discern between noise and the presence of a tag.

A Visual Basic executable handles all communication with the readers and includes a setup function that sends a series of commands to initialize the readers and initiate data polling.

Software/Data Processing

The system relies on two layers of software to complete the experience. The first layer, handled by Visual Basic, manages the continuous stream of data delivered by the RFID readers. Visual Basic simultaneously writes the data to disk for future recall and processes positive tag hits, converting them

into Cartesian coordinates. A lookup table drives this conversion by assigning unique x and y coordinates for each data position on each line of data sent by the reader.

These coordinates are passed to Flash, the second layer of software, which handles the specific program logic. Translating user movements into actionable behaviors is handled by Flash, which also describes the visual and auditory expressions of the installation.

Platform Construction

The building block of the platform is a 2-foot by 4-foot unit containing 8 independent antennas. Each antenna covers 1 square foot using a cloverleaf configuration.

All 8 sets of antenna leads terminate at a common point on the platform. Termination points are designed to efficiently reach the center point of a cluster of four units. The RFID hardware including antenna multiplexers is placed at this intersection with four components required to drive the full-sized platform.

– *128 separate RFID read zones*
The platform is comprised of 16 indi-

vidual units to produce a 16-foot x 8-foot area at 7 inches high. The platform houses four RFID readers driving 128 independent antennas (read zones). RFID tags placed in both shoes of each participant.

– *265 unique tag positions*
When a foot is placed between two individual read zones, both readers detect the tag and provide the means to interpret 265 tag locations, roughly double the number of read zones.

– *1,953 interpreted user center points*
The number of recordable user locations is further increased because a tag exists in both shoes of a user. This provides two separate tracking points, allowing the system to calculate the user center point between the right and left tags.

System Logic

The following definitions were developed as the underlying rules for the evaluation of socialization based on discernible user behaviors and movements. These rules, combined with the specific program logic, determine how the system responds.

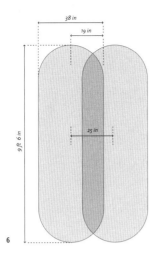

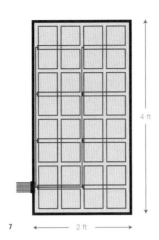

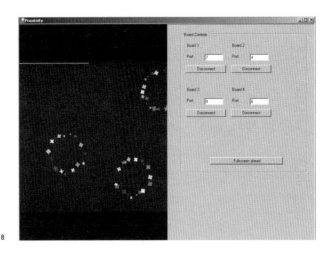

6 7 2 ft 8

5. The final visual study for "Social Circles" program running on the "Proximity Lab" platform.

6. Diagram from study to test feasibility of overlapping regions created by separate RFID fields.

7. A single platform unit contains eight independent antenna loops.

8. Setup view of the Visual Basic executable shown with the embedded Flash file.

– *Personal space*: A half-circle with a two-foot radius exists at the user's center point. The shape is rotated based on user direction to remain in front of the user.
– *Intimate encounter*: Occurs when a user's personal space intersects with that of another user with the intersection occurring for at least three seconds.
– *Intimate departure*: Occurs when the intersecting areas of two user's personal spaces no longer intersect with a tolerance of three seconds to reconnect without ending the encounter.

While initial experiments deal with personal space as a fixed and uniformly sized area, the potential to dynamically define and adjust personal space on an individual basis based on the actions or inactions of the individual is compelling. This logic will be explored in future revisions of the experiment and may take a variety of forms including the reduction of personal space for relatively non-social users, requiring even closer proximities to trigger encounters.

These events have various effects on the user socialization ratings, which are calculated continuously as users interact with the system. Socialization value is calculated with the following expression: $socVal(K) = (encInit^2 \times encUn \times depSoc^4 \times encDur^{1/2}) / depNon^2$. The resulting socialization values are used as the primary vehicle to determine the behavior of the floor-projected visualizations.

It should be noted that this system was simplified for the initial release of Proximity Lab, which uses total accumulated interpersonal interaction time to assess individual socialization value.

KINESTHETICS AND BEHAVIOR

If the changing positions of participants are the primary input for the system, then the visual material projected onto the platform floor is the primary output.

This dynamic visual layer exists to reveal the nature of social activity on both individual and collective levels. To leave room for subjective interpretation and a more expressive experience, imagery should be more abstract than literal.

Rendering Socialization

The key component to visualization is the direct relationship between the socialization value (socVal) of users and the formation and kinetic activity of visuals at user locations. This relationship exists to provide users with a direct, if subjective, window into the general operational rules and behavior-derived data that is collected and used by the system.

This window is a two-way conduit connecting users with the system. It focuses the user's attention on the cause and effect nature of proximity in social interaction—within the walls of this installation and hopefully beyond.

Sound Exploration as Conceptual Tool

I found great clarity can occur when the structural and conceptual possibilities of sound are considered early in the creative process. Moreover, it had a profound influence on the conceptual and visual development of my work.

I had struggled with the visual language throughout the development of the program

9

10

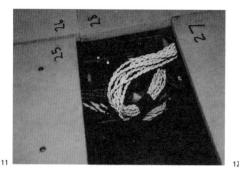

11

12

13

logic. I had fleshed out the general system rules and was unable to find meaningful solutions that would connect image and kinetics to the overall concept. An advisor suggested shifting to the exploration of sound and the solution materialized in a matter of days.

I began by recording violin notes and phrases. I was immediately drawn to the faster, higher-pitched plucked sounds over the low bowed notes I had originally envisioned. This lead to varied sound experiments including rice spilling into glass bowls and colliding marbles. Certain sounds seemed to connect with the concept of socialization.

While making these recordings, I noticed the sound of ice cubes rattling in my drink and heard the sound of computation and randomness. It focused my sound experiments and suggested the first clear visual forms for the program. My next recordings included tapping metal measuring cups and experimenting with digital samplers to diversify instrumentation.

A molecular aesthetic emerged. I envisioned participants surrounded by small circles as they navigated the platform. The molecules are in motion, orbiting around participants, reacting as if excited when users approach one another.

By recording and analyzing a wide range of sounds including variations in timbre, tempo and composition, I was able to consider how specific events and variables could be expressed. Manipulating tempo and reversing certain recordings revealed structural possibilities that would not have been otherwise apparent. A rapid succession of Kalimba notes played forward and backward created respective acoustic compliments of two users approaching and departing.

These event-driven phrases are heard against the backdrop of similar notes, whose tempo is directly related to the amount of movement by the group. The result is cohesion of visual form, behavior and sound and a newfound respect for the conceptual value of sound.

OBSERVATIONS

Proximity Lab was operational for ten days in the Stephen D. Paine Gallery in Boston in April 2005. Over this period, I had an opportunity to observe several people from 3 year-olds to 60-somethings interacting with the platform. I observed users exploring the system without instruction and had the opportunity to explain the underlying principles and mechanics of the system to others. I watched as bystanders observed others interacting with the system.

After nearly three years of work on this project, seeing the first participants interact with the system was quite a thrill. In a moment, the gap between pure conceptual exploration and first-hand observation was filled.

General Observations

1. Age appeared to be a significant factor in the willingness or reluctance of users to engage the system.
   – Kids aged 4-12 generally engaged the experience without hesitation
   – Some refused to interact with the system even at the encouragement of others; most were men over the age of 50

9. A serial data cable is connected to one of four RFID
readers.
10. Special slippers fitted with
uniquely tuned RFID tags allow
the system to locate users on
the platform.
11. RFID readers and antenna
loop connectors where four
platform units meet.
12. The wiring beneath a
platform unit.
13. Detail of the eight wires
terminating at a common point.

2. Individual motivation appeared to play
a significant role in how satisfied users ap-
peared to be with the experience.
  – Users that were mainly interested in
    "playing" and having fun with the
    system were unaffected by the lack of
    instruction and undisclosed workings
    of the system
  – In some cases, I observed users spending
    extended periods of time investigating
    the system through experimentation,
    examination and play
  – Many users appeared dissatisfied with
    the lack of information disclosed about
    the exhibit

3. The vast majority of participants and
bystanders I observed showed great interest
and curiosity and were eager to participate
and learn about the project.
  – Dialogue was frequent among partici-
    pants; several theories about the me-
    chanics of the system were expressed
  – The lack of instruction and information
    seemed to increase curiosity and dia-
    logue about the system

– Participants who were given a basic
  overview of the exhibit appeared more
  comfortable and satisfied with their
  relationship with the system

4. Many users attempted to interact
with the system based on their own false
assumptions about the mechanics of
the system.
  – Pressure sensitivity was the most
    frequent misconception about how the
    system works and led to specific types
    of movement and interaction by users
    (i.e. exaggerated steps, forcing weight
    onto the platform surface)
  – Some users observed others on the
    platform without noting the special
    slippers required and joined the
    interaction without hesitation wearing
    their own footwear before becoming
    aware of this requirement
  – For some, the lack of understanding
    of system mechanics seemed to make
    them uneasy and less willing to engage
    the system more fully

5. Users who invested more time on the
platform generally showed a more complete
understanding of the system.
  – Some system rules remained
    undiscovered to all users I observed
  – Other users were able to form more
    complete understandings of the cause
    and effect relationships governed by
    the system after extended periods
    of interaction

Design Flaws

1. Differences in the interaction rules and
system response between the two programs
was problematic for many users.
  – For example, participants who viewed
    others using the Loop Holes program
    before participating with Social Circles
    program carried their knowledge of the
    user-system relationship over based on
    first-hand observation
  – These users immediately arrived at
    false conclusions about cause and effect
    that influenced their interaction
  – Many were able to overcome this bar-
    rier and revise their understanding of
    the system with further interaction
  – Others were unable to overcome this

and their frustration seemed to diffuse
their motivation for further exploration

2. Logic for sound spot reconfiguration in
Loop Holes program flawed
  – The cause of sound spot reconfiguration
    (random for first three loops, targeted
    to least interactive user in last three
    loops) created unnecessary confusion
    about system mechanics
  – The original approach (progressive
    degrees of relocation based on least
    interactive user) may have decreased
    confusion
  – Leveling or standardizing reconfigura-
    tion behavior across all six loops would
    have likely decreased confusion further

3. Purely iconic approach to main menu
flawed.
  – Relying solely on the visual forms
    and kinetic properties to represent the
    two programs on the main menu was
    problematic
  – The main menu looked so similar to the
    programs themselves that most users
    were unaware of the distinct function
    the main menu served
  – Users generally triggered a program
    unknowingly since they had no knowl-
    edge of the functional differences be-
    tween menu and running programs

4. System failed to clear user positions at
the end of sessions causing the false identification of tags on the platform.
  – This created auditory and visual
    responses not based on actual partici-
    pant interaction and created confusion

CONCLUSIONS
Proximity Lab was operational for only
ten days. To say the experiment provided
only limited opportunities to draw broad
conclusions would be an understatement.
However, the installation is supported by
several iterative tests, prototypes and nearly three years of development, discussion
and critique from faculty, peers and advisors. It is against this backdrop that I offer
the following conclusions.

1. The absence of explicit instruction is
generally not a barrier for participation

- However, when system complexity is moderate or high, lack of instruction can limit the extent to which users can interact with the system
- Disclosure and instruction needs to be balanced to (1) minimize the appearance of complexity when users first encounter the system, and (2) clarify fundamental concepts and introduce the seeds of possible interaction to users

2. The basic principles of advertising and communication design are echoed in the management of exploratory system experience.
- attract: the first step involves getting users to take note and investigate further; requires an emotional, sensory appeal
- engage: requires action on the part of the user; involves tapping into user's existing interests and desires
- retain: user actions must translate quickly into payoff; discoveries must be made early, benefits realized if user is to invest additional time

3. Personal experience plays a leading role in (a) a user's willingness to engage exploratory systems, and (b) the extent to which users can modify and develop their understanding of the systems.
- Noteworthy differences exist between initial engagement and exploration
- While children may generally show no reluctance to engage such experimental systems, they lack the ability to consider the more complex relationships, mechanics and possibilities that the system may provide
- Older adults are most likely to observe but not participate, perhaps being more dependent on disclosure and instruction to overcome reluctance to participate in front of others

4. The ability for people to observe others exploring systems plays a critical role in how users understand and interact with exploratory systems.
- Enables observers to begin formulating and modifying their understanding of the system
- Provides precedence; can decrease anxiety about performing in public

- It creates opportunities for some to interact with more immediacy than is possible with conventional computer interfaces

Beyond Observation

Important lessons have been learned from observing users interacting with Proximity Lab. Most noteworthy is the need to balance ambiguity and instruction to leave room for individual interpretation impeding usability. Some level of clarity is advisable even with exploratory, open-ended systems. Still, the underlying promise of elevating user experience and opportunity for discovery by empowering users to take a leading role in the exchange is compelling.

Interactive experiences that allow users to innovate and create new relationships with the system—re-interpreting and redefining the interface—achieve the highest levels of discourse and collaboration between the architect and participant.

While specific context and content is important, it is possible to independently evaluate the opportunity for self-directed interaction and discovery offered by the interface architecture. Consider the following levels as a tool for such evaluation.
- *Level 1*: Ambiguity favored over instruction to promote self-directed interaction and discovery
- *Level 2*: Users can interact in a variety of ways (multi-dimensional interface)
- *Level 3*: Architect relinquishes control to extent that users are able to invent new methods of interaction at moment of use; discrete levels of observation and system logic employed to extend interaction possibilities; users can create new relationships with system

A (Revised) Appeal to Designers

In an early draft of this paper, I spoke preachingly about the need for interactive design professionals to rethink conventional interfaces and input devices. In the weeks that followed this draft, I had the opportunity to fully experience the work that goes into experimental systems involving fabrication and custom engineered electronics and complex data integration and processing.

While this basic sentiment holds, I do have a new perspective on the issue. I have a better understanding of why experimental systems like Proximity Lab are not embraced more often. The truth is that it requires a combination of skills, multidisciplinary collaboration and extremely generous time frame and budget. This is as rare in academic circles as it is in the commercial design community.

There are several examples of innovative work in this space, but the steep hill of coordinated multidisciplinary expertise and technical know-how prevents it from entering the mainstream design practice.

For the foreseeable future it will remain on the fringe, inspiring some to think beyond the conventions of mass media communications and computing and perhaps influencing the next generation of integrated interface systems. Momentum is building in artistic and commercial design communities where best of breed interactive systems are easily identified for what they lack—a keyboard and mouse.

LOOKING AHEAD

Proximity Lab is a fully functional hardware and software system. As such, it seems obvious that work should continue on this experimental interface platform. While the future of Proximity Lab is uncertain, there are several possibilities that I intend to explore. I have considered two main possibilities for the next generation of this system.

Participatory Museum Exhibit

One of the early application concepts for Proximity Lab involved an exploratory installation for kids. A modified version of the platform may be appealing to local venues like The Boston Children's Museum and The Museum of Science. Proposals to these museums are in the works, including recommended modifications to program logic and industrial design based on the focus of the institution and visitor demographics.

Collaborative Academic Initiative

As we ask how users will interpret their role with the system, we should be similarly interested in how other artists and architects make use of it. Their unique experiences and influences will shape the aesthetic and structural choices they make. To what extent control is shared, guarded or relinquished by these architects is of great consequence to the collective experience.

Based on an open source model, the platform could be made available to graduate and/or undergraduate students in progressive academic programs. The platform could travel from school to school, accumulating an archive of authored interactive experiences reflecting the intellectual territories and experiential and aesthetic goals of the "guest architects" who hosted the platform.

ACKNOWLEDGEMENTS

I would like to thank thesis advisor Jan Kubasiewicz for his tireless consultation, honest critique and friendship. Thanks to adjunct advisors Joe Quackenbush and Teresa Nakra and to George Creamer for financial and logistical support. Thanks to Rich Fletcher and Jennifer Clay of TagSense, Inc. for their work engineering the RFID technology. Thanks to Dave Fullam and Phil Stephenson of Hookumu Inc. for their generous efforts in software development.

For More Information

To learn more about *Proximity Lab* visit www.proximitylab.org.

REFERENCES

Walkable Systems

- Smart Floor, *Petracolor*
  www.petracolor.de/FC/Flying.html
- Interactive Walkways, *Electroland*
  www.electroland.net
- Untitled 5, External Measures Series, *Camille Utterback*
  www.camilleutterback.com/untitled5.html
- External Measures, *Camille Utterback*
  www.camilleutterback.com/externalmeasures2003.html
- Arc Tangent, *Camille Utterback*
  www.camilleutterback.com/arctangent.html
- Boundary Functions, *Scott Snibbe*
  www.snibbe.com/scott/bf

Socially-based Physical Interactive Systems

- Blowing Gently..., *Antenna Design*
  www.antennadesign.com
- The Emperor's New Clothes, *Antenna Design*
  www.antennadesign.com

Participatory Exhibits

- CECUT Project, *MIT Interrogative Design Group*
  web.mit.edu/idg/cecut.html
- VorWerk, *Petracolor*
  www.petracolor.de/vorwerk/vorwerk.html
- Tissue Installation 2002, *Casey Reas*
  www.bitforms.com/artist_reas8.html
- Floccus 2002, *Golan Levin*
  www.bitforms.com/artist_levin2.html
- Meshy 2002, *Golan Levin*
  www.bitforms.com/artist_levin4.html

Publications

Kepes, Gyorgy, ed. *The Nature and Art of Motion*. New York, Braziller, 1965.

Lunenfeld, Peter, ed. *Digital Dialectic: New Essays on New Media*. New York, Routledge, 1997.

Manovich, Lev. *The Language of New Media*. Cambridge: MIT Press, 2001.

McCullough, Malcolm. *Abstracting Craft: The Practiced Digital Hand*. Cambridge, MIT Press, 1998.

Wilson, Stephen. *Information Arts*. Cambridge, MIT Press, 2002.

Price, Sara, and Yvonne Rogers. Cognitive and Computing Sciences, University of Sussex, Brighton. *Let's get physical: the learning benefits of interacting in digitally-augmented physical spaces*.

Wisneski, Craig, and Hiroshi Ishii, Andrew Dahley, Matt Gorbet, Scott Brave, Brygg Ullmer and Paul Yarin. *Ambient Displays: Turning Architectural Space into an Interface between People and Digital Information*. Tangible Media Group, MIT Media Laboratory, 1998.

kod book interactive

KATE NAZEMI

Class of 2006

sum.c #include int main (int argc, char *argv[]) { int i; int sum = 0; for (i = 0; i <= 100; i++) sum + = i * i; printf ("The sum from 0 .. 100 is %d\n", sum);}sum. s .text .align 2 .globl main .ent main 2 main: subu $sp, 32 sw $31, 20($sp) sd $4, 32($sp) sw $0, 24($sp) sw $0, 28($sp) loop: lw $14, 28($sp) mul $15, $14, $14 lw $24, 24($sp)] addu $25, $24, $15 sw $25, 24($sp) addu $8, $14, 1 sw $8, 28($sp) ble $8, 100, loop la $4, str lw $5, 24($sp) jal printf move $2, $0 lw $31, 20($sp) addu $sp, 32 j $31 .end main .data .align 0 str: .asciiz "The sum from 0 .. 100 is %d\n" sum.nolabels addiu sp,sp,-32 sw ra, 20(sp) sw a0,32(sp) sw a1,36(sp) sw zero,24(sp) sw zero,28(sp)lw t6,28(sp) lw t8,24(sp) multu t6,t6 addiu t0,t6,1 slti at,t0,101 sw t0,28(sp) mflo t7 addu t9,t8,t7 bne at, zero, -9 sw t9,24(sp) lui a0,4096 lw a1,24(sp) jal 1048812 addiu a0,a0,1072 lw ra,20(sp) addiu sp, sp, 32 jr ra move v0, zero 00100111101111011111111111110000010 10111110111111000000000000101001010111110100100000000000001000 00101011111010010100000000001001001010111110100000000000000000 01100010101111101000000000000000001110010001111101011110000000 00000111001000111110111000000000000000110000000000011100111000 00000000011001001001011100100000000000000000000100101001000000 01000000000011001011010101111010100000000000000000111000000000000000 00000000111100000001001000000011000011111100100000100001000101 00001000001111111111110111101011111011100100000000001100000 11110000000100000100000000000001000111110100101000000000000110 00000001100000100000000000011101100001001001000001000000010000 11000010001111101111110000000000010100001001111101111101000000 00001000000000001111100000000000000000001000000000000000000000 0100000010001001111011110100000000000001000000000

Digital code is the requisite material used by scientists to process information and produce results, and now by artists who use it as a creative tool. Here, we find a link between two seemingly disparate disciplines. But the connection goes deeper than shared material and the challenge is how to communicate it across the linguistic divide.

Kod Book Interactive is a gesture driven interface and a printed book. Both domains complement each other well: the interface allows participants to explore the visual and aural elements of code, while the book provides a historical foundation for learning. Together, these methods blend the nonlinear, dynamic, and unique explorative attributes of interactive digital media with the linear, static, and analytic properties of the printed book for a complete multi-sensory experience.

Each method of representation rigorously investigates various levels in, and representations of, a programming language in order to relate it to the broader context of human experience and learning. This is observed in the following ways: 1. Translation—code to computer, fixed language of science to the fluid language of poetry, visual to sound; and 2. Relationships—size, weight, value, contrast, rhythm, space.

1. These characters represent the first step in translating the programmer's instructions into specific tasks the computer can perform – in this case, to count from 0 to 100. Before code language can be interpreted by the microprocessor, it is reduced through the substitution of mnemonics and operational commands. This translation is SILENT, PRIVATE and EXACT.

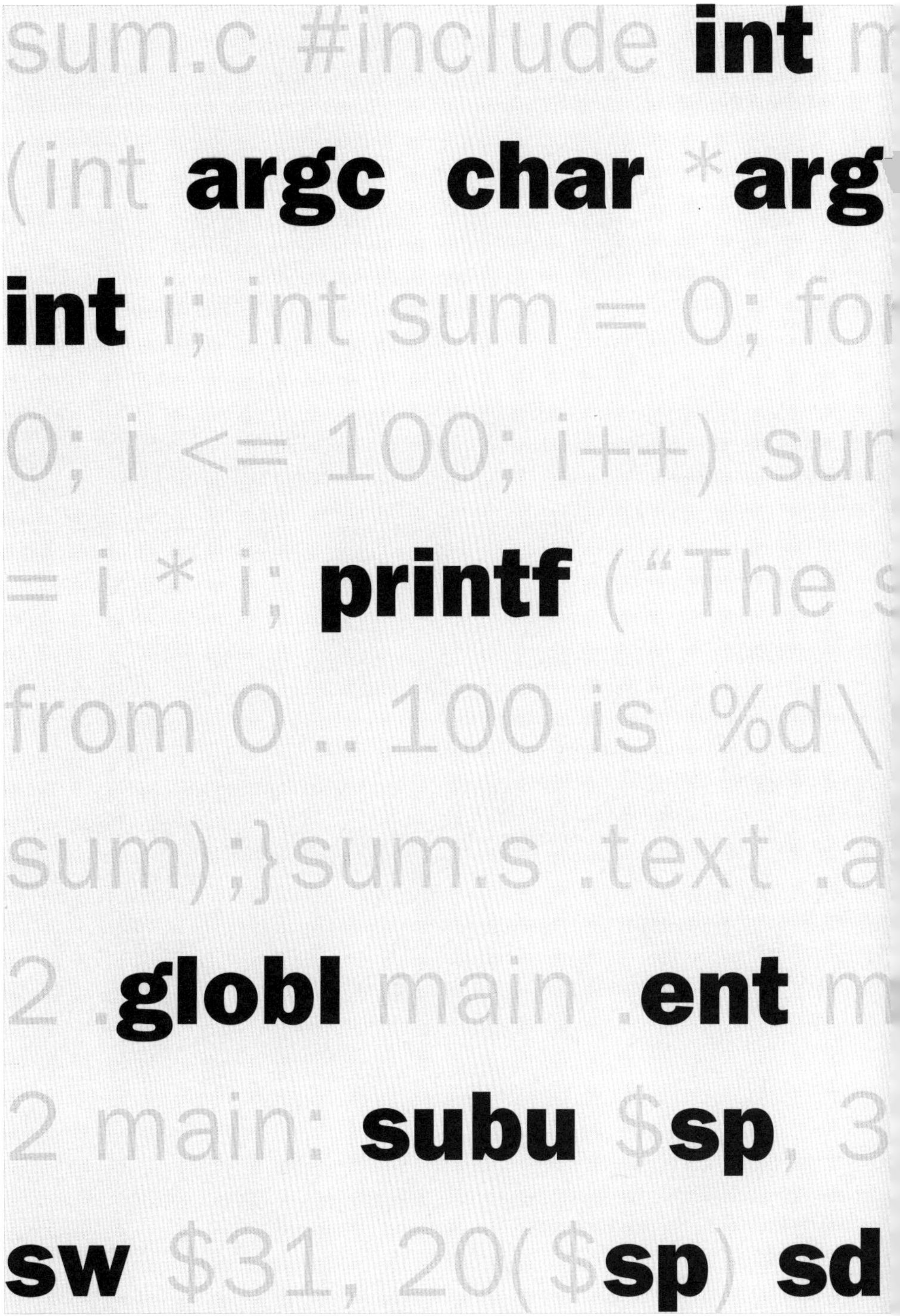

sum.c #include **int** m

(int **argc char** * **arg**

int i; int sum = 0; for

0; i <= 100; i++) sur

= i * i; **printf** ("The s

from 0 .. 100 is %d\

sum);}sum.s .text .a

2 **.globl** main **.ent** m

2 main: **subu** $sp, 3

sw $31, 20($sp) **sd**

1

OVERVIEW

Kod Book Interactive: Book is a soft-covered book measuring 6x9. The book is an analytical examination of the transformation of the scientific language of code to the poetic interpretation of "kod."

Kod Book Interactive: Interface, was developed in flash and runs on a touch screen monitor. Participants, presented with a continuous flow (left to right) of "kod," are encouraged to explore the poetry through touch. Interactive specifics are discussed later under the heading "Relationships."

TRANSLATION

To translate is to transform. This process is one of conversion for the purposes of learning and understanding, and takes on many forms. In one sense, to translate is to express in another language precisely the original sense. In another, to translate is to "convey from one form or style to another" (American Heritage Dictionary). In accordance with this definition, *Kod Book Interactive* uses the processes of translation to identify and communicate unique connections between the diverse languages of science and art.

Code to Computer

What do the many expressions of code look like (or even sound like)? What connects the process of translation from human thought down to the interpretation of binary code by the microprocessor? Where does one expression begin and another end?

Given the relative secrecy that code operates in (its activity is invisible to most computer users), the search for answers suggests both an analytical and creative approach.

Beginning analytically, code is expressed in several distinct forms before being interpreted by the microprocessor. Take for example the following line from the highest level language of code:

```
sum.c #include int main (int argc, char *argv [])
```

These characters represent the first step in transforming the programmer's instructions into specific tasks the computer can perform—in this case, to count from 0 to 100. Curiously, high level language is considered closest in relationship to human linguistic communication.

Before high level language can be interpreted by the microprocessor though, it is reduced to assembly language through the substitution of mnemonics and operational commands:

```
sum.s .text .align 2 .globl main .ent main 2 main: subu $sp, 32 sw
$31, 20($sp)
```

This translation is silent, private and exact. Finally, assembly language is reduced to binary code, called machine language. This lowest level language has the smallest vocabulary, yet is largest in volume:

```
00100111101111011111111111100000101011110111111100
0000000001010010101111101001000000000001000001010
11111010010100000000010010010101111010
```

And to think that this three step transformation takes place in the blink of an eye and in complete silence! (code courtesy of Professor James Larus, The University of Wisconsin)

Perhaps well understood by the computer programmer, the degrees of abstraction apparent in the translation of code make this language difficult to understand. Therefore, code remains elusive to the many who depend on it for creative work. It is with this assumption that the search to convey code in more approachable forms begins.

Language of Science to Language of Poetry

One of the best ways to understand something better is by breaking it down into smaller, more manageable parts. A visual language offers countless creative ways to express complex information, and is where the transformation of code from a language of science to a language of poetry starts.

The expressive and communicative potential of this traditionally silent and purely computational material begins with the isolation of unique letter combinations from each line of code:

```
sum.c #include int main (int argc, char *argv [])
sum.c #include int main (int argc, char *argv [])
```

This process of isolation, when applied to the entire programming language, detaches code from its original sense and creates a reduced vocabulary subject to a new set of parameters and a different kind of analysis. Code, in its new context, is freed from a silent and fixed form, and transformed into a rhythmic array of visual language:

int   in*t* argc **char** argV

The parameters that govern this visual language originate with the Avant-garde artists of the 1920s who pioneered the reduction and restructuring of language to form new relationships to space and time, and thus new ways to perceive and create meaning. Of particular influence are the concrete poets "who reduced words to their elements of letters (to see) and syllables (to hear)." (*Concrete Poetry: A World View*) This approach to language came from a belief that accepted grammatical-syntactical standards were inadequate to express certain ideas of the time. It is in this sense that the transformation of code from a scientific to a poetic language makes a historical connection to the Avant-garde artists.

Visual to Sound

When we read—internally or externally—we give voice to the world of words. Tapping into multiple layers of perception, phonetic poetry (a subcategory of concrete poetry) explores this simultaneity of sound and visuals.

By forming relationships between typography and sound, both visual and aural communication channels help translate the scientific language of code into its new poetic form. Letters are seen and syllables are heard, reinforcing a unique relationship not unlike the ones taught in early childhood. It is this union between sight and sound that delivers the message over time.

2. Code enables us to do complex and robust things. Yet code as a language is simple, small, and fixed. After isolating and emphasizing different letter combinations unique to code, I began to see its expressive promise.

int

argc char arg

int

printf

globl **ent**

subu sp

sw **sp sd**

2

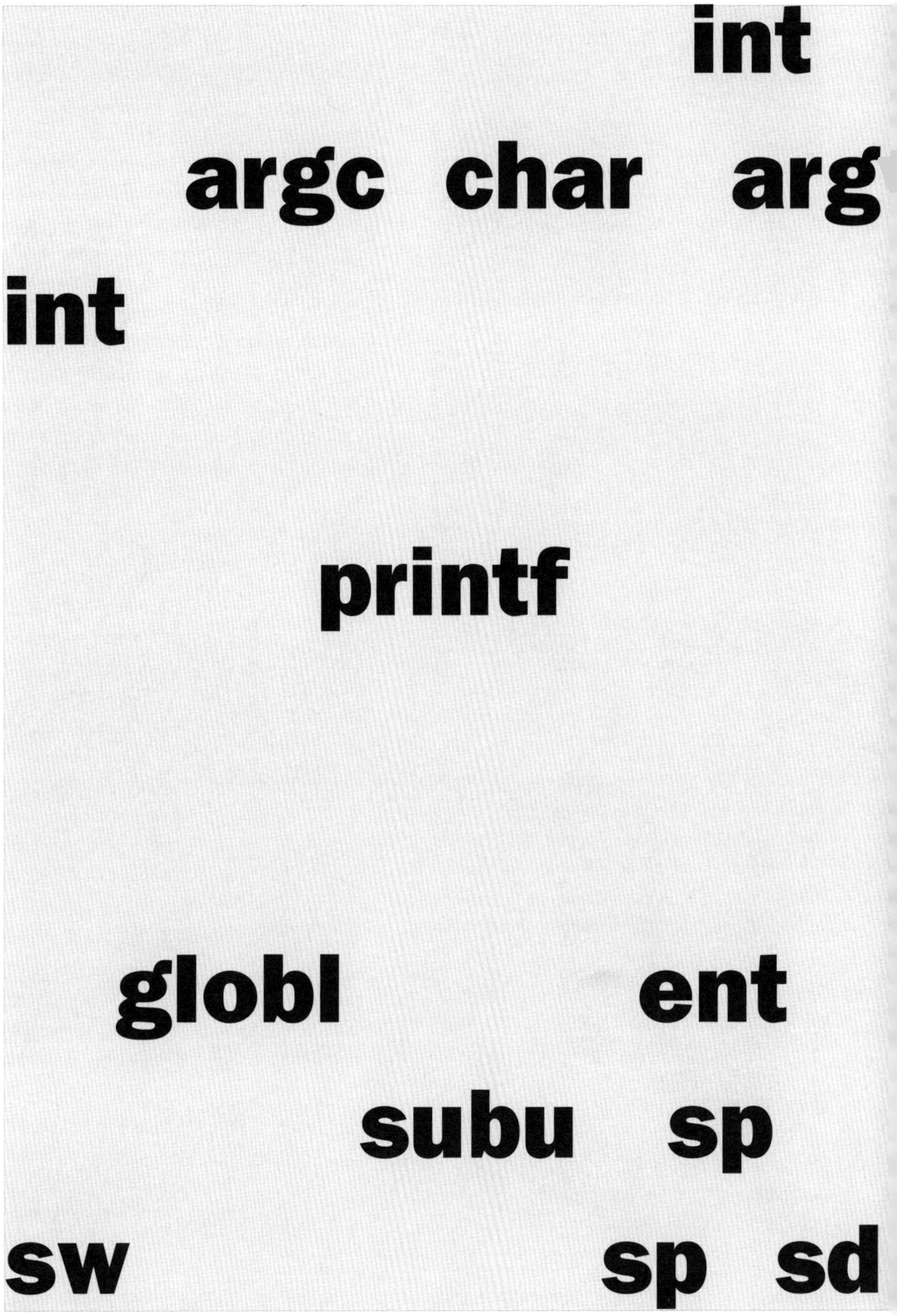

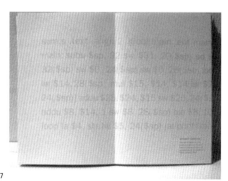

RELATIONSHIPS

To relate is to connect. *Kod Book Interactive* fuses traditional formal elements in design: scale, contrast, rhythm and space, with properties of dynamic media: modularity, variability, and time, to make clear visual and aural connections between content and form. In unison with the poetic language of "kod", this creates an environment for learning and understanding.

Integral to *Kod Book Interactive: Interface* is the typographic scale of "kod." Here, distinctions in typographic size distinguish inactive typography—small type flowing from left to right—from active typography that, when touched, scales in relation to the volume of the word heard. Here, a the following relationship between scale and sound are formed: the larger the word, the louder the pronunciation. Another relationship between scale and sound is found in the rate of word flow: the larger the word, the slower it moves from left to right. These variations in typographic scale and sound create contrast and rhythm in the interactive environment.

Adding to a sense of contrast and rhythm are the vocal expressions of the two typefaces chosen: Mrs. Eaves and Franklin Gothic. The voice of words set in Mrs. Eaves (a feminine typeface) is female, while Franklin Gothic (a masculine typeface) is male. Within each voice, alterations in pitch range from high to low depending on speed.

Space and time are also explored through the developing user relationship within the interactive environment. Through the touch of a hand, changes in size, content organization, and time are investigated. The fluid gestures of a hand allow participant the freedom of isolating certain words and re-organizing them within the given space. The time line of events can also be paused to allow a more thorough investigation.

CONCLUSION

What began as a modest experiment in how to communicate the language of code across a linguistic divide has opened the door for future explorations in multi-sensory and multi-methods of communication.

This past spring, *Kod Book Interactive: Interface* was a featured exhibition at the 2005 Boston CyberArts Festival. It received a warm response and helpful feedback, much of which is reflected in this fall's exhibition: *The Language of Dynamic Media*.

Kod Book Interactive: Book was also featured in the 2005 AIGA BoNE Show and awarded a Certificate of Award.

I would like to thank my advisor, Jan Kubasiewicz, and all DMI faculty and friends for their continued guidance and support.

NOTABLE RESOURCES

Prof. James Larus, The University of Wisconsin, Madison, Computer Sciences

Mary Ellen Solt, *Concrete Poetry: A World View* (1968, Indiana University Press)

3. By analyzing the sounds of speech and the symbols that represent these strange arrangements of letters, I was able to hear how different syllables could be emphasized in relationship to different typographic attributes. Here, code is freed from a silent and fixed form, and transformed into a loud, spacious, and rhythmic array of phonetic poetry.

4, 5. Kod Book Interactive: a gesture based interface. Code flows from left to right. Words are "caught" by the hand as they scale up in size and pronounciation is heard. Images taken at this year's Boston CyberArts Festival.

6, 7. Kod Book Interactive: 6x9 printed book. Cover and inside spread shown. Images taken at this year's AIGA BoNE Show.

3

te + hands

KEIKO MORI

Class of 2005

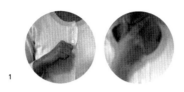

てをつかってかいわをたのしむ。

手を使って会話を楽しむ。

INTRODUCTION

TE + Hands is a text-based online communication system where the maximum of four users use hand gestures as an important vocabulary in their communication. It provides the users a library of images of hand gestures. The system is not only for a communication purpose, but also for a learning purpose. I designed the system to be used by Japanese people and American people. "TE" means hands in Japanese. It prepares a library of Japanese hand gestures for Japanese users and a library of American hand gestures for American users.

I decided to introduce only two cultures in order to limit the scope of this case study. I chose Japan and America because of my familiarity with these cultures. In this system, users learn the use and the meanings of each other's hand gestures during their conversation.

In addition to the on-going conversation mode, *TE + Hands* provides an archive mode which allows the users to see the structure of their conversation. The users can interact with it and gain knowledge about their communication while performing various filters.

WHY HAND GESTURES?

What would happen if we were asked to have a conversation without using our hands at all? We would still be able to communicate. However, we would find it much harder to express our minds and emotions. In our real-space communication, we often use hand gestures along with our spoken words to emphasize or to support

them. We also use the gestures alone to make nonverbal expressions. For example, when a speaker refers to him/herself, he/she points to his/her chest with a spoken word, "me," "my," or "mine." In this case, the hand gesture emphasizes and confirms the spoken word. The speaker can show he/she is thinking by stroking or touching his/her chin without saying anything. In this case, the hand gesture works alone as a statement. Therefore, hand gestures are important nonverbal expressions for speakers in communication. [1]

They are also important to listeners. For listeners, hand gestures work as visual cues of what is spoken. Chinese letters in written Japanese works just the same. In Japanese, we can write anything only using "Hiragana" which is one of the three characters we have. However, we write some words in "Kanji," a Chinese character, instead of in "Hiragana." Compared to reading what is written all in "Hiragana," it is much easier for us to read when some words are written in "Kanji." This is because "Kanji" works as visual symbols/pictures to our eyes. Instead of reading, we are able to visually catch the words written in "Kanji," which makes our reading process much quicker and easier. [2]

In our communication, listeners perform the process by looking at the speaker's hand gestures. For example, when a speaker points at his chest, the listener understands this verbal gesture to mean that he is talking about himself.

CULTURAL DIFFERENCE IN HAND GESTURES

Hand gestures vary from culture to culture. In Japan, we touch our nose with a index figure when we say "me," "my," or "mine." Our gesture for thinking is crossing arms. This gesture might seem to be offensive to American people. Misunderstandings occur when a gesture means something in one culture and something else in another. For example, Japanese gesture for "Come here" is similar to the American gesture for "Go away." In TE + Hands, users go through the process of guessing, asking, and teaching gestures during their communication. [3]

GESTURE LIBRARIES

For each culture, the system provides a library of 28 hand gestures including an image showing no hand gesture. When the user logs into the system, he/she chooses one of the system's gesture libraries. There are a female gesture library and a male gesture library for each culture. The white empty circle shown in the library is for the users to to upload their own gestures. The users can customize the placement of the gestures. [4, 5]

Filtering in Gesture Libraries

There are three circles of gestures in a gesture library. The largest circle contains all the gestures, the second biggest circle contains 20, and the smallest circle contains 10 of all the gestures. The system learns the user's behavior from his/her previous history and stores the most-used 10 gestures into the smallest circle and the most-used 20 gestures into the second biggest circle. The user can do this manually if he/she wishes. The user can perform the filtering by simply dragging the handle towards the center of the circle to change its size. This filtering is convenient to hide the gestures the does not use that often. [6, 7]

On-going Conversation Mode

The users can send entries with or without texts. This is the same as how we use gestures in our real-space communication. Silence, therefore, speaks and has a meaning in this system. I am using a table as a visual metaphor for the big gray circle placed in the middle of the interface. The users are color-coded as are their entries. The users' entries appear and float on this table for a while and gradually disappear. The shape of the circle visually creates a sense of fairness and equality in their communication. This circular form can also flexibly handle the different numbers of users. In the prototype, I am showing a case of four users having a conversation and a discussion. [8]

Creating Topics

A conversation always starts with someone creating a topic. The three empty circles the users see initially on the table are topic circles that haven't been created. The user can create a topic by typing in what he/she wants to talk about with the other users and clicking the topic maker icon. Then, the entry floats on the table and gets attracted to one of the empty topic circles. Then the topic circle becomes filled in light gray and moves to the center of the table. All the users' entries that talk about this topic float on the table and vanish into this topic circle after a while. When a new topic is entered,

5

Japanese gesture library

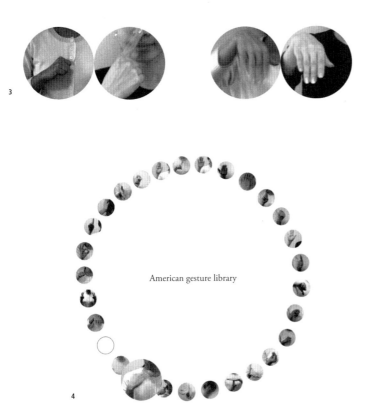

3

American gesture library

4

6

7

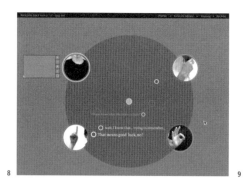

8

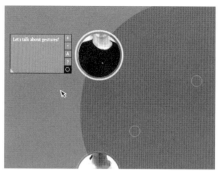

9

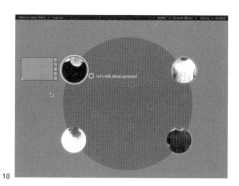

10

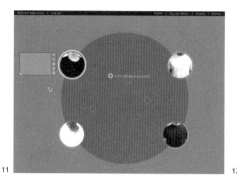

11

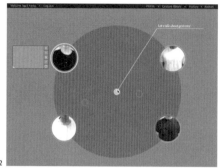

12

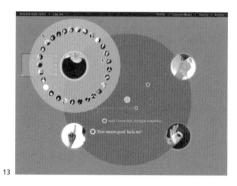

13

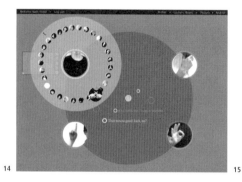

14

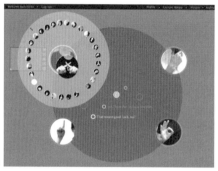

15

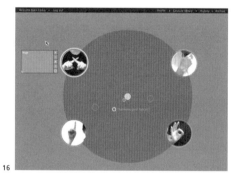

16

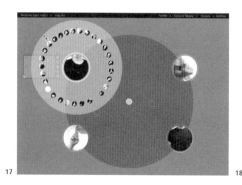

17

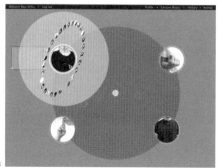

18

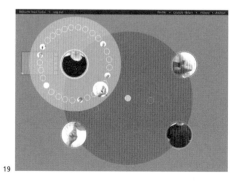

19

it becomes a new topic circle and the previous topic circle gets pushed away from the center of the table and becomes dark gray in color. Another empty topic then appears on the table. The users can see a content of each topic circle by rolling over it. [9 – 12]

Choosing a Gesture

During a conversation, the user can open his/her gesture library by clicking on his/her gesture circle. To choose a gesture, he/she clicks the gesture or drags it into the gesture circle. Clicking the gesture circle again closes the gesture library. To get back to the default image of no hand gesture, the user simply drags the current gesture out of the gesture circle. [13 – 16]

Creating Regular Entries

When the user wants to send his/her comment about the topic, the user can do so by choosing a gesture and typing a comment in the input field. The user can also create an entry only with a gesture. In this case, only a circle in the user's color gets sent out to the table. The created entry always appears over the user's gesture circle, moves out of it, stays right next to it on the table for a while, and vanishes into the topic circle.

Collecting the Other Culture's Gestures

The users can collect gestures of each other's culture. This is the result of their learning activity in this system. If the user is Japanese, his/her American gesture library is initially empty. The user can collect all the American gestures that have appeared in the conversation. His/her American gesture library sits behind his/her Japanese gesture library. To reveal the American gesture library, the user flips the Japanese gesture library by keep dragging the handle across to the bottom-right. The user can use the collected gestures in his/her future conversations. [17 – 19]

Capturing Other Users' Entries

The users can agree, disagree, ask questions, and answer the questions by capturing each other's entries. The user can capture someone's entry by simply clicking it while it is floating on the table. When it is captured, it creates its own copy. The copy moves to the user's gesture circle and stays there until the user attaches his/her entry to it.

To attach an entry, the user types a comment in the input field and selects one of the icons; +, -, A, and ?. If the user wants to agree with the captured entry, then he/she selects the icon, +. After his/her entry is attached to the captured entry, they float together on the table for a while and vanish into the topic circle. [20 – 24]

History

The system provides a history of their conversation as a list of entries. In the history window, the entries are grouped by the topic entries. The user can see the gesture of each entry by rolling over its color circle. Let's say an entry A captured an entry B during a conversation or a discussion. Then in the history window, the user sees two color circles for the entry A; a bigger circle of the entry A and

a smaller circle of the entry B. Rolling over the smaller circle highlights the entry B in the list of entries in the history window. [25]

ARCHIVE MODE

This mode allows the users to see the structure of their conversation. It maps out their entries and creates an interactive conversation map. In this mode, the users can not only learn about the relationships between their entries but also can gain specific information and knowledge about their conversation by performing various filters. [26]

Filtering 1: Magnifying Glass Tool

The users can perform three kinds of filters in the archive mode— zooming in and out with a magnifying glass tool, hiding certain entries with a closing-eye tool, and hiding entries by certain users. Zooming-in filters the conversation map since one can have only a part of the map shown big in the space of the interface. Inside of the magnifying glass, it shows the amount of zooming-in or zooming-out. One can keep zooming in up to 300% and zooming out to 25%. When the map is zoomed in more than 150%, a small navigation map appears in the interface to prevent the user from getting lost in the space.

There are two ways the user can see a gesture and a comment of each entry. When the user rolls over a color circle, a balloon comes out from it and shows the gesture and the comment. The other way is through the history window. When the user rolls over one of the entries in the list, the same entry in the conversation map gets highlighted in the space. The user can highlight the entry in the history window by rolling over the one in the conversation map. [27 – 30]

Filtering 2: Closing-Eye Tool

With the closing-eye tool, the user can filter out certain entries in the conversation map. For example, when the user uses the tool over a topic circle, all the entries that belong to it become invisible. When the user uses it over one of the main entries, the main entry and all the entries that belong to it disappear as well as all the entries that come after it. The closing-eye tool works like a stamp. When it is used, it leaves its trace as black closing-eye icons. By leaving them, it tells the user where the hidden entries are. The user can reveal the entries by clicking those icons. [31 – 34]

Filtering 3: Individual Users

The last one is filtering the entries of individual users. The user can perform this filtering by deactivating a circle/circles under "User" in the side bar. This filtering is suited if the user is interested in the entries by a particular user/users. The user can focus on and learn the relationship between his/her entries and the particular user's/ users' entries. This also allows the user to see who was interested in which topic. [35 – 37]

Gesture Database

Gesture database is another feature in this archive mode. The database organizes the gestures appeared in the conversation individually in a chronological order. It filters out all the comments, so the

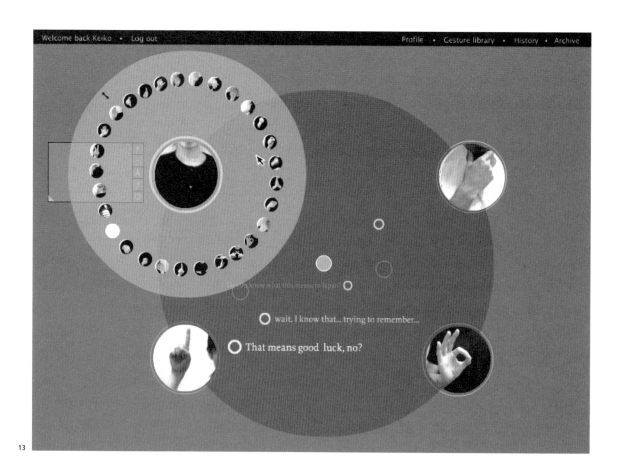

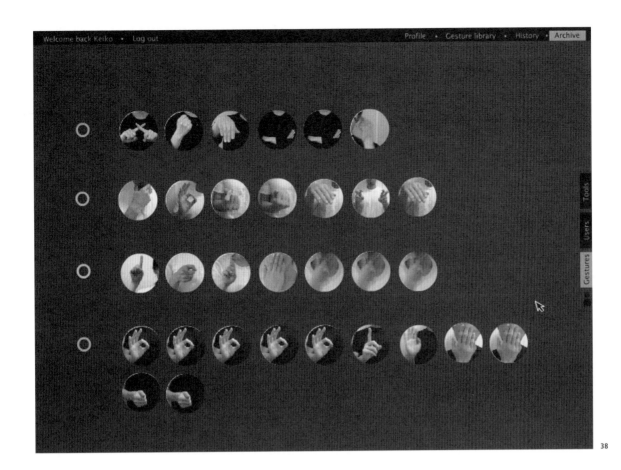

38

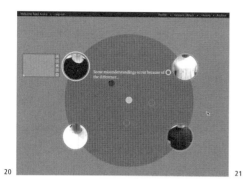

20

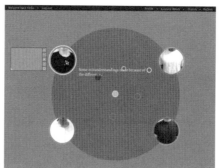

21

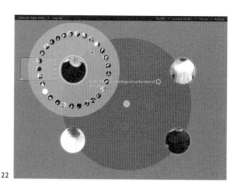

22

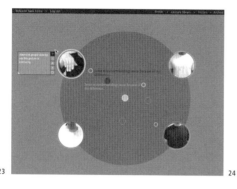

23

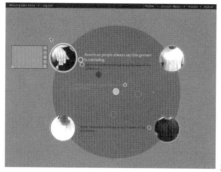

24

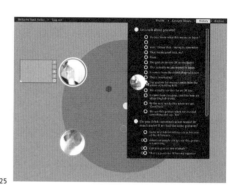

25

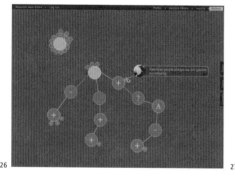

26

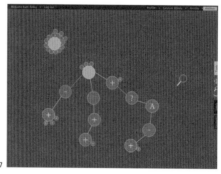

27

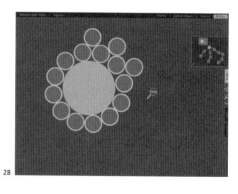

28

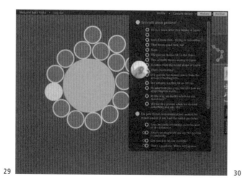

29

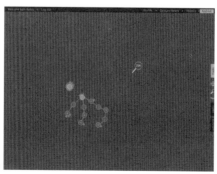

30

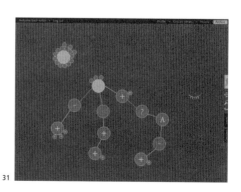

31

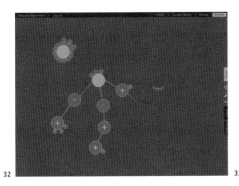

32

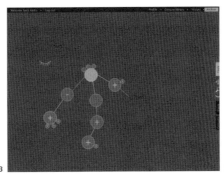

33

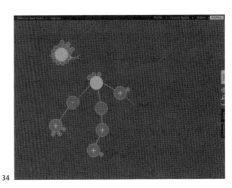

34

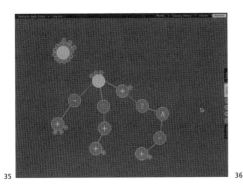

35

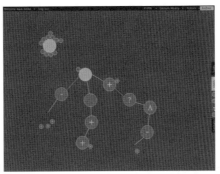

36

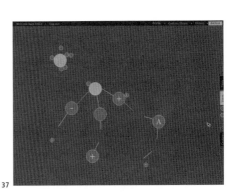

37

user can focus only on the gestures. From this data, the user can learn about each user's way of communicating with hand gestures. The user can also see the other culture's gestures he/she collected in the conversation. [**38**]

CONCLUSION

There are still some interface issues, such as the size of the gesture circle. It should take more space since it is the most important vocabulary of communication in this system. *TE+Hands* handles hand gestures as visual symbols for the text-based communication. The system speaks this unique language instead of only recreating our real-space communication.

The system is successful also because it allows the users to see the structure of their conversation. In the on-going conversation mode, the users see how they respond to each other through their captured entries. The archive mode provides an interactive conversation landscape with the three filtering tools. The user can customize his/her filtering by performing them together. Filtering is the key to allowing users to have a unique experience and to gain specific knowledge about that experience and interaction.

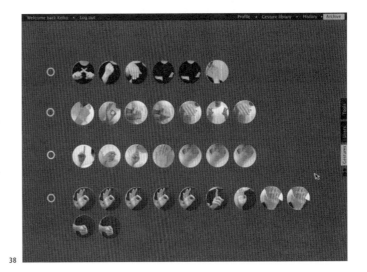

38

animation, motion and education

JULIA GRIFFEY

Class of 2005

"If our bodies know something our minds do not, can the knowledge in our bodies help out our minds?"

BODY OVER MIND

Books and articles about athletics and dance often refer to the practitioner's "physical memory" or "muscle memory." When we perform a physical movement several times, our body remembers the feeling. Eventually we do not need to even think about what we are doing and our bodies perform automatically. In a recent article in *Running and Fit News*, the author encourages runners to do leg exercises with resistance bands. His contention is that the runner's muscles will remember the motion and push harder when running. (Yessis, 2003)

HOW MOVEMENT HELPS LEARNING

If our bodies know something our minds do not, can the knowledge in our bodies help out our minds? Helen Gummerseimer thought so. Mrs. Gummerseimer was my second grade teacher who taught us the "pronoun-a-la-go-go" to help us learn our pronouns. It was a simple little dance—a couple of hand gestures and some steps forward and back—that went along with a rhythmic chanting of "I, You, He, She, It, We, You, They." Thanks to Mrs. Gummerseimer, I will never forget my pronouns.

Other educators besides Helen Gummerseimer subscribe to the philosophy of using physical motion to help kids learn. The Washington Center for Learning is a non-profit agency with the mission of helping primary and high school teachers with educating students in reading, writing, math and language. They developed KTM (Kinematics Teaching Methodology), a system that "uses a whole body's motion in space as a medium for translating abstract concepts to the concrete." Mathematical dances that use timing, direction changes, and distance to reinforce mathematical concepts are one example of how the KTM philosophy is applied. (www.washington-centerforlearning.org)

On a purely physiological level, when we move, we are better learners. Exercise shunts oxygen to the brain, increasing the blood flow to this area by 20%. (http://www.utexas.edu/student/utlc/making-grade/physical.html) This makes us more alert, allows us to think more clearly, and aids in committing new concepts to memory, which essential for learning. (Peterson & Bryant, 1999)

Exercise also helps memories to "stick". In his book, *The Owner's Manual for the Brain*, Dr. Pierce Howard recommends exercising shortly after learning new material to help remember it. "After a learning episode of an hour or so, take a break and do something to pump up your epinephrine levels; walk about, do isometrics, climb some stairs, do laundry, move some boxes—anything that will generate epinephrine and norepinephrine to help fix the memory." (Howard, 1994)

Perhaps the most prominent theorist to link movement and learning is Harvard education expert, Howard Gardner. In his book *Multiple Intelligences: The Theory in Practice*, Gardner explains that people can have strengths in seven different types of intelligences: linguistic, logical-mathematical, spatial, musical, body-kinesthetic, interpersonal and intrapersonal. Once a person's intelligence strength is identified, it can be used as a learning avenue for content that is typically associated with a different type of intelligence.

I found this phenomenon fascinating and set out to build interactive experiences especially suited to users with high aptitudes in body-kinesthetic intelligence (people that have good control of body movements and are able to perform specific movements when required and are able to solve problems using their body). While movement would be a key part of these experiences, their content would not be movement related. My theory was that the movement would facilitate the learning of the non-movement related content.

WHY AN EXHIBIT?

After considering other settings, I decided that an educational, computer-based, interactive, movement-driven experience would fit best into an exhibition space. One reason is that the educational goal of an exhibit is specific; it is a one-time learning experience. Therefore, the project would not have to address multiple educational objectives.

A movement-driven, interactive learning experience would also be consistent with the changing role of museums, as physical experiences tend to foster a social atmosphere. Exhibit designer Maeryta Medrano explains that, while "in the past, people tended to view museums as equivalent to schools, more and more they have become places where people have a kind of shared social experience." (Winn, 2003)

THE BARN OWL PROJECT

Background

The *Barn Owl Project* is an animated, movement-driven, interactive exhibit designed for the Franklin Park Zoo. It teaches children about barn owls through animation and interactive physical activities.

The idea for the project emerged after a meeting with zoo staff. They had an interest in teaching children about birds or owls. They also had a space at Franklin Farm in which they could host an exhibit.

Franklin Farm is an area at Franklin Park Zoo where children can interact with farm and barn animals. It includes a large barn and several outdoor pens for chickens, sheep, goats and other barn animals. When I first visited, there were placards about the animals but no interactive exhibits in the space.

Why Barn Owls?

Inside the barn at Franklin Farm there were two barn owls residing in an elevated cage. Despite a sign informing visitors to "Look Up!" to see the barn owls, they were easily missed by the casual visitor. Creating an exhibit dedicated to these creatures would finally bring them the attention they deserved.

Barn owls make an interesting subject for an interactive, animated movement-based exhibit. They are distinct looking animals from which a unique character could be created. Their behavior is also fascinating. They are nocturnal and rely on their super-sensitive hearing to do all their hunting at night. Barn owls also mate for life.

"Anything that gets the kids engaged—that's not a passive learning experience where maybe they are just reading or being lectured to—anything that involves them learning in a more dynamic way has a better chance to leave more of an impression."

— Anthea Lavalle, Director of Education at the Franklin Park Zoo

HOW IT WORKS

The exhibit is based on the life of an adult barn owl named Larry. [1] In the program, Larry talks about his life and then gives the user an opportunity to participate in games that mimic his life experiences. There are five interactive, movement-driven activities interspersed with six pieces of linear animation. The interactive experiences are: hatching, feeding, flying, warming the nest and hunting. The games are fairly simple. Most are timed experiences where the user

has to accomplish a goal within a certain period of time.

The mat in the exhibit is comprised of seven pads (labeled A-D and 1-3), and the arrangement of the pads facilitates the playing of all of the five games.

Hatching Interactive

In the hatching interactive, the user must break Larry, the unborn chick, out of his shell by jumping on pads that represent his legs, wings and egg tooth. The challenge in this game is that the user needs to press the pads at the right time and also move very quickly. [2]

Feeding Interactive

In the feeding interactive, the user must help Larry compete against his four other siblings to get fed. To move Larry in front of one of his siblings, the user needs to select the pad associated with the sibling immediately in front of him. The user must be quick because sometimes Larry is pushed back by another chick. If and when he makes it to the mother barn owl, he must

3

4

squawk to get fed before another one of his siblings pushes him out of the way. Larry needs to eat four rodents in one minute in order to be successful at this task. [3]

Flying Interactive

The flying interactive begins with the mother barn owl perched on the barn window with a young Larry. [4] When she nudges him off of the window sill, the user must make Larry fly by doing quick jumps on three of the pads. If he is not successful within 3 tries he loses the game.

Defending the Nest Interactive

In this interactive experience the user takes on the role of Lulu, the female owl. She has two jobs: 1. keep the eggs warm and 2. fend off predators during the egg incubation period (one minute). To keep the eggs warm, the user must touch the pad corresponding to each egg, frequently and lightly. To prevent the predators (a cat, snake and raccoon) from attacking the eggs, the player must use her attack button. Predators that return more than once need to be fought off more

aggressively than the first time they are encountered, which means that the user has to press the pad more than once. This forces Lulu to be away from her nest longer, which makes the game harder as time goes on. If one of the eggs is attacked by a predator or gets too cold, the user loses the game.

Hunting Interactive

In the hunting interactive, the user takes on the role of Larry trying to capture his prey (a rodent). Each location corresponds to a pad. When the user hears the sound corresponding to a location, she must quickly choose the correct pad. If she does this quickly enough, the owl catches the rodent. The owl must capture four rodents within one minute. [5]

"Welcome to Franklin Farm! I'm Larry, and I'm here to teach you what it's like to be a barn owl. Just keep watching, and I'll let you know when to move!"

PROCESS

For the linear animation between the interactive experiences, the script needed to be

factual but light and conversational in tone. Reliable references as well as feedback from my zoo collaborators assured a truthful script. Establishing the appropriate tone was more challenging, requiring several revisions of the script.

A colleague with acting and voice-over experience played the role of the narrator, Larry the barn owl. He truly gave life to the character. His skillful reading made the script sound natural, light and jovial. [7]

A paper prototyping session helped determine how the interactive experiences would work. The goal of this process was to simulate the real experience as much as possible by acting out the parts of the computer and the user. From this experience, we discovered that many of the games could be simplified.

In creating the animated content, lessons learned in previous projects drove the direction of the piece. To teach users how to play the game, I took advantage of the flexibility of the animated medium. For example, in some cases, I show what is happening on the screen at the same time as I illustrate what should be happening on the

mat. I also utilized fluid and unexpected transitions to a greater extent in an effort to hold the viewer's interest between games.

Programming the interactive experiences required extensive testing. Some of the games worked well when playing them with a keyboard, but not initially with the mat. For example, in the flying game, it was easy to make the owl fly if you were pressing keys on the keyboard. Making the owl fly by jumping on the mat was much more difficult. I had to alter the variables controlling the level of difficulty several times after watching users attempt it on a mat.

ASSESSMENT

This project is a true culmination of all I have learned at MassArt. It's been rewarding to combine my fascination with body memory and animation into such an educational piece.

The *Barn Owl Project* was installed in the gallery at the New England Institute of Art as part of the Boston Cyberarts Festival in April 2005. It resided at the Franklin Park Zoo for one month during the summer of 2005. This allowed me to watch many different people experience the exhibit.

These observations validated my concept. Participants really had to move! Some got quite sweaty and attributed failures in the game to being out of shape. While some adults were initially shy about playing, many lost their inhibitions once they were absorbed in the game. Children, on the other hand, approached the physical challenge with enthusiasm and wanted to play again and again.

The exhibit was also successful at fostering a social atmosphere. Observers would help the player by yelling out what pad(s) he should hit. Sometimes children played the game collaboratively. For example, when testing the Defending the Nest game, on brother-sister team split duties, one monitoring the attack button while the other warmed the eggs.

In the midst of all the fun, by participating in these perceptual experiences, players gained an appreciation for what it is like to be a barn owl. One player reported that she never thought warming a nest would be difficult. Many were surprised to learn how barn owls hunted, and how many rodents the owl needed to capture. I do not believe that the participants would have this level of understanding if the format of the exhibit were more traditional.

the "zhi" project

JUN LI

Class of 2000

1

The "Zhi" project is an experiment in creating a function-driven, intuitive, interactive teaching tool, conveying an innovative pedagogy for teaching Chinese characters.

Chinese characters are complex relative to other writing systems. Roman letters give relatively precise information on pronunciation, but no information on meaning. In contrast, Chinese characters give less precise pronunciation information, but do give information on meaning.

It's often said that each Chinese character is a picture, but in the scholar XuShen's dictionary, only four percent of Chinese characters are actually pictographs, one percent are simple ideographs which suggest an abstract meaning directly, and thirteen percent are logical aggregates which combine the meanings of different characters to create a new meaning. Although pictographs, ideographs and logical aggregates indicate the meaning of characters by their forms, none of these three categories gives any hint as to pronunciation.

The pictophonetic method was developed to create new characters by combining one element indicating meaning and the other sound. More and more characters have been made this way and today such pictophonetic complexes comprise more than eighty-three percent of all Chinese characters. Therefore, learning the structures of pictophonetic complexes has become one of the crucial aspects of the Chinese writing system. For beginners, especially adults, understanding this structure enable them to enlarge their vocabulary at a much faster pace.

In language learning, interaction between teacher and student is important. Effective language learning requires feedback, which

2

3

1, 4. Introductory screens (stills from animation).

2, 3. "How to use this program" section, includes the diagram of information architecture representing the structure of the CD-ROM, which serves as an overview of the content.

5. Main interface based on "Zhi" character and its components. Pronounciation of each character is triggered by mouse-over.

6. "Zhi" character front page has access to the following menus: "Character in Combination," "Stroke Order," and "Historical Evolution" as well as to global navigation.

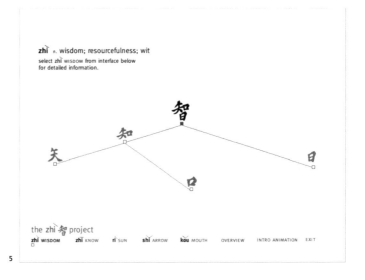

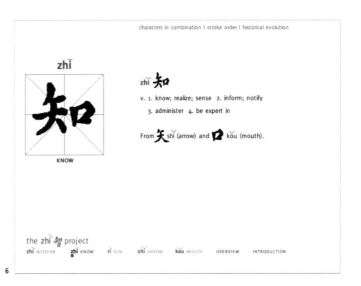

is a form of interaction. In the past few decades, there has been a shift in focus from teaching to learning, from the teacher to the learner. Learner-centeredness requires respect for and accommodation of individual backgrounds and learning styles. It gives the learner control in material selection/sequencing and the pace of progress. Interactivity, properly used, facilitates learner centered teaching methods. However, with over a billion people speaking Chinese, the most common ways of learning Chinese remains traditional: textbooks, tutors and tapes.

In recent years, with the escalating development of computer technology, many computer assisted language-learning programs have been produced. For learning Chinese, digitized audio makes possible to include the demonstration of pronunciation. Digitized video provides an effective way of showing how Chinese characters have changed over time. The teaching of a character's stroke order and direction can be achieved by animation, which was formerly achievable only with a human instructor. Random and rapid access contributes to easy learner control.

The intention of my interactive teaching program is to create an environment in which it is easy to explore the structure of Chinese characters, to see why they look they way they do, and how they relate to each other. The emphasis of this tool is placed on the structure of pictophonetic complexes, which combines radical and phonetic components. Each character, far from being an arbitrary collection of strokes, is a combination of well defined components, which may themselves be characters. A component may suggest either the meaning or the pronunciation of a character. The process

7. "Ri" character front page.

8, 9. "Historical Evolution" menu of "Ri" character.

10. "Character in Combination" initial menu of "Ri" character.

11, 12. "Character in Combination" menu of "Ri" lets the user dynamicaly change radicals and learn difference in pronounciation (triggered by mouse-over).

13, 14. "Stroke Order", "Show Me" menu of "Ri" "character (stills from animation).

15. "Stroke Order", "Let Me Try" menu allows the learner to practice brush strokes within the grid.

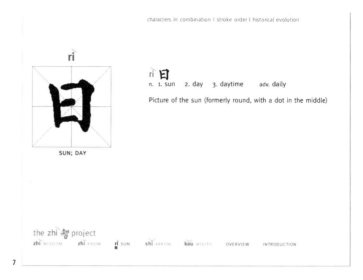

of learning Chinese characters becomes increasingly logical and efficient as the user sees and understands this structure.

The structure of Chinese characters is an essential part of learning those characters, especially when the students are adult beginners, and structure should be introduced at the beginning of the curriculum. The process of learning Chinese characters may therefore entail increasing logic and efficiency, rather than just heavy tasks of memorization, as the beginners grasp the "radical-phonetic" method.

Interactivity is a crucial strength of the new technology, by virtue of the fact that the user can gain control of learning and become an active participant in the learning process. Multimedia is also considered truly revolutionary for language pedagogy. The sound and graphic capabilities of the computer not only have improved presentation they have also made possible what conventional textbooks cannot do.

This project received the Distinction in Communication Design category of the Willy Guhl Prize at the "Design Preis Schweiz 2001" (Swiss Design Award 2001) in Lagenthal, Switzerland.

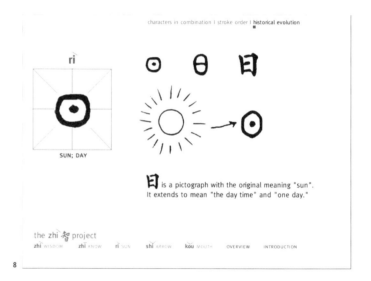

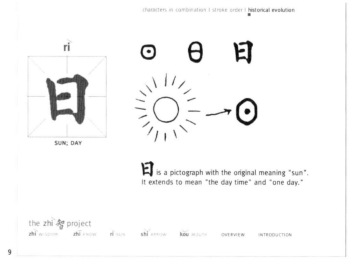

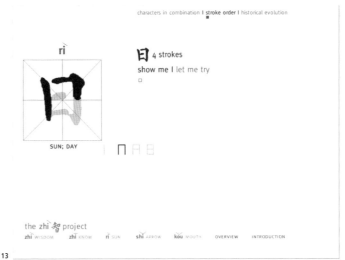

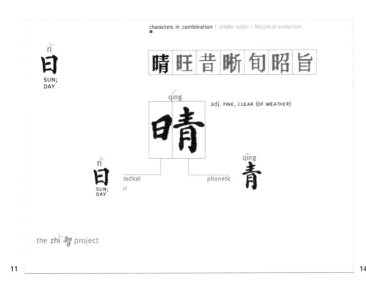

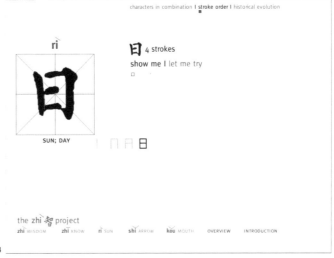

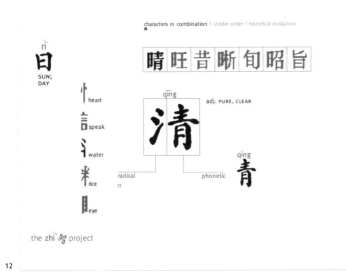

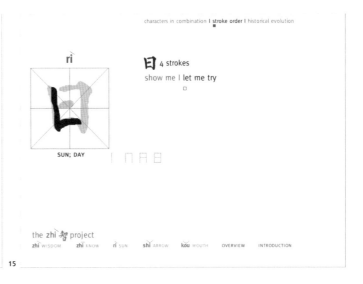

envisioning the human brain: a case study for dynamic interactive visualization in human brain research

FENYA SU

Class of 2002

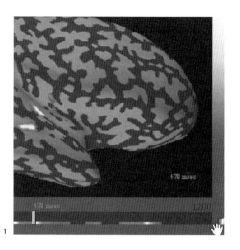

1

1. Timeline signal indicator
2. Interactive small multiples:
opacity slider and scale slider
3. Interactive small multiples:
marker

This thesis proposes dynamic interactive visualization for researchers to explore a large amount of spatiotemporal data. The proposed dynamic interactive visualization uses multiple representations which can increase the understanding of spatiotemporal information. The researchers can make comparisons among images and facilitate the searching of desired information more efficiently.

This thesis discusses three groups of concepts. The first concept, timeline signal indicator, is an essential building block to enhance temporal information. Timeline signal indicator, facilitates the locating of desired temporal points. The second concept, interactive small multiples, facilitates and simplifies the comparison between time instants using multiple images. The third concept, spatiotemporal probe, facilitates the display of complete time series of a specific brain point within brain structure.

The six experiments discussed in the following section were created in order to illustrate the concepts of a. timeline signal indicator, b. interactive small multiples,

and c. spatiotemporal probe. The interface issue is not discussed in this instance.

CONCEPT A: TIMELINE SIGNAL INDICATOR

The advantage of timeline signal indicator is that it provides a constant reference color bar on the timeline with average power indices. In the experiment, the color bar shows the signal of temporal lobe over the span of the entire movie. Potentially the area of timeline signal indicator can be customized by the researchers according their tasks. With the color indication on the timeline, it is easier for researchers to identify the location of the onset point, the points of maximal and minimal activity. [1]

CONCEPT B: INTERACTIVE SMALL MULTIPLES

The concept of interactive small multiples proposes a solution to display the image of each time instant individually and simultaneously without overlapping. Interactive small multiples amplifies, intensifies and reinforces the meaning of images.

Several visualization issues are solved as a consequence of introduction of the

components of interactive small multiples: b1: opacity slider, b2: scale slider, b3: marker, b4: time zoom, and b5: draggable time. Opacity slider helps to resolve the difficulty of observing signal over multiple images obscured by repetitive brain structure in the background. Scale slider controls the size of image by zooming in and out to accommodate the amount of image on screen. Marker provides tools to create regions of focus on multiple images as the reference for comparison. Time zoom allows researchers to display a range of image in a customized temporal definition by specifying the start, the end, and the interval. Draggable time allows researchers to drag images freely to provide a non-sequential method of displaying images.

Concept B1: Opacity Slider

The inflated brain in the background helps the researcher to identify the anatomical location of activity. However when seeing them in small multiples, the same brain structure may obscure the minor dynamic changes of the spatial distribution of the auditory functional responses. The opac-

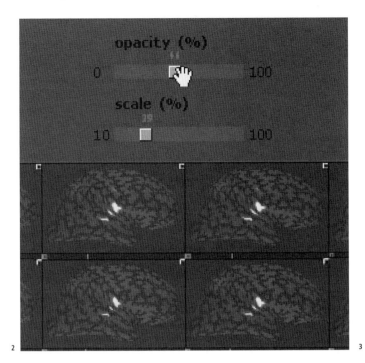

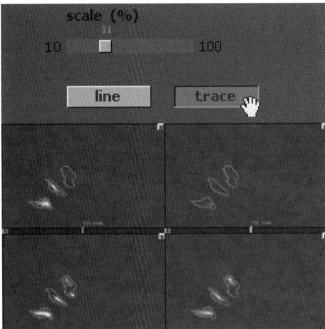

2

3

ity slider allows researchers to control the transparency of brain structure, which appears repetitively in small multiples. By using opacity slider, the static structural brain becomes insignificant and the dynamic changes of functional activations become visually significant. Opacity slider helps brain researches to observe temporal changes of brain activities. [2]

Concept B2: Scale Slider

When there are too many images displayed in the limited screen space, the individual image may be too small to be examined thoroughly. For example, at a specific time instant, researchers may need anatomical brain structure to understand the spatial distribution of the activity. The inflated brain partially alleviates the difficulty of identifying anatomical structure hidden inside the folded brain. The advantage of scale slider is to allow to control of the size of an individual image. A larger image allows more accurate spatial distribution of the functional activities (such as distinguishing the activities at gyrus or sulcus). A smaller image allows more snapshots of

brain movies to be displayed simultaneously on the screen. The trade-off in selecting appropriate scale of an individual image can be achieved dynamically using the scale slider. [2]

Concept B3: Marker

Image comparison is a powerful tool of visualization by providing references to highlight differences. When comparing power activity between images, brain structure in the background provides anatomical reference for comparison. In principle, the user can select one key image to create localized markers. The identical markers will be displayed simultaneously at all shown small multiples to facilitate the comparisons between images. Creating localized markers can be done by using either line tool or trace tool in this concept. Line tool allows researchers to outline freely. Potentially there will be several pre-defined basic geometrical shapes and anatomical landmarks (eg: sulci and gyri) to generate localized references. Trace tool automatically outlines the area of functional activation in one key image selected by researchers. The

same trace will appear on other small multiples automatically. Marker provides alternative customized and automatic tools as reference for comparison. This reference is especially useful when the brain structure in the background is invisible. [3]

The following concepts b4 and b5 are proposed to provide alternative linear and nonlinear dynamic image display. Rather than showing all images from the beginning to the end defined by the original brain movie, these two concepts allow the user to select images of interest for detailed exploration.

Concept B4: Time Zoom

Time zoom allows researchers to specify the starting point and the end point of the small multiples. This is equivalent to using a fixed temporal resolution while varying the observation window to explore the data within an interval of interest. This visualization makes researchers focused on the interval without being distracted by other time spans. Additionally, the temporal resolution can be modified to allow efficient visualization of fast varying responses

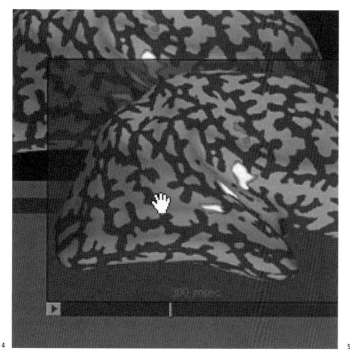
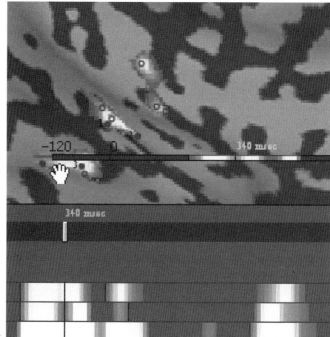

4. Interactive small multiples:
draggable time

5. Spatiotemporal probe

and slow changing responses. For example in the experiment, a finer temporal resolution (smaller interval value) generates slow changing responses while a coarser temporal resolution (larger interval value) generates fast changing responses.

Concept B5: Draggable Time

Instead of displaying all the images in the time sequence defined in the original brain movie, researchers can drag any image of any sequence directly from movie player and place them next to each other. This concept enables an efficient way to compare two or more snapshots of brain activities. Draggable time [4] is the implementation of nonlinear browsing as compared to the conventional brain movie browsing and time zoom, which are completely linear. The advantage is based on 1. selecting interested time instants, which can be more than two, and 2. displaying these brain images side by side for the convenience of comparison on spatial distribution and the signal intensity.

CONCEPT C: SPATIOTEMPORAL PROBE

Time-signal plot is a popular tool used by many brain researchers to show the changes of signal power over time. The advantage of time-signal plot is to appreciate the temporal properties of z-score directly. However, the spatial information regarding the exact location of rendered brain structure, as well as the topological relationship between brain locations, are completely invisible. The disadvantages of losing spatial information can be partially solved by the brain movie, which shows concatenated spatial information. Spatiotemporal probe [5] is a concept trying to combine the benefits of these two visualizations. First, researchers locate a point or a region. Highlighted location brings a color bar to provide instant information regarding the complete time series of the activity associated with that location. With the color bar, researchers are able to review the complete temporal activity of a single brain location in the reference to all brain locations simultaneously.

To further help the comparison of brain activity at multiple brain locations, this concept also provides the functionality to drag the color bar beneath the main window. This process can be repeated to collect color bars from different brain locations aligned with each other and to the timeline. Spatiotemporal probe provides a visually convenient way to perform qualitative comparison between brain locations without the spatial constraint of the original brain movie.

In implementation, the time series of the brain location can be encoded by either color bars or time-signal plots. The color bar was chosen to maintain consistency with the concept of timeline signal indicator. Furthermore, time-signal plots require in general a larger area to show the complete information, which might obscure the brain activities at other brain locations at this time instant. Nevertheless, time-signal plots provide more precise quantitative information compared to color bars. Therefore users can potentially switch these two options on demand.

INTEGRATION OF FUNCTIONALITIES IN DYNAMIC INTERACTIVE VISUALIZATION: A USER SCENARIO

In the case study, the researcher uses the brain movie generated from MEG with external auditory stimuli to explore the brain responses to external acoustic 40Hz clicks.

Specific questions of interests include 1. the identification of brain regions sensitive to the provided auditory stimuli, 2. the temporal information regarding the onset and the maximal responses of auditory area, 3. the transition of brain activity from the onset to the maximal response, 4. exploration of subtle changes of functional activity with anatomical landmarks, 5. locating the representative local responses within auditory area, and 6. comparing the activities of theses representative locations across time. This includes the integrated manipulation of the original data in the brain movie in spatial 1, 5, temporal 2, 6 and spatiotemporal 3, 4 domains.

Given the original brain movie, traditionally the researcher has to drag the slider bar of the brain movie to find the onset and the maximal power. With timeline signal indicator [1], the researcher immediately locates the onset and the maximal power of brain activity. To compare images of these two temporal instants, with this interface the researcher can use the playhead back and forth to enable the contrasting of functional activities at these two instants. To avoid this repetitive process, the researcher uses draggable time [4] to display the image at 210 msec and the image at 600 msec in parallel. This leads to the examining the signal transition between 210 msec and 600 msec. Instead of dragging them one by one from the brain movie, time zoom allows the researcher to specify 210 msec as the start point, 600 msec as the end point and 10 msec as the temporal resolution (i.e. interval). As a result, 40 images corresponding to the selected interval are displayed on-screen. Each image includes time-invariant brain anatomy and time-varying functional activities at different time instants within this interval. The repetitive brain anatomy obscures the subtle changes of functional activity coded by colors. To avoid visual distraction due to brain anatomy, opacity slider [2] is used to adjust the transpar-

ency of the brain structure. Consequently, color-coded brain activity thus becomes visually significant. To further investigate the details of functional activities, scale slider [2] is employed to magnify the size of individual small multiples within this 390 msec interval. Subsequently, the researcher utilizes marker [3] to outline the signal of the image at 210 msec in order to elucidate the change of activities using 210 msec as the reference of comparison. The identical activity outlines are shown within all small multiples accordingly. To explore representative responses at distinct brain locations, spatiotemporal probe [5] is used to provide the complete signal fluctuations at selected brain locations. By placing the color bar encoding activities at indicated locations, the researcher can perform direct comparison of brain activity at these places.

CONCLUSION

The thesis proposed the dynamic interactive visualization to facilitate the manipulation and exploration of large-size and high-resolution spatiotemporal brain imaging data. Based on a combined MEG/fMRI auditory project conducted in Mass General Hospital, the data can be explored dynamically and interactively to reveal the spatial features, including the anatomical location and distribution of the functional activity, as well as temporal features, including the onset and duration of brain activations.

The dynamic interactive visualization contains three major concepts: timeline signal indicator, an enhancement of temporal information by providing temporal references to the brain activity, spatiotemporal probe, an interactive tool to facilitate the display of complete time series of a specific brain point with brain structural reference, and interactive small multiples, a collection of multiple images to facilitate and to simplify the comparison in spatial and temporal domain. Specifically, interactive small multiples depends on five components to amplify, intensify and reinforce the meaning of images. They are opacity slider, scale slider, marker, time zoom and draggable time. All together they resolve the difficulty of observing signal over multiple images obscured by repetitive brain structure in the background, accommodate the amount of

image on-screen, create regions of focus on multiple images as the reference for comparison, allow researchers to display a range of image in a customized temporal definition by specifying the start, the end, and the interval, and provide a non-sequential method of displaying image by dragging.

The reviews from two researchers in the discipline of the brain mapping confirmed the effectiveness and the improved efficiency in data investigation provided by the dynamic interactive visualization. The three proposed concepts are useful to compare different activities and regional functional responses in either scientific or clinical applications. The reviewers confirmed that the integration of these three concepts in dynamic interactive visualization streamlined the conventional process to a single set of spatiotemporal brain imaging data, which can be presented freely in spatial and temporal domain in the limited space.

The reviewers suggested alternative options in spatiotemporal probe by both color-coded probe as well as time-signal plots in order to provide more quantitative information. The reviewers also suggested a future study to provide multiple subject comparisons. This would require a new computational technique in order to build credible transformation between subjects. Provided with data and the mapping between subjects, most concepts proposed in the thesis could be readily applied to perform data exploration and comparison.

visual elements of motion capture

SAM MONTAGUE

Class of 2003

We rely on our senses to gather data on the external environment around us. Our nervous system continually processes this data to create a perceptual "picture" of the world outside ourselves. In the course of our tool-making evolution, we have developed technologies that not only extend our physical abilities but also extend the range of our natural senses. Through the microscope we see an infinitely small world. Through the television we see live pictures from any corner of the globe. What is fascinating is the ability of technology to capture events in space-time that are beyond the sensory capacity of our natural vision. Certainly Leonardo da Vinci had a keen eye and remarkable drawing skills, however like many artists he had visual limitations. Leonardo da Vinci could not be expected to accurately render a world hidden by the fourth dimension. In order for us to understand the dynamics of an object in motion we must use technology that can capture and represent motion that is either too fast, or too slow, too small, or too large for us to observe with the unaided eye. Without this technology, our natural visual perception renders much of the fourth dimension invisible. With the invention of technologies in the nineteenth century that could visually record events by capturing instances in time, we ushered in a new revolution in visual communication. These motion capture technologies enabled us to visualize kinetic forms that were previously obscured by the normal passage of time.

Before I began my study of motion capture representation, I was struck by the similarities of contemporary motion representations in film, photography, computer-generated imagery (CGI) and video, and with the work of the motion capture pioneers like

Eadweard Muybridge and EJ Marey. For instance, the technique for the "Bullet Time" special effect developed by John Gaeta for the movie *The Matrix* and the galloping horse motion study conducted by Eadweard Muybridge over a hundred years earlier are very similar. The complexity of the technology has increased—Muybridge used 12-24 cameras in an array and Gaeta used over 100 cameras—however the basic concept behind the visual reconstruction is the same. Each representation is merely a parametric change of the same basic visual elements. It was interesting to think that the roots of a cutting edge special effects technique originated over 100 years ago. By making a parametric change, Muybridge and Gaeta created very different visual experiences for the viewer. From this observation I began to explore two basic questions. Are there fundamental visual elements that are universal for all motion capture representations and could these visual elements be codified into a common language for all motion representations?

By studying hundreds of examples, both historical and contemporary, I developed a way of identifying and diagramming the basic visual elements that are fundamental to all motion capture representations. These elements were described and illustrated an interactive prototype. [1–6] The prototype includes many examples that I researched to formulate my visual elements diagram. These examples were organized into a matrix. [4] so that it would be possible to click on each one to expand and visually display each representation. The other purpose of the motion matrix was to use the motion elements and their parameters as filters to help sort and clarify the myriad of representational possibilities available to the designer. [5] The prototype also went beyond the motion elements diagram and included key historical references as well as physiological issues associated with motion perception. [3, 6]

CODIFYING THE VISUAL ELEMENTS

The crux of my investigation was to codify the major elements of motion capture representation. However, before developing an organized structure of motion representation, it is important to note that the ability to perceive motion is a construction of the mind. An example of this mental motion construction is the famous Times Square news "Zipper" that first appeared in 1928. The words describing news events seem to miraculously move across the New York Times building when the thousands of light bulbs in the display remain stationary. The display designers knew that by correctly timing the flash of each stationary bulb, the "Zipper" display would trick the viewer's brain into constructing a coherent motion of letterforms that does not physically exist. The real magic is not the technology that we use to recreate motion but our brains ability to construct the apparent motion in a variety of forms.

The codification of visual elements begins with a simple definition of motion. For motion to occur, an object must go through some sort of change in position and or form through space and time. Therefore, we can define motion this way.

Motion is the displacement of objects through space and time.

To put this definition into context, we can watch a figure skater jumping and spinning *(Object + Displacement)* while the camera

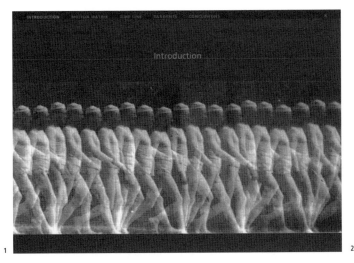

1

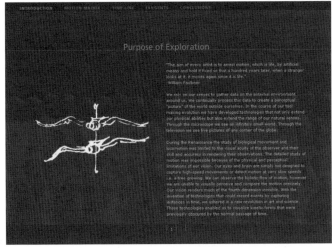

2

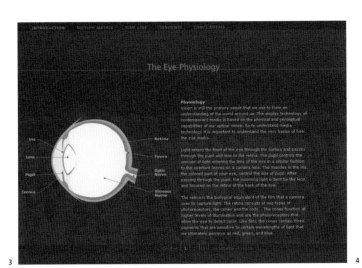

3

4

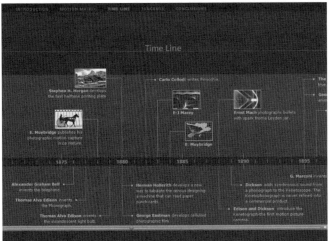

5

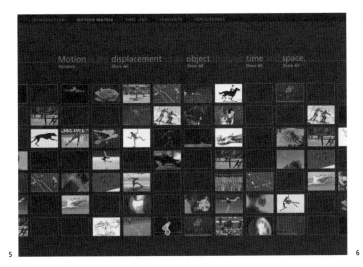

6

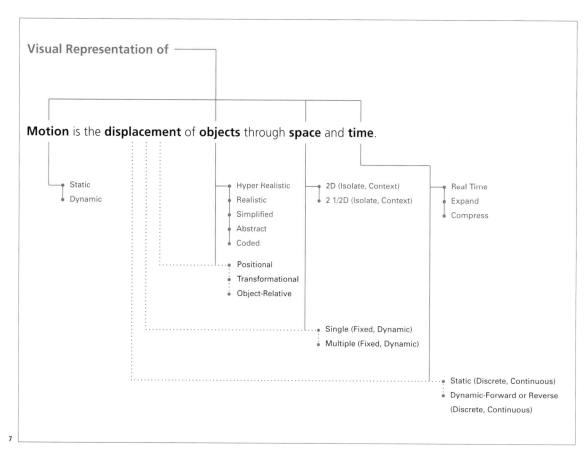

Visual Representation of

Motion is the **displacement** of **objects** through **space** and **time**.

- Static
- Dynamic

- Hyper Realistic
- Realistic
- Simplified
- Abstract
- Coded

- Positional
- Transformational
- Object-Relative

- 2D (Isolate, Context)
- 2 1/2D (Isolate, Context)

- Real Time
- Expand
- Compress

- Single (Fixed, Dynamic)
- Multiple (Fixed, Dynamic)

- Static (Discrete, Continuous)
- Dynamic-Forward or Reverse (Discrete, Continuous)

7

zooms out and tracks with the action *(Space + Displacement)* as the video camera records the action *(Time + Displacement)*. By using this definition, we can isolate the key elements of visual representation—Motion, Displacement, Objects, Space, and Time. We can take this definition and diagrammatically illustrate [7] the connections and interrelationships between the basic visual elements and each element's parametric range.

In the diagram, the visual representation of motion can be depicted either statically or dynamically. An object can be represented either realistically or in some form of abstraction. The representation of object displacement can either be positional displacement, transformational, or object-relative. The representation of space involves two methods; 2-D and 2½-D. 2-D refers to a flat representation whereas 2½-D is defined as implied depth such as we see in a perspective drawing. Attached to the representation of space is the attribute of frame of reference that serves as a comparison between the desire to isolate a particular action or the desire to provide a context of motion with other objects. Space displacement is concerned with the point of view. Point of view can be characterized as single or multiple and contain the attributes of being fixed or dynamic. Time can be represented as real time compressed time or extended time. Time displacement can be characterized as Fixed or Dynamic and have the attributes of continuous, discrete or a combination of both. The designer can manipulate the parameters of these elements in order to achieve different informational and or expressive goals.

CASE STUDY

While some of the parametric terminology in the diagram builds upon familiar representational descriptions, others require a more thorough explanation that is beyond the scope of this article. We can however, look at a case study I developed [8–15] based on Gjon Mili's famous photograph of Picasso drawing a centaur with a light (1947). This case study exemplifies how varying parameters of each element can fundamentally change the content expressed and the viewer's experience of the representation.

In the original photographic image [15], Mili has captured on a single frame of film a static visual representation of motion. Objects in his photograph are represented in a realistic manner and the image reveals a positional change in the light that Picasso is holding. Space is depicted in 2½-D and through a single fixed point of view. The line that forms the shape of the Centaur represents the continuous representation of the time that Picasso took to actually draw the shape with light. The image of Picasso himself represents the discrete interval of time when he began his drawing. So this photograph combines both continuous and discrete attributes of static time displacement to render time. This combination of discrete and continuous attributes reveals the shape of the centaur and the author of the motion, Picasso. Mili's motion capture reveals the structure and pattern of Picasso's motion in a way that would not be possible with the unaided eye.

To illustrate the point of how the modification of parameters fundamentally changes the meaning and content of a representation, I animated Mili's static image to simulate what the visual experience would be like if you had personally witnessed the event. Using Flash, I abstracted Picasso's light into a single white dot (object parameter) and reanimated the motion in a simulated real time discrete visual representation of time. The space parameter was modified to a 2 dimensional representation by removing the background. The result was a dot that seemed to randomly float around the screen. This dynamic recreation roughly simulated how the natural event appeared to a person watching Picasso, however the simulation did not reveal the recognizable pattern of the motion. [8]

The variation continued with the animation of the white dot however the time displacement attribute was changed to continuous in order to reveal the true intent of the motion. [8–12] With this representation the purpose of the motion is reviled however there is another level of information missing. To add the final level of important information, the motion artist, Picasso, is revealed through an object transformation. [9–15]

These explorations were finally stitched together into one movie to demonstrate how varying the parameters of the basic elements fundamentally change the type information revealed and visual experience of the representation.

BENEFITS OF CODIFYING VISUAL ELEMENTS

By identifying these elements and describing their attributes we can better understand the representational parameters used to envision motion. These elements of motion representation can be thought of in the same way that we use the basic elements of typography. Designers can control location, letterform, size, leading, kerning, color etc. to convey meaningful content. The elements of motion capture function in the same manner. Like the basic elements of type, these elements provide representational variables for design possibilities. They are used in endless variation to create a unique visual expression.

It is easy to assume that technology completely controls the nature of the representation. However if designers can see beyond the superficial limits of the technology then we can control the representational language of the technology instead of the technology controlling us. EJ Marey's interest was the study of biomechanics. For him, photography was a tool to unlock the secrets of motion. He was always trying to enhance the capability of photography to match the continuous representations of his mechanical graphic inscriptors. The abstraction of the human figure was Marey's visual solution to the problem of maintaining true object displacement while increasing the frequency of the images taken. His early experiments that captured realistic images resulted in a figure field confusion caused by the multiple figures superimposed on one negative. By dressing his assistant in a black suit with white stripes, Marey was able to achieve his scientific objective of reducing motion into an elegant graphic notation. He was able to see past photography's limitation by suppressing the representational essence of the technology. Marey did not limit his view of photography to the relm of pure realistic representation. The lesson for the communication designer is that the informational goal should rule the visual expression not just the predetermined solution of the technology.

8

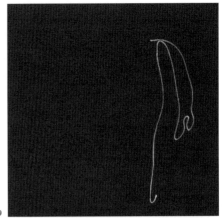

9

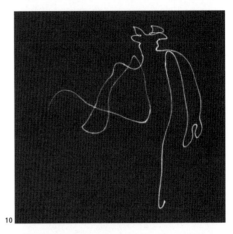

10

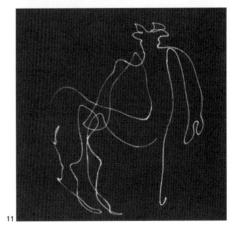

11

Contemporary technologies like Dartfish's SimulCam or Orad's Virtual Swimmer take advantage of digital image manipulation to modify time and object displacement in order to broadcast sporting events with new informational depth. SimulCam creates virtual object relative displacement by superimposing two separate time displacements into one simultaneous event. The result is that the TV viewer can easily compare object-relative displacement of two Olympic alpine skiers and see where the race was won or lost. While the clarity of the representation is not perfect, the visualization of showing two separate skiers running the same course simultaneously is very interesting.

Virtual Swimmer transforms time into an abstract linear object that moves up and down the pool at world record pace. This allows the viewer to see exactly where the swimmer is in relation to the world record. Orad's innovation is transforming time from a coded representation into an abstract representation (yellow line) that can be superposed onto the video image of the event. Time is no longer a flashing blur of numbers but a tangible element that enables the viewer to envision the athletes' performance through object-oriented displacement.

These are just a few examples of how the variables of the basic motion elements can be manipulated to achieve a certain visual expression. The hope is that by codifying these elements designers can identify and understand the parametric range of possibilities for captured motion representation and communication. The result is a primer of the universal elements that a designer can manipulate in order to generate a clear visual explanation of objects in motion.

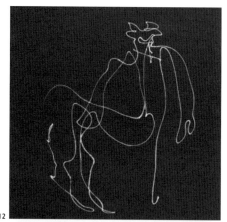

12

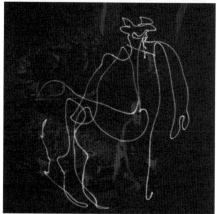

13

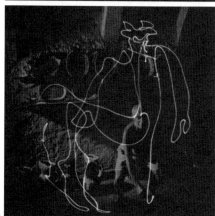

14

15

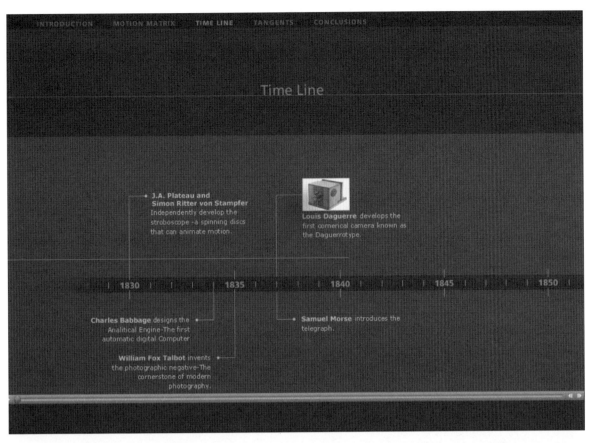

Time Line

J.A. Plateau and Simon Ritter von Stampfer Independently develop the stroboscope -a spinning discs that can animate motion.

Louis Daguerre develops the first comerical camera known as the Daguerrotype.

1830   1835   1840   1845   1850

Charles Babbage designs the Analitical Engine-The first automatic digital Computer

Samuel Morse introduces the telegraph.

William Fox Talbot invents the photographic negative-The cornerstone of modern photography.

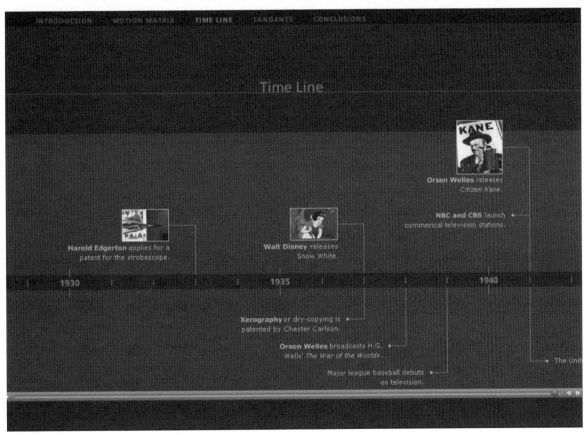

Time Line

Orsen Welles releases *Citizen Kane.*

NBC and CBS launch commerical television stations.

Harold Edgerton applies for a patent for the strobescope.

Walt Disney releases *Snow White.*

1930   1935   1940

Xerography or dry-copying is patented by Chester Carlson.

Orson Welles broadcasts H.G. Wells' *The War of the Worlds*.

Major league baseball debuts on television.

The Unit

defining gesture: a visual dictionary for american sign language

SUE-ELLEN LAMB née JOHNSON

Class of 2004

DESIGNING THE FINAL PROTOTYPE

The *Defining Gesture* project is comprised of two interconnected parts—the "Search" interface and the "Definition" interface. After mapping out the functionality for both interfaces, it was time for the final visual design. My first task was to make the interface pieces seem like other computer-based tools—media players, CD-rom games and demos, and even Instant Messenger—by softening corners/edges, and giving some modularity. A consistent visual language also needed to be finalized.

THE SEARCH INTERFACE

I began the final design by focusing first on the Search interface. I knew that the toolbars needed to be separated into elements that would seem "stacked" on top of each other in the same screen real estate. There would be tabs or buttons available for each section, so everything would be accessible, no matter which was "on top." In this final version, the entire block of toolbars would be one moveable element. I also planned that the search results would be a separate interface element.

I then created the icons for the system. They would identify categories of information—the Hand Shape section, the Motion Path Section, and the Facial Expression section, as well as the options within each section. I then built a shell of the interface that would show that each section was a different piece, but all part of the same whole. Having already defined how the different pieces would interact wth each other, I then worked to fine-tune the functionality of each section separately. [1]

The Main Search Interface Area

Since the main area with the model is the focal point of the system, I decided to place it on the top left of the interface, to indicate that the toolbars, etc. were supplemental to it. In this section, users can manipulate the model to recreate a sign, as well as choose which model to work with, and turn the grid on or off. The Reset button in this section will remove all changes that have been made in all toolbars and bring you back to the beginning of the search. The Reset button in each toolbar are more specific, and will only remove changes made from that toolbar.

The Handshape Toolbar

The Handshape Toolbar is used to identify particular handshapes, or general categories of handshapes, that are used in signs. This toolbar contains 34 handshape options divided into three categories. In order to use space most efficiently, and to avoid overwhelming the user with too many choices, each category is represented by just three samples, with an option to view all handshapes in each category as needed. Once the user decides which shape or hand shape category is correct, there are various ways to indicate the choice. [2]

One way is to select a handshape or handshape category icon from the toolbar and drag it onto the appropriate hand on the model, where it will "snap" into position. The model's image will then change to show the chosen handshape. If a category icon is used, a small version of the icon will remain on the hand to indicate the category.

If the user clicks on the hand to select it before dragging the icon to it, the hand will be highlighted in green, but it is not necessary to do so.

Instead of dragging, the user may also either click first on the model's hand and then on the shape or category icon, or vice-versa. The chosen icon will then automatically move to the hand and snap into position. In all cases, when a user rests the mouse over a handshape icon, a larger image will appear to give the user a better view of the shape.

The Motion Path Toolbar

The purpose of the Motion Path toolbar is to identify the "gesture" of a sign—where the hands move in relation to the body. Through a long process of experimentation, I was able to simplify the categories of motion to four—straight line, wavy line, arc and circle—that could be identified using icons in the toolbar.

There are two ways to identify a motion path. First, the user can click on the type of motion in the toolbar, and then click once on the hand used, click again on/near the model where the path begins, and click a third time where the path ends. The system will then draw the chosen type of path between those points. The starting point is represented by an open square, and the end point by a closed square.

The user may also "draw" a motion path using just the mouse. First, the user can click on the appropriate hand, then click and drag the hand from the start to end points in space near the model, or click once at the start and once at the end points of the path. By default, the system will draw a straight line between the points. [3]

Once a path is drawn, the user may manipulate it using two methods. First, each path includes a small "handle" at its midpoint. Users can click and drag this handle in any direction, and the path will curve in response. If the desired path has more than one curve in it, the user can also rest the mouse near one half of the path (until a small curved-line icon appears at the top of the cursor), and then drag the section of the path into a curve. The midpoint stays in place, so the user can create a "wavy" or "bumpy" path.

One of my goals is to make the use of this system as intuitive as possible, so at any point, no matter how a path was drawn or has been manipulated, any method can be used to edit it. For instance, a path that has been changed by using the "handle" could then be clicked on (selected and highlighted in green), and then the user could click on an icon in the toolbar to change the qualities of the path. [4]

As I thought about all the options to offer in this toolbar, I realized that I could include the "Motion in Place" option in this tool, rather than having two separate toolbars. "In place" is defined as moving within one section of the space near the body (as defined by a customized three-dimensional grid), rather than between two different sections. If a motion is "in place," the user can check the correct box to indicate this. In addition to this option, there are check-boxes to indicate whether the same motion is made by both hands, and whether or not the motion is repeated.

The Facial Expression Toolbar

The Facial Expression toolbar is used to indicate specific facial expressions made during the sign that contribute to its meaning. This toolbar contains options for the eyes and the mouth. It works in the same way as the Handshape Toolbar. The user can select options by dragging an icon onto the head, by clicking on an icon and then on the head, or by clicking on the head and then on an icon. The only difference is that in the Facial Expression tool bar, more than one quality can be attributed to the head—one eye option and one mouth option. [5]

Search Results

When the user has finished identifying sign characteristics, and clicks on the "Find the Sign" button at the bottom of the main interface window, a Search Results module will appear. This module will contain thumbnail images of the signs that fit the criteria specified by the user. When moused-over, these thumbnail images will play previews of the signs. To see a full definition of one of the signs, the user will click on the thumbnail. This will open a definition screen on top of the search interface. [6]

The information in the search interface will not change when the definition opens, and so the user can go back and open definitions for more of the signs in the search results, or reset and start over, without losing the first defintion.

In addition to these visual tools I have developed, I have also included a small text-search option in my interface. This will allow my project to be a true "two-way dictionary" that users can also depend on when they simply want to know the sign for a particular English word or phrase.

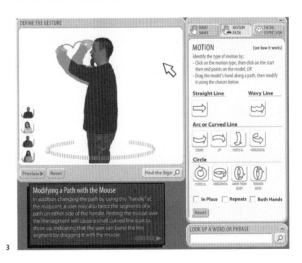

1. The default search interface with Handshape Toolbar showing.
2. Identifying a hand shape. Left hand selected, hand shape category expanded, hand shape detail shown.
3. Identifying a Motion Path. Model seen from left side, path defined by drawing.

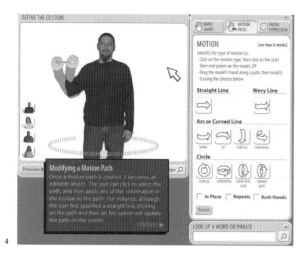

4

5

THE DEFINITION INTERFACE

When I started to create the interfaces for this project, in addition to the "search" interface, I also needed to map out what kind of information the user would be accessing, and how it would be displayed. Based on my understanding of ASL from taking classes, reading, and speaking with experts, I was able to identify a number of particular pieces of information that would combine to create a full "definition" or description of each sign.

My definition interface would need to include:
– The English word or phrase that corresponds to the sign
– A written description of how the sign is made
– An interactive motion graphic of a person making the sign
 – both alone and in the context of a sentence
– Options to see the sign performed by different people to help understand the nuance and subtle qualities of signed language
– Distinct images of the various parts of the motion or shape of the sign that go together to create the whole sign
– Links to definitions of the other signs used in the "context sentence" motion graphic
– Links to definitions of other signs that are related to the defined sign by shape, motion, sign family, or meaning

It was clear that my "definition" interface could be as innovative as my search interface. The New Media elements of motion and interactivity could help to educate users about the nature of the language. There could be many paths to information through and from the definition interface, not just through the search interface.

The Best Use of Video

Because of the visual nature of ASL, I realized that the motion graphic/video part of my definition interface should provide a great deal of interactivity and detail. In addition to being able to view the video of the sign being made, the user could view a zoomed-in detail video of the sign, as well as the sign in context. The user would be able to see each of these parts being performed by different people. A progress bar could also be dragged at a user's desired speed in order to focus attention on any part of the sign. In addition, the sentence would be displayed below the video in both ASL and English to reinforce the differences between the grammar of the two languages.

Cross-Referencing

The connections between related signs seemed to be an opportunity to reinforce the elements that made up my database, and their organization. To do this, I created a grid, or chart, that would show which of the related signs had various elements in common—so a user could see which signs were more closely related on what basis, and learn the differences between relation based on different characteristics.

The Final Definition Interface

First, because the interactivity of the video module included a detail view of the sign, and could be replayed at any speed by the user, I decided that the series of still images of the sign's component parts (that I had included in my initial list of required elements) was unnecessary, and removed that information. I also updated the "Similar Signs" area. It would now include thumbnail images of the signs that could be moused-over to play previews, exactly like the search results section. [7]

The final design of the entire project had become more modular, with each element becoming a separate entity that could be manipulated and moved as the user desired. This carried over to the definition interface in a few important ways. I had already decided that each time a user opened a definition, it would create a new window, so that a user could compare signs to each other easily by viewing them side by side on screen. To maximize use of space in these situations, I added an option to the definition screen. It would offer two views—the default view with all of the information, and a minimized view that would hide the textual and similar-sign information on the left side of the screen, showing only the interactive movie and sentences.

To give users even more flexibility for using space on screen, I also provided the option to minimize the entire definition for a sign. When a definition is minimized, it will show up as a small window header that snaps to the search results section of the interface, and can be maximized for viewing as desired.

By making these changes, I was able to integrate the definition interface much more seamlessly with the search, so that users could more quickly become comfortable with the entire system.

4. **Editing a Motion Path.** Path selected, "handle" being dragged by mouse.

5. **Identifying a Facial Expression.** Dragging an option to the head.

6. **Search Results.** Path shown on model, results module with matches appears below.

7. **Definition Interface.** Definition appears on top of search interface with all options showing by default. Can be moved or minimized, and search options and results still appear in search interface.

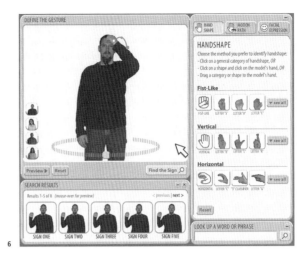

6

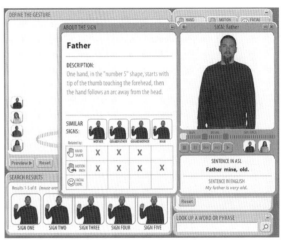

7

american sign language online learning tools

DONG-KEUN JANG

Class of 2001

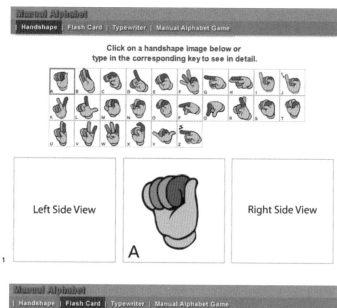

LEARNING AMERICAN SIGN LANGUAGE ALPHABET

Online learning activities under the "Manual Alphabet" menu consist of four types of interactive tools:

Handshape

Users can learn the manual alphabet handshapes through this activity. This tool allows users to display a handshape by typing an alphabetic character on the keyboard or clicking on the small handshape images in the window. To make it clearer for users to see how fingers move, I have color coded each finger. Reviewers of this tool pointed out that some Handshape images were difficult to read correctly when seen from one direction. To address this issue, I created three different views of each handshape. Except for the navigation menu buttons, all of the graphics were created as vector images. [1]

Flash Cards

This tool supports interactive practice of memorizing handshapes by a person at the computer. When a single user uses the tool, computer shows a random handshape and displays English character when the user types the correct key on the keyboard. Upon hitting the next button, computer displays another random handshape. Multiple users can use this tool to practice with each other, with one user selecting a question, and another responding to it. When key is pressed, the corresponding handshape is displayed on screen, and clicking on the image displays the English character. [2, 3]

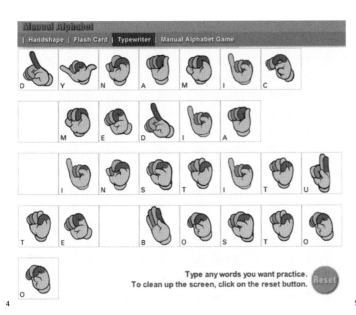

Type any words you want practice.
To clean up the screen, click on the reset button.

Reset

4

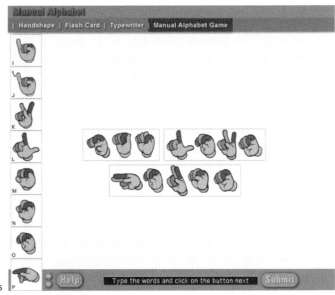

Help   Type the words and click on the button next   Submit

5

Correct   Incorrect

Why? Unlike English adjectives in ASL generally follow the words they are describing. Instead of signing "Old Book," for example, you would sign "Book Old." It's as though you're saying "the book that is old."

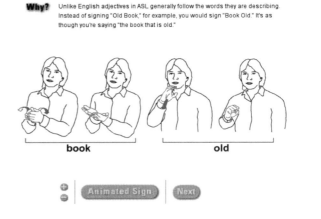

book   old

Animated Sign   Next

6

Typewriter

This tool is useful when practicing words consisting of several handshapes. When users key in words of their choice, the corresponding handshapes are displayed on the screen. These images help users practice finger spelling. Clicking the reset button allows them to key in a new word. [4]

Manual Alphabet Game

This tool aims at helping users improve finger spelling. Upon the start of the game, several finger spellings show up, and fall slowly down screen. Users need to type the correct words into a text box. Users who correctly typed in all the words for corresponding finger spelling go up to the next level. Users also can get help by clicking on the help button, and handshape figures from A to Z are displayed on the screen. [5]

LEARNING AMERICAN SIGN LANGUAGE ADJECTIVES

In American Sign Language, an adjective usually comes after the noun it modifies. For example, "black dog" in English is signed as "dog, black" in ASL, because of the influence from old French Sign Language.

There are three exceptions to this rule: first, when a compound noun is made of two nouns or an adjective and noun, the modifier sign comes before the noun. For example, the order of ASL signs for words like "Christmas tree" or "dark room" is the same as that of English. Second, when two signs are put together to make a new sign, the modifier comes before the sign being modified. For example, Teach + Person means Teacher, and White—Rain means Snow. Third, when a qualifier or quantifier is used with nouns, and in this case, modifier is a facial expression or hand gesture. For example, the intensity of the color Blue, Light Blue, Blue, Dark Blue can be added with facial expression and movement of hand.

Online learning activities in its Grammar section have three submenus, and one of them—the "Practice" button—brings up an interactive tool, which allows users to practice particular word combinations. [6]

It is another game that users can use to assess their understanding level. Users are put to a test that requires them to tell if the order of the ASL for certain English words is correct or not. In response, an explanation on why the illustrated example is correct or incorrect, including an option to see animated signs in continuous sequences.

Manual Alphabet 1

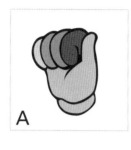
A

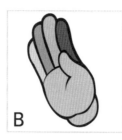
B

C

D

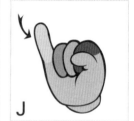
E

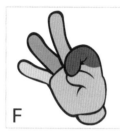
F

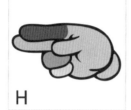
G

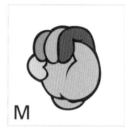
H

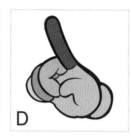
I

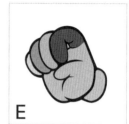
J

K

L

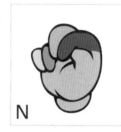
M

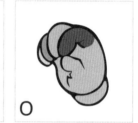
N

O

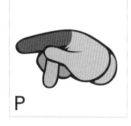
P

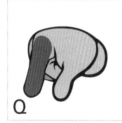
Q

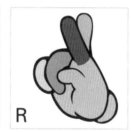
R

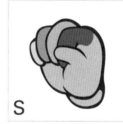
S

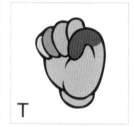
T

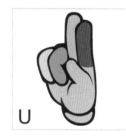
U

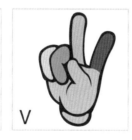
V

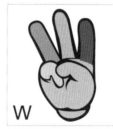
W

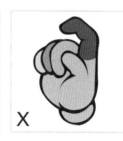
X

Y

7
Z

Fold here to make it as a flash card ▼

8

ANALOG METHODS INTEGRATION

During many presentations of the project, users and critics contributed many interesting questions that resulted in my thinking about offline, or analog alternatives to online activities. Suppose some family members who wish to use the resources, but do not have access to computer. Perhaps other family members would try to make hardcopy printout of the web content. However, online interactive games, cannot be printed out therefore their access is limited. The following is my alternative solution for a situation like this.

Color Coded Gloves

As an equivalent of the online "Manual Alphabet" teaching tools, I developed the color-coded glove. I believe color-coded gloves will benefit deaf children, as well as their families. Instructions on making and using the gloves are included in "User's Tutorial."

Since babies depend on their parents as the source of almost all the information they acquire, the use of the color-coded gloves by the parents has a chance to become more effective than any computer software program or TV learning program.

Users' Tutorial

Each of the sub-contents under the ASL section has its own Users' Tutorial. For example, the "Manual Alphabet" page has a Users' Tutorial in PDF format [7] and the "Flash Card" chapter contains PDF images of each handshape sign with a line at the center, so folding it turns the page into "real" Flashcard. [8]

motion + sound

motion + sound

EVAN KARATZAS

CARLOS LUNETTA

KEIKO MORI

KAROLINA NOVITSKA

ELIF OZUDOGRU

HARUN RAZITH

FENYA SU

MIKE WIGGINS

ELIF OZUDOGRU

Elifman
2003
sound mix by Elif Ozudogru

KAROLINA NOVITSKA

Crossword
2005
music by Telepopmusik

FENYA SU

Cucurrucucu Paloma
2000
music by Gaetano Veloso

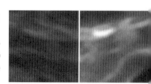

A graduate elective course, *Design for Motion and Sound,* and an undergraduate elective course, *Dynamic Typography,* were specifically created to intensify the study of time-based structures and compositions. Meaning is created through an exploration of image, sound, time and motion in linear and non-linear narrative structures.

This section of the book presents nine short movies developed in response to a project entitled *Sound + Sight,* offered in multiple sections of both courses, taught by Jan Kubasiewicz between 2000 and 2005, in collaboration with the following co-instructors: Teresa Marrin Nakra (2004), Evan Karatzas (2003) and Isabel Meirelles (2002).

Students were asked to explore the visual representation of sound, pacing, and rhythm.

The first step of the process was to mix or compose a sound sequence. That represented a major challenge for many students, since sonic design requires an expertise far beyond the usual scope of visual designers.

The following step was to analyze this sound sequence and to identify various dimensions of contrast in time-based structure. That led to creating a visual map or a diagram of the sound sequence—an initial step in studying the basic correspondences of different vocabularies. Finally, the students developed visualizations as their final deliverables—short movies.

The ultimate goal was to create a *cinematic* (visual/sonic/kinetic) experience by exploring rhythmic and synchronous as well as arrhythmic and asynchronous relationships between image, sound and motion.

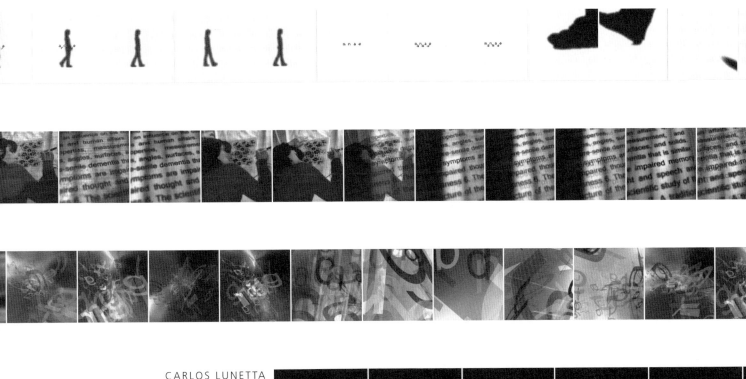

CARLOS LUNETTA

The Near Dorian Experience
2004
music by Carlos Lunetta

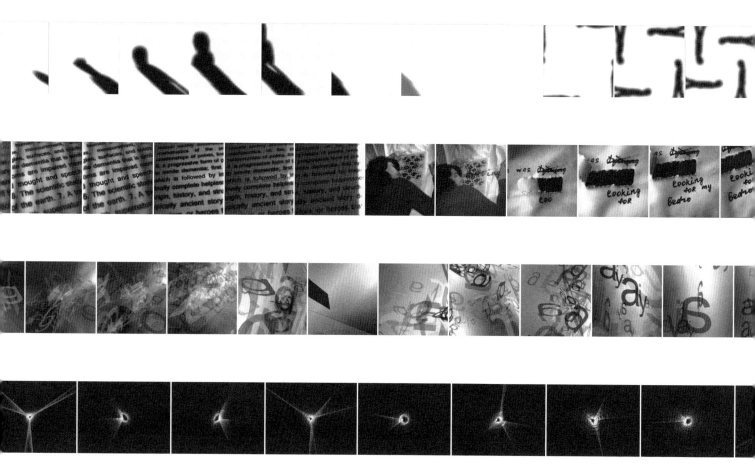

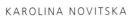

KAROLINA NOVITSKA

Phonopera
2005
sound mix by Karolina Novitska

KEIKO MORI

6
2005
sound mix by Keiko Mori

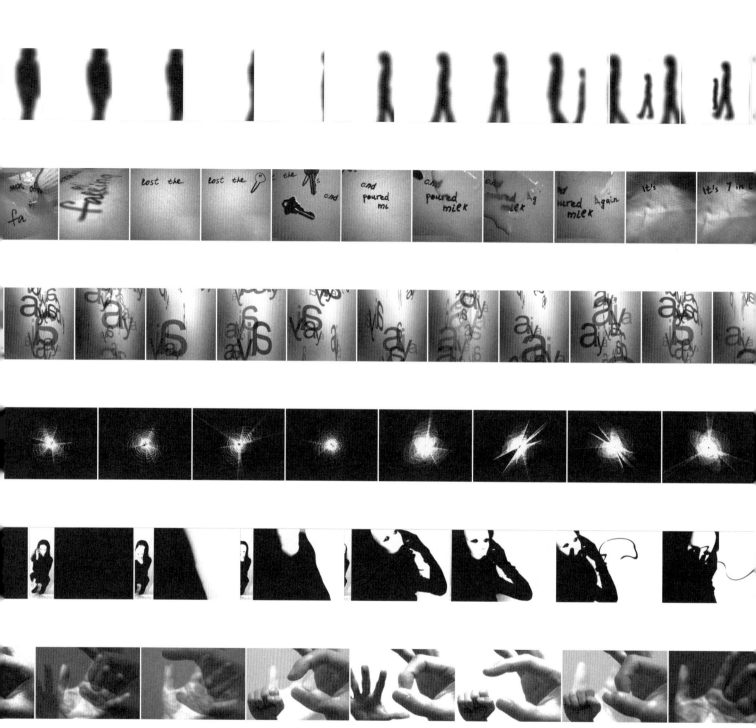

EVAN KARATZAS

Sambadrome
2003
music by Funk n' Lata

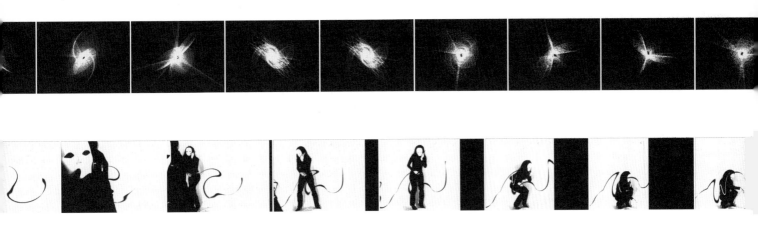

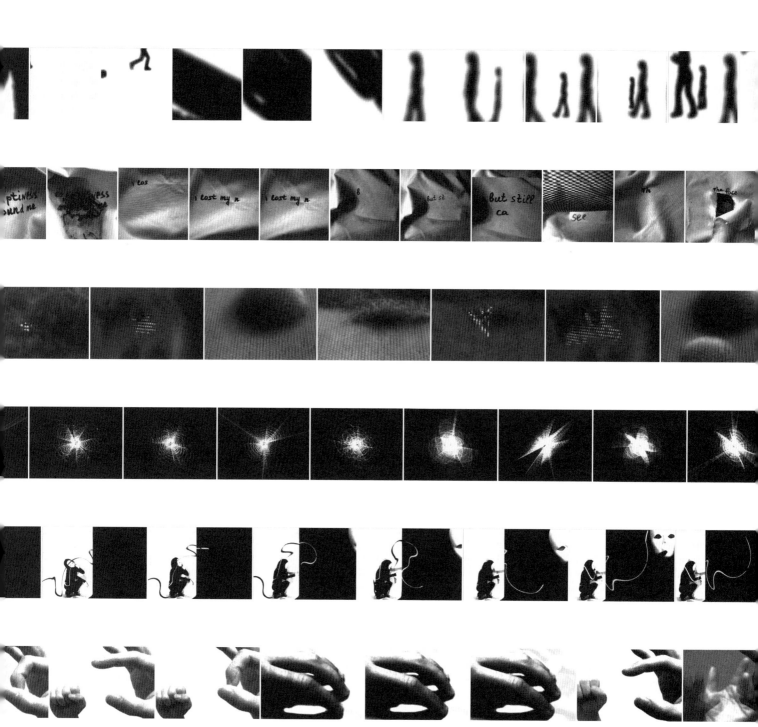

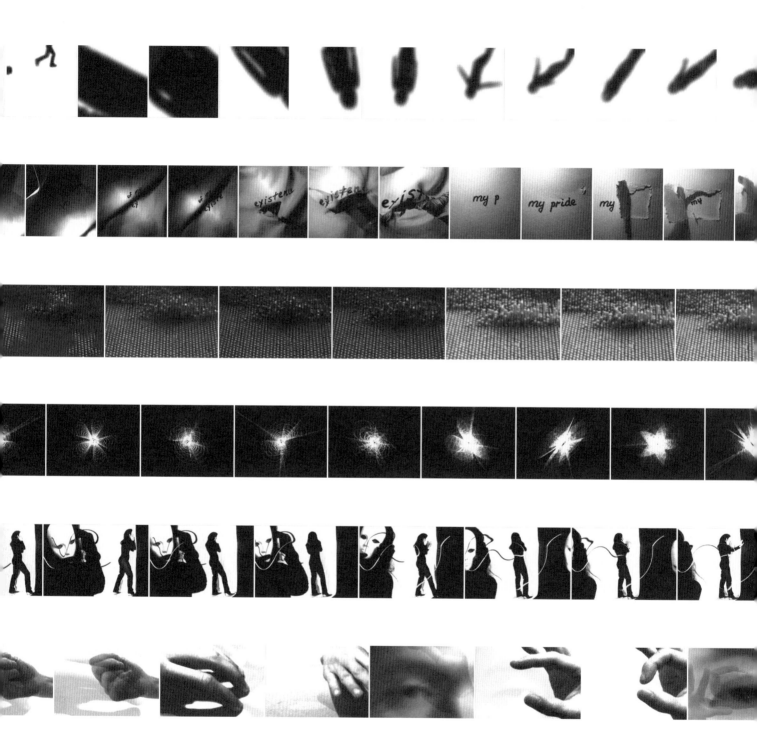

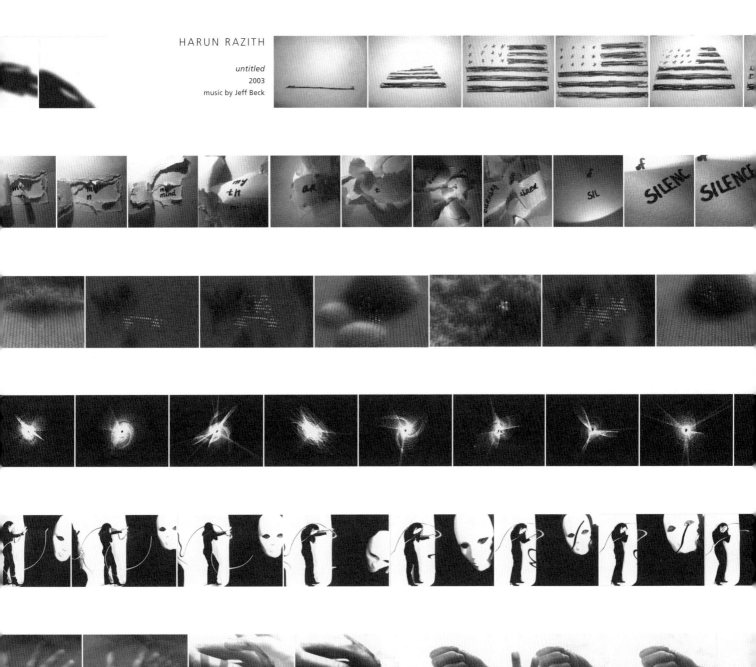

HARUN RAZITH

untitled
2003
music by Jeff Beck

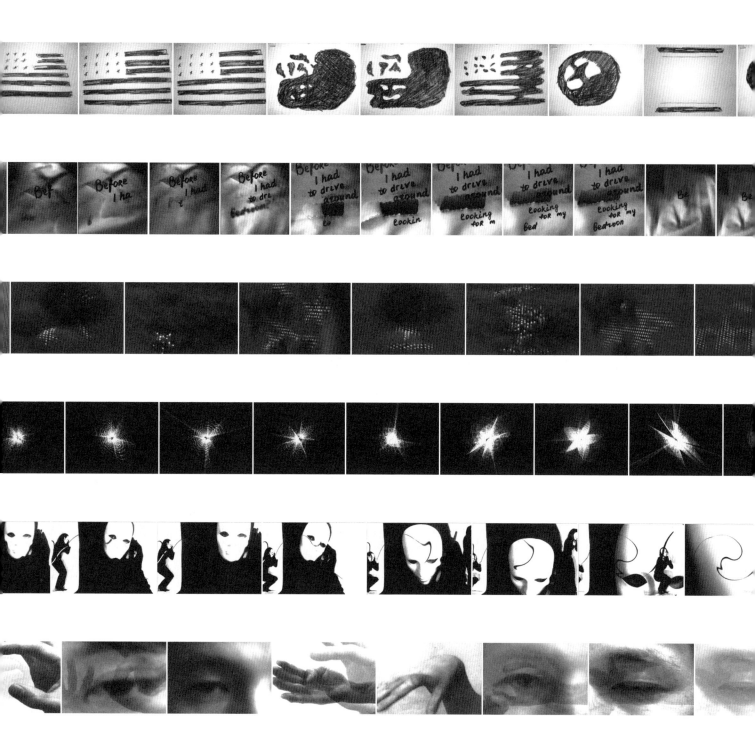

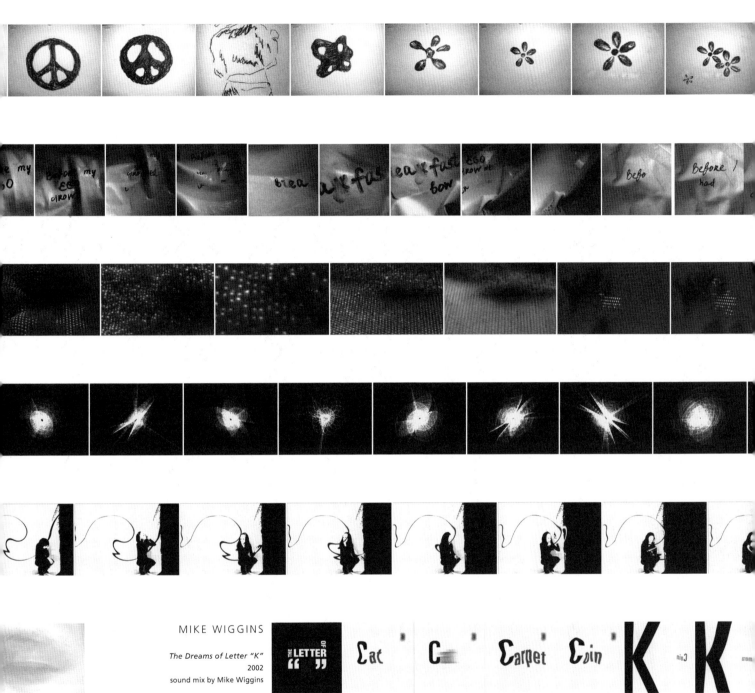

MIKE WIGGINS

The Dreams of Letter "K"
2002
sound mix by Mike Wiggins

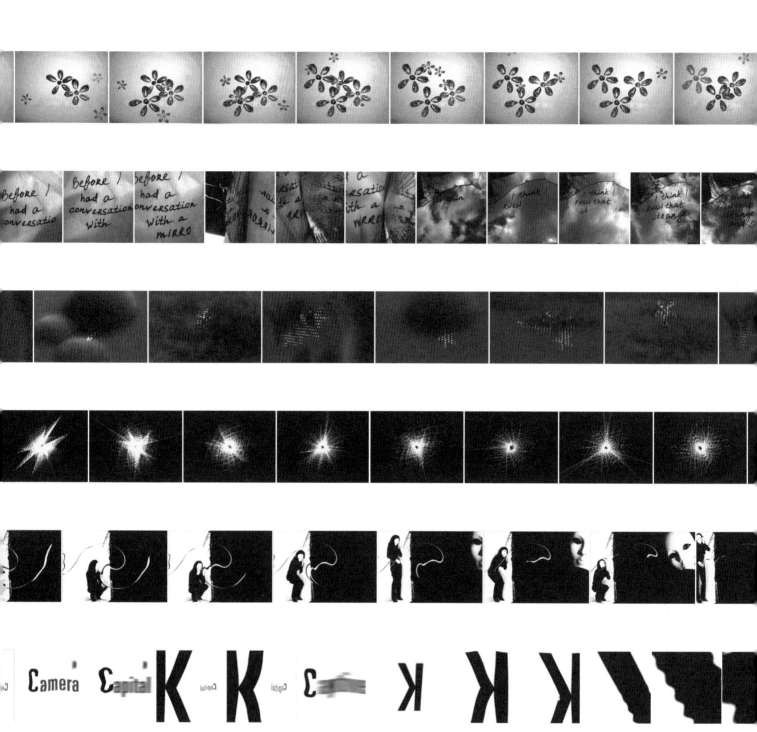

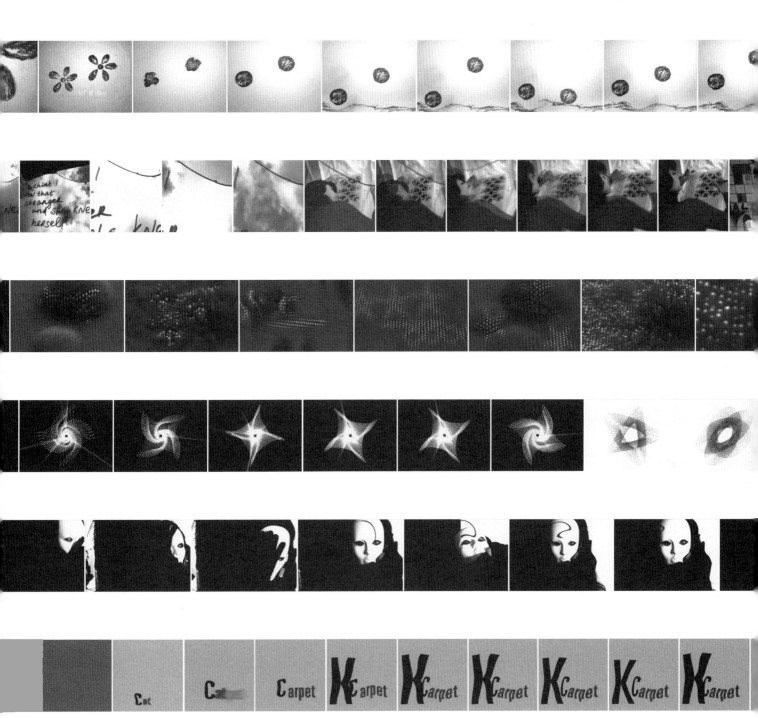

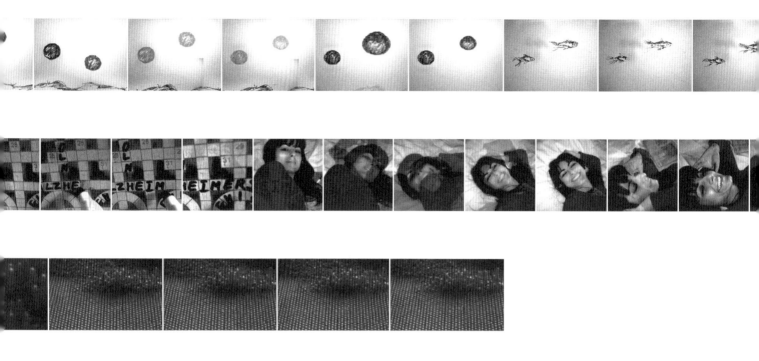

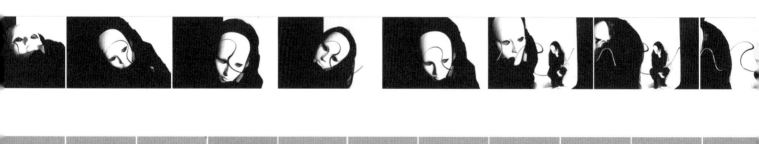

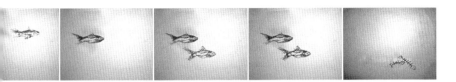

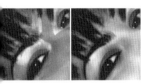

EVAN KARATZAS

CARLOS LUNETTA

KEIKO MORI

KAROLINA NOVITSKA

ELIF OZUDOGRU

HARUN RAZITH

FENYA SU

MIKE WIGGINS

collaborations

madamimadam

ISABELLA STUART GARDNER MUSEUM

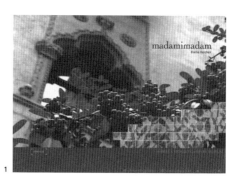

The *madamimadam* project was a team effort between graduate students Heather Shaw and Mike Wiggins; in close collaboration with the Gardner's curator, Pieranna Cavalchini, and the artist, Elaine Reichek. *Madamimadam* was a virtual exhibition of Reichek's works in the Gardner.

"Unlike any previous show at the Museum, madamimadam *is a virtual exhibition. Working while the galleries were closed to the public, Reichek briefly installed her samplers among the works in the Gardner's permanent collection.* madamimadam *comprises a group of images of this temporary installation that can only be seen through this digital project. In this virtual exhibition of her work amid Mrs. Gardner's collection, the artist subtly overcomes restrictions in Mrs. Gardner's will, which stipulates that her installation can never be altered."*

— www.gardnermuseum.org/madamimadam/index.asp

Madamimadam is unique in that our task was to create a web-based documentary of something that never happened. It is a complete fabrication of an exhibition that will never come to physical manifestation, and must always remain in the digital realm. The first task was to capture Elaine's work placed in the museum. Mike and I spent two weeks videotaping Elaine's work at the Gardner. We had to shoot while the museum was closed, which entailed shooting all day on Mondays and other weekday mornings from 8-11am. This was an interesting experience as we were not professional camera technicians nor film students. We rented high-end digital cameras (Sony PD-150) and had a weekend to learn how to use them before our first shoot on Monday. I remember the first few days we struggled with heavy tripods, walked everywhere in the museum by escort (even to the bathroom) and wondered if the video we were capturing would be good enough. By the second week we were tripping over the cameras and walking around the museum loosely chaperoned.

Our next course of action was to start conceptualizing our approach to the interface. A digital dialogue began between Mike and myself, strategizing concepts and ideas. We needed to develop the look and behaviors of interface, as well as an identity for *madamimadam*. Through our dialogue our concept began to center around the element of mutation; work had been added to the collection, against the will of Mrs. Gardner, and then removed before anyone had a chance to witness that this mutation had taken place. It was our job to document this mutation, and particularly the relevance of Elaine's pieces to the rooms in which they resided. Elaine's sixteen embroideries explore themes involving creation and reproduction, using quotations from a wide range of sources: the Bible, Milton, Mary Shelley, Charles Darwin, Ray Bradbury, and film director David Cronenberg. Her work was placed with careful con-

2

3

4

1. Interface for virtual exhibition "madamimadam."

2 – 4. Homepage "mutates" based on mouse movements; changes from the garden, to Elaine's work, to a pixilated abstraction of Elaine's work.

sideration, relating to other artifacts in the room on both visual and conceptual levels. The virtual exhibition needed to convey these subtleties via the video editing and interface design.

MADAMIMADAM IDENTITY

There is an interesting connection between Ms. Reichek's medium and the medium of the computer screen, in that each stitch creates the whole, just as individual pixels constitute imagery on-screen. "...embroidery is in any case closer to the pixel method of constructing images than to traditional painting; yet it is at the same time a method of the hand, and inherits a tradition that can compete with painting for longevity." (www.gardnermuseum.org/madamimadam/index.asp) Her work is built like pixels, yet it has the touch of the artful hand. Mike and I wanted to convey this in our design, and particularly how the interface behaved.

Madamimadam became a site rich in photography, videos and interactivity. The video proved successful (despite our inexperience) and many beautiful still shots came out of our two-week session as well. These stills were used as background imagery that randomly changed after several seconds. This was a conscious decision on our part: to keep the viewer intrigued as to where Elaine's pieces are in the museum, and to reflect the sense of instability within the actual space. When browsing the museum, visitors have the impression things are constantly changing due to the sheer mass of objects. Within each glance something new is noticed. The navigation is laid out as a configuration reminiscent of the court-

yard; however, the links around it have no bearing on the location of the rooms in the actual museum. Again, these elements were built into the interface to maintain ambiguity in the placement of Elaine's work. *Madamimadam* has no beginning and no end, although once a person views all of Elaine's work then they would technically be "finished."

In working on the *madamimadam* project, much of our thesis research was put into practice. For example, the construction of this site proved to us that interface and content should tie together conceptually. The smallest interface details that make *madamimadam* conceptually rich. For instance, when the viewer chooses to close a movie clip, the box scales down to the smallest pixel, and then slowly fades away. Although this detail may go unnoticed by some, it ties into the concept of dealing with the pixel, even on a very small scale. All these conceptual elements are key to this particular project.

Secondly, we learned that the artist, curator, Mike and I are clearly the authors of the virtual exhibition. By authorship I mean that we made distinct choices as to what the user can interact with, and how. Decisions such as the interface having no beginning and no end. The viewer has choices for viewing; however they are not able to change the story or become a "character" within the virtual exhibition.

As authors of this piece, we found that participating in the entire process adds so much long-term value. Spending countless hours videotaping helped us to develop a strong intimacy with Elaine's work, as well as with the permanent exhibits. Long dialogues with the artist helped us to understand her motivation with

madamimadam
Elaine Reichek

the dutch room

Isabella Gardner entertained in this room among works by Rembrandt, Rubens, Van Dyck, and Zurbarán. Empty frames mark the places of several stolen paintings.

close

ISABELLA STEWART GARDNER MUSEUM

about the project   about the artist

5

5. Navigation (left) is reminiscent of the courtyard; on rollover a brief description of the room and Elaine's piece pops-up.

6. "DNA" by Elaine Reichek. Image shows video playing (left), and additional information about the piece (right).

this exhibition project. Conversations with the curator, Pieranna Cavalchini, enabled us to walk the forbidden courtyard, film in roped-off rooms, and "zoom in" on some very precious artwork. That was all part of a day's work, and yet it was such a privilege at the same time.

All of this helped us to wrap our minds around the information we were delivering. I doubt we would have the same approach to the site if someone else had videotaped the work, and left the rest up to us. This is one of the most important things we learned form this experience.

Finally, we learned to value the great benefits inherent in collaboration. For the conceptual strength of this piece was generated throughout our close collaboration with Pieranna Cavalchini and her expertise, and Elaine Reichek and her vision.

Madamimadam was awarded First Prize, category CD-ROMs, by the American Association of Museums 2005 Museum Publications Design Competition.

Presence:
The Ephemeral
in Focus

ISABELLA STUART GARDNER MUSEUM

In 2001 the British collaborative artists Heather Ackroyd and Dan Harvey were invited by Pieranna Cavalchini, Curator of Contemporary Art, to the Artist-in-Residence Program at the Isabella Stewart Gardner Museum (ISGM), Boston. While at the ISGM Ackroyd and Harvey produced a series of works that resulted in three projects: the exhibition *Presence* (Oct 2001-Jan 2002), the CD-ROM *Presence: The Ephemeral in Focus* (2003), and a video (2004).

The CD-ROM *Presence: The Ephemeral in Focus* was designed and produced by Isabel Meirelles and Fenya Su at the Dynamic Media Institute.

THE MEDIUM: CD-ROM

There are two major challenges facing the design of art CD-ROMs that reproduce physical artwork. One is to reconcile the absence of the physical reality and sensory nature of the works with the mediated and interactive environment of the electronic medium. The other is to transform a medium that has limited storage capacity into unlimited ways of exploring the artwork.

Presence: The Ephemeral in Focus was designed with these two challenges in mind. In the attempt to integrate the viewer with the image and to enhance the viewer's interactive experience of the artwork, strategies of immersion and participation were employed as the conceptual framework for the interface design. The goal was to reduce the sensory and psychological distance created by the mediated presentation of images and to activate the view-er's own memories and associations, changing an objective presentation of the data into a subjective exploration of the artwork.

THE ARTISTS AND THE ARTWORK

Ackroyd and Harvey gained international recognition for the use of grass on works that span public art, installation, photography, and landscape design. From growing skeins of seeds on abandoned sites to using the photosynthesis process to record large photographic images, the seedling grass is used as a means to explore themes of transformation, of transience, of growth and decay.

During the four weeks of September 2001, the artists transformed the Special Exhibition gallery at the ISGM into their studio, germinating and growing seven organic photographs, the same space where later they exhibited to the public.

In the discussions with the artists and the curator it became apparent that there was an opportunity to broaden the content beyond the works produced at the ISGM towards a more thorough representation of their oeuvre. It was decided to produce a CD containing a total of 35 works (7 from the *Presence* exhibition and 28 early pieces) and that it would somehow include edited footage documenting the artists' process and an interview, both filmed during their residency.

THE DESIGN OF THE CD

We conceived of a product that would parallel Ackroyd's and Harvey's artistic process in dealing with germination, growth and de-

1. CD-ROM packaging: cover.
2. CD-ROM packaging: disk image.

cay. The idea was to design an interface in which each work would become the locus of the viewer's experience. And the associations and memories raised by the works would become the connectors to personal narratives. How to thread the narratives together is the viewer's choice.

The interface design centered on two major concepts. One was to engage the viewer in the artists' work and to enrich that aesthetical experience with related and supplemental multimedia material. In order to achieve that, all information was structured around individual works. Video was edited into 34 clips specifically connected to the works.

The other was to enhance the viewer's choices in the exploration of Ackroyd's and Harvey's artworld. Content is organized in a non-hierarchical data-structure and is accessed by means of a nonlinear double navigational system.

Ultimately, the CD-ROM *Presence: The Ephemeral in Focus* invites an almost infinite variety of readings, of sights, of experiences. It encourages the viewer to explore Ackroyd's and Harvey's oeuvre through personal narratives shaped by the viewer's own choices—what is viewed, perceived, watched, heard. To paraphrase Cavalchini, "it teaches people to look."

ACKNOWLEDGEMENTS

This is a condensed version of a presentation by Isabel Meirelles at the 2004 Festival Audiovisuel International Musées & Patrimonie (International Audiovisual Festival on Museums and Heritage), National Palace Museum, Taipei, Taiwan.

The CD-ROM Presence: The Ephemeral in Focus was awarded Honorable Mention, category CD-ROMs, by the American Association of Museums 2004 Museum Publications Design Competition.

3

4

3. Screen shot of the interface: new window with extra information about the "Presence" exhibition.

4. Screen shot of the interface: new window with extra information about the artists Heather Ackroyd and Dan Harvey.

5. Screen shot of the interface: the work "Mother and Child."

6. Screen shot of the interface: the work "The Script."

7. Screen shot of the interface: the work "The Script."

5

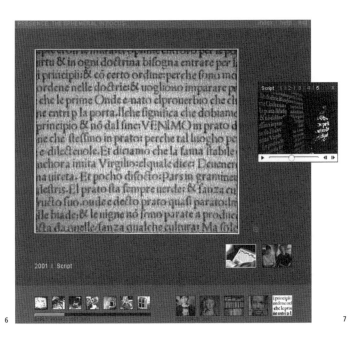

6

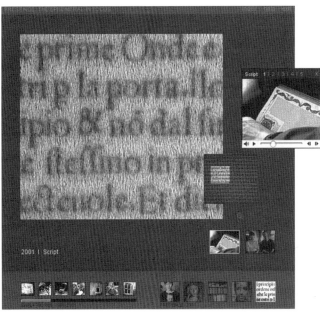

7

scratch
MIT MEDIA LAB

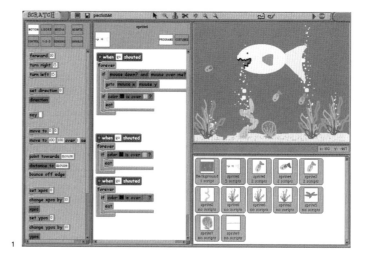

1

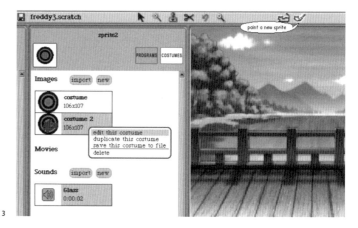

3

In July 2004, the Lifelong Kindergarten group and the Dynamic Media Institute began collaborating on a comprehensive redesign of the Scratch application. Graduate students from DMI work closely with Mitchel Resnick and Scratch team members at the Media Lab to improve architectural, visual, and usability aspects of the evolving Scratch platform. This collaboration continues after more than a year of active research and development, and the two programs are discussing ways to expand the partnership.

Scratch is a programmable toolkit that enables kids to create their own games, animated stories, and interactive art—and share their creations over the Internet. Scratch takes advantage of new computational ideas and capabilities that make it easier for kids to get started with programming (lowering the floor) and to extend the range of what kids can create and learn (raising the ceiling). The ultimate goal is to help kids become fluent with digital media, empowering them to express themselves creatively and make connections to powerful ideas.

Scratch is designed specifically for youth at Computer Clubhouses, an international network of after-school centers for youth (ages 10-18) in low-income communities. Scratch is grounded in the practices and social dynamics of the Clubhouses, adding programmability to the media-rich and network-based activities flourishing there.

Children create their own Scratch programs by snapping together graphical building blocks, each representing a different command or action. They learn important computational ideas as they dynamically transform photos, mix in sound clips and drum beats, and integrate inputs from real-world sensors.

Developed by the Lifelong Kindergarten research group at the MIT Media Lab (led by Mitchel Resnick) in collaboration with KIDS research group at the UCLA Graduate School of Education & Information Studies (led by Yasmin Kafai), Scratch builds on the Squeak programming language developed by Alan Kay and an open-source community of colleagues.

RESOURCES

http://llk.media.mit.edu
http://llk.media.mit.edu/projects/scratch
http://www.computerclubhouse.org

THE SCRATCH TEAM

Mitchel Resnick
John Maloney
Natalie Rusk
Brian Silverman
Amon Millner
Evelyn Eastmond
Margarita Dekoli
Ioana Fineberg

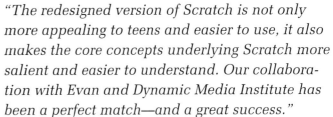

"The redesigned version of Scratch is not only more appealing to teens and easier to use, it also makes the core concepts underlying Scratch more salient and easier to understand. Our collaboration with Evan and Dynamic Media Institute has been a perfect match—and a great success."

—Mitchel Resnick, Acting Head, MIT Program in Media Arts and Sciences, Director, Lifelong Kindergarten group at MIT Media Lab

"Mitchel's team has created something that goes far beyond a breakthrough programming platform for young people. They've developed a creative community that feeds on collaboration and discovery and it provided us with a continuous feedback loop that allowed the interface to support and extend functionality in unexpected ways."

—Evan Karatzas, Scratch Interface Design Lead, Dynamic Media Institute

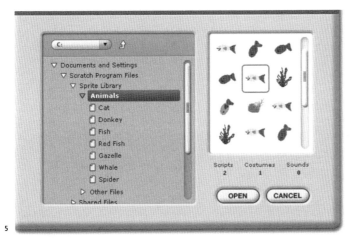

1. The original Scratch workspace.

2. The redesigned workspace included significant changes to toolbars, panel selection and the grouping of program functions.

3. Costumes panel and rollover tips before the redesign.

4. Redesigned costumes panel and rollover tips.

5. The redesigned file browsing panel.

6. File browsing before the redesign.

massaging media conference

THE MASSACHUSETTS

COLLEGE OF ART

- *massaging media* was the title and the theme of the ATE (Art, Technology, Experience) conference.
- *massaging media* was a one-day event presented by the Dynamic Media Institute at MassArt in collaboration with AIGA (American Institute of Graphic Arts) Boston Chapter, hosted by Jan Kubasiewicz and Judith Richland (MFA 2003) at the Massachusetts College of Art.
- *massaging media* was a forum of artists/practitioners (filmmakers, performers, dancers, musicians, designers, writers, and illustrators) as well as theorists in culture, education, architecture, and philosophy.
- *massaging media* was a collaboration, a dialog, a discourse, a lecture, a performance, a multi-disciplinary experiment, a multi-sensory experience and, "...a process of subliminally sniffing out environmental change." (Marshall McLuhan)

The conference project was set up in the form of the Dynamic Media Institute 3-credit graduate elective studio, coordinated by Judith Richland. This unique, project-based course with clearly defined goals attracted a strong group of participants. Soon, a leadership team emerged. The core members of the team were: Leila Mitchell, Mike Wiggins, Heather Shaw, Julio Blanco, Geraldine Garrido, Claudia Baeza, and Carlos Avila, with additional help from Richard Streitmatter-Tran, Dusan Koljensic and faculty members Brian Lucid and Gunta Kaza.

For details of the conference program, names of speakers and performers, please read the massaging media flyer reproduced on the following page or visit www.massagingmedia.com

massagingmedia > november 23

1. "Fearless Transmissions" by Krzysztof Wodiczko
2. massaging media website
3. "Immersion Music Techniques for the Professional Performer" by Teresa Marrin Nakra
4. massaging media collateral printed material

The first annual **ATE conference**, *massaging media*, is a collaboration, a dialog, a discourse, a lecture, a performance, a multi-disciplinary experiment, a multi-sensory experience and, for all of us, " ... a process of subliminally sniffing out environmental change." (Marshall McLuhan)

The ATE conference explores where we are, and what we EAT as a culture with regard to new media. It will be about ideas. No shameless self-promotion is allowed. You will feel that you ATE plenty.

ATE conference participants:

Henry Jenkins, *Director of the Comparative Media Studies Program at MIT. Cultural theorist in new media. Author of "From Barbie to Mortal Combat: Gender and Computer Games."*

Chee Pearlman, *Design / Editorial Consultant. Columnist for the New York Times and former Editor of ID Magazine.*

Nancy Bauer, *Professor of Philosophy at Tufts University, teaches philosophy with film and feminist philosophy.*

Mitchell Resnick, *Director of Lifelong Kindergarten research group at the Media Lab at MIT and developer of the StarLogo environment and Lego MindStorms.*

Krzysztof Wodiczko, *Director of Visual Arts Program at MIT, heads The Interrogative Design Group at MIT.*

Sandy Stone, *Founding Director of ACTLab / Convergent Media program of the University of Texas. Filmmaker, rock 'n roll music engineer, neurologist, cultural theorist and performer.*

Maira Kalman, *CEO, VP and Secretary, M&Co. Illustrator and Author of: Unfashion: A Designer's Strip Tease. Co-Illustrator of the New Yorker's "New Yorkistan" cover.*

Rick Meyerowitz, *Illustrator for the National Lampoon, numerous magazines and books, and co-illustrator of the New Yorker's "New Yorkistan" cover.*

Glorianna Davenport, *Principal Research Associate Director of Interactive Cinema, MIT. Pioneer in new methods of digital media: "Evolving Documentary" "Very Distributed Storytelling."*

Aisling Kelleher, *PhD candidate, Interactive Cinema at MIT (Media Lab). Developing software for video publishing online.*

Teresa Marrin Nakra, *Artistic Director of Immersion Music, Inc., conductor, composer, and inventor of the "Digital Baton" and other digital technologies for musicians.*

Joanna Kurkowicz, *Violinist, Concertmistress of the Boston Philharmonic, the Boston Modern Orchestra Project, and the Vermont Symphony.*

Sangita Shresthova, *Dancer/ Choreographer, trained in Nepalese classical dance, Bharat Natyam, and South Indian Martial Art. Her performances incorporate visual projections and sound.*

Jeffrey Huang + Muriel Waldvogel, *Partners, Convergeo. Designers of new architectures and media that combine physical and virtual technologies.*

The purpose of the AIGA is to further excellence in communication design as a broadly defined discipline, as a strategic tool for business, and as a cultural force.

The AIGA is the place design professionals turn to first to exchange ideas and information, participate in critical analysis and research, and advance education and ethical practice.

For more information about AIGA Boston, upcoming events or becoming a member, please visit the AIGA web site at *boston.aiga.org.*

Interested in becoming a Sponsor? Sponsors provide AIGA with much appreciated and needed financial support. We encourage our members to keep our sponsors in mind when their services might be required. To speak with the AIGA about sponsorship opportunities please contact us at 781.446.9082.

Sponsors
GMUND Paper
North America *gmund.com*   GMUND

Hewlett Packard *hp.com*

Patrons
Printing and Paper:
Deschamps Printing Company
Salem, MA *deschampsprinting.com*

Technical Assistance/Equipment:
Tech Superpowers, Inc.
Boston, MA *techsuperpowers.com*

Poster Design:
Heather Shaw
Mike Wiggins
Dynamic Media Institute

Event Committee
Mike Wiggins, Leila Mitchell, Heather Shaw, Claudia Baeza Hochmuth, Dusan Koljensic, Carlos Avila, Julio Blanco, Geraldine Garrido, Cindy Zoppa, Dai-Min Cheng, Richard Streitmatter-tran, Dana Moser, Jen Hall, Brian Lucid, Gunta Kaza and Kate Brigham.

art.technology.experience.

The Conference:

Saturday, November 23, 2002
a week before thanksgiving!
9:00am - 5:00pm

Massachusetts College of Art
Tower Auditorium
621 Huntington Avenue
Boston, Massachusetts 02115

Hosts:
Jan Kubasiewicz,
*Professor and Coordinator of
Graduate Design Program
Dynamic Media Institute at MassArt*

Judith Richland,
*President, Richland Design Associates
Former President AIGA Boston*

Introduction
9:00-10:00   Coffee/knowledge transfer*
10:10-10:40 Lecture
10:40-11:10 Performance
11:10-11:20 Break
11:20-11:50 Lecture
11:50-12:20 Performance

12:20-1:30   Lunch/knowledge transfer*
1:30-2:00   Lecture
2:00-2:30   Performance
2:30-2:40   Break
2:40-3:10   Lecture
3:10-3:40   Performance
3:40-5:00   Soft drinks/knowledge transfer*

*schmooze/networking

Fees and Registration:

☐ Register before 11/15 **($135)**   ☐ AIGA member register before 11/15 **($100)**   ☐ MassArt Student register before 11/15 **(FREE)**
☐ Register after 11/15 **($150)**   ☐ AIGA member register after 11/15 **($115)**   ☐ MassArt Student register after 11/15 **($15)**

Name _____   Email _____   Telephone _____

Please make your check, payable to : AIGA Boston/ATE Conference
Mail your nonrefundable check to AIGA Boston/ATE Conference, 17 Station Street, 1st floor, Brookline, MA 02445. Seats are limited! For information please visit: **massagingmedia.com** or **boston.aiga.org**. All checks for reserved seats must be received by November 18, 2002. Your canceled check is your receipt.

wally gilbert:
an exhibition of
photography

THE MASSACHUSETTS

COLLEGE OF ART

1. The 120-page, hard-cover catalog entitled "Wally Gilbert: An Exhibition of Photography" was produced in conjunction with the exhibition. The catalog designed by Lynn Faitelson, (MFA 2005) and Jan Kubasiewicz, was included in the American Institute of Graphic Arts, Boston 2005 Best of New England Juried Show.

In the Fall of 2004, the Dynamic Media Institute presented an exhibition of photography by Wally Gilbert in the Patricia Doran Graduate Gallery at the Massachusetts College of Art, curated by Jan Kubasiewicz.

Gyorgy Kepes commented once that: "In our day, the artist and the scientist are almost never the same person." This exhibition represents one of those rare exceptions. Wally Gilbert the photographer is the same person as Professor Walter Gilbert, the accomplished scientist, and for him the computer, a tool of scientific research, becomes a tool of exploration in the domain of the visual arts.

The photography of Wally Gilbert aligns with our beliefs at the Dynamic Media Institute, that creativity in art and science share more similarities than differences. Perhaps even more interesting is the shared excitement surrounding new imaging technologies in art and science, which restates the fundamental synergy between creativity and technology that underpins the very origins of the Massachusetts College of Art.

An excerpt from *A Conversation with Wally Gilbert:*

JK Over the years, your interests have spanned mineralogy, astronomy, chemistry, biology, mathematics, and theoretical physics—virtually the entire foundation of science. What skills, acquired in your professional life as a scientist, contributed to becoming a photographer?

WG Indeed, in my professional career, I worked in a large number of scientific fields. First I was a theoretical physicist, very close to pure mathematics, and then later I became an experimental scientist working in biochemistry in a biological laboratory. Then I became more of a computer scientist, doing computer based analysis of genes, going back—after thirty years of laboratory work in molecular biology—to my roots as theoretician. I have both types of skills—the intellectual skill needed in mathematics and theory and the manual dexterity needed to work with one's hands in the laboratory. My personal history of experimental activities might have directed me to painting or to sculpture, to use my hands. But the tool of my later theoretical research was the computer, and that is why I feel so comfortable with digital photography.

thesis abstracts

thesis abstracts 2005

Claudia Baeza

Social as Interface: The Conceptual Design for a Mobile Learning Environment for a Museum

advisor: Brian Lucid

This thesis explores how handheld mobile devices can expand and augment the informal learning opportunities offered by museums. Using constructivist pedagogy as the guiding principle for fostering high level thinking, my work brings together characteristics of museum environments, wireless technology, and learning theory to create user-centered learning tools, that are participatory, experiential and interactive.

The foundation for high level-learning faculties inside a museum has three foci: collaboration and participation; experience; and social interaction. In my research I analyze each of these elements in the context of user scenarios, prototypes, and interface.

The goal is to develop learning tools that children in middle school can use during a visit to the Museum of Fine Arts (MFA) in Boston. My explorations will focus exclusively on the Egyptian galleries at the MFA in order to use a specifically designed curriculum developed by the MFA educational staff.

Lynn Faitelson

Making a Human Mark: Bridging the Gap between Traditional and New Media

advisor: Jan Kubasiewicz

My thesis investigation attempts to synthesize tactile, material objects and electronic technology into discrete new media objects using sound, light, video, and the human form as mediating tools.

The principles of new media design are discrete representation, numerical representation, automation, and variability, and these precepts make manifest the human condition. Coming from the field of traditional graphic design, where static images deliver a two-dimensional message, I have been encouraged to explore space, volume, time, and dimension using tools that take advantage of and emphasize all of our human senses. Communication design has become a hybrid of complementary technologies and media, and designers are uniquely positioned to create work that reflects life and humanity.

In this thesis investigation, I have tried to bridge the gap between traditional graphic design and new media design, bearing in mind that while the visual dialect and idiom may change, there is always unity across diverse fields.

Julia Voellinger Griffey

Animation, Motion and Education

advisor: Brian Lucid

This thesis is an exploration of human motion, education, and animation, their relation to new media, and to one another, culminating in the creation of an animated, movement-driven, educational exhibit for the Franklin Park Zoo.

Animation, human motion, and education intersect in many ways. Human motion can be better understood when rendered through the medium of animation or analyzed with new media applications. New media systems can give the user an experience of motion. Animation with its flexibility and simplicity can facilitate education.

My interest is in making the user's movement integral to an animated, interactive, new media learning experience. There are many benefits to such a project. Movement enhances our physical health; it also enhances our learning. Studies show that when we move, we improve circulation to our brains and become better learners. In moving, we tap into our physical memory, which helps us with recollection and retention.

When movement is part of a game, it fosters a social atmosphere. Incorporating animation to this movement and learning experience adds joy as well as clarity.

Evan Karatzas

Proximity Lab

advisor: Jan Kubasiewicz

Dušan Koljenšić

Application for Building Content-Aware Scientific Graphs

advisor: Jan Kubasiewicz

Carlos Lunetta

The Articulation of Visual Experiences through Algorithm

advisor: Jan Kubasiewicz

Keiko Mori

Digital + Human Communication

advisor: Brian Lucid

Proximity Lab is a participatory installation that investigates the role of physical proximity in interpersonal communication and interfaces that promote self-directed exploration. The exhibit is an experimental interface platform designed to visualize and reinterpret relationships between users and the mediated spaces they occupy.

The platform is an 8-foot by 16-foot walkable surface fitted with radio frequency ID (RFID) technology. Participants wear shoes fitted with RFID tags, enabling the system to track and record their positions in real time. Images projected directly onto the floor are accompanied by stereo sound as a continuous response to the actions and interactions of participants. *Proximity Lab* has the unique ability to discern the individual identities of participants, regardless of how or where they move. Conceived as an experimental physical interface system, it allows architects with diverse intentions and aesthetic goals to create repeatable experiments in physical interaction.

The study explores the relationships between disclosure and participation. Do increased levels of participation and collaboration occur when users are allowed to innovate and create new relationships with the system? Is approachability and participation adversely affected when system rules are aggressively withheld?

Observing users interacting with *Proximity Lab* has yielded important observations. Most noteworthy is the need to balance ambiguity and instruction to leave room for individual interpretation impeding usability. Some level of clarity is advisable even with exploratory, open-ended systems. Still, the underlying promise of elevating user experience and opportunity for discovery by empowering users to take a leading role in the exchange is compelling.

In November 2002 I spent a day in one of the molecular biology labs at Boston University observing researchers working at their computers. I was surprised to see that the programs they were using to present their findings were standard graphic design applications: Illustrator, Photoshop, and QuarkXpress. They explained that just about every published piece of scientific findings involved creating graphs using these design tools. No graphics software tailored to their specific needs —the presenation of data rather than visual formatting—existed. My aim is to develop an application for molecular biologists that facilitates separation of form and content, as well as a visual interface that allows them to quickly and accurately build scientific graphs.

On the back-end, using XML, the application will provide a platform for embedding actual scientific data into elements of the graph, making them searchable and indexable, among other things. On the front-end, the application will aid in the separation of the science from the design—choosing the right element vs. choosing what that element should look like.

The Articulation of Visual Experiences through Algorithm explores the concepts and possibilities computation presents as a creative medium for design.

This thesis investigates the relationship between code and visual language. From this relationship, a new vocabulary of new media will emerge, driven by ideas that stretch their existence simultaneously through all means—visual, aural, verbal, haptical, temporal, and logical.

My methodology was based on discrete experiments native to the computational medium that investigated a range of topics including: musical intervals; generative and interactive form systems; interactive op art; database visualization; and the plastic components of time.

Computer-mediated communication systems today focus too much on convenience, on speed and efficiency, and filter out the important elements of human communication, such as physical space, gestures, emotions, and individuality.

In the field of new media, anything can become information. Your experience in reading this becomes information. The sound you hear while reading becomes information. The shift in your attention from reading to hearing becomes information. Information is the raw material of things, events, actions, and thoughts in our world. Our job as new media designers is to take this information and translate it into a form or into an experience, which will then become a user's knowledge.

In this process of translating information into experience, it is important to be aware of what we gain and what we lose through the available channels of digital communication. For instance, in the currently existing online communication systems, the dynamic nature of human communication gets flattened, and so many rich nuances are filtered out.

My thesis explores the questions and issues indicated above. Using dynamic mapping, I investigate how designers can inject some of the richer nuances of human communication into online communication systems.

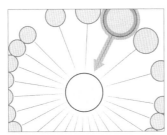

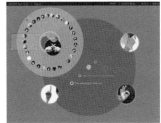

2005

Christine Pillsbury

**Interactive (N.)arrative:
An Alternative Approach**

advisor: Jan Kubasiewicz

Harun Razith

**Culture Bots: Implications of Cultural
Content in Computer Gaming**

advisor: Brian Lucid

Stephen Spiridakis

**Data Shadow: Remixing our Public and
Private Selves in the Age of New Media**

advisor: Brian Lucid

Narratives are not merely written—they have a long history of being visualized and performed. Narratives are an essential part of the human condition for both the author and the reader; both create subjective interpretations of a story. It is this subjective point of view that makes a narrative unique and immersive.

Every narrative, in any medium, is already interactive in a implicit sense: a reader must decode the author's subject. But the promise of Interactive Narrative is that the user can influence the narrative in such a way as to create discourse that would otherwise not exist. This is not to say that Interactive Narrative requires the user to be the author. Interactive narration is but one possible path that this medium can take.

Between the points of Barthes's *Writerly Text* and Janet Murray's *Holodeck* lies a spectrum of possibilities. The age of hyperlinks and non-linearity has reached its apex. It is now time to think about the possibilities of the procedural structure, presentation, and visual language of future narratives. To do so, one must again revisit the definitions of authorship, narrative, interactivity, and participation. Authorship and participation are not necessarily analogous. To interact, one must have something to interact with. And, between the overly simplified and exorbitantly theoretical definitions of narrative, a practical definition exists.

Computer games have the latent potential to communicate significant issues beyond mere entertainment. My thesis explores the implications of coupling problems of higher social and cultural value with the conventional design elements of role-playing games. The main objective is to allow the user to gain "first-hand" experience of a subject from multiple persepectives without taking away the usual fun of a conventional game. The interactive projects offer users various levels of character role-playability. With the ability to see through someone else's eyes, users are prompted to empathize with the character's, emotions and point of views. Therein lies a the path to heightened socio-cultural learning and richer, value-based gaming experiences.

The goal of my thesis is to design work that explicitly communicates the negative effects of new technology on our privacy, and further, on our public and private identities.

My thesis uses technology in various social experiments in a reflexive manner to illustrate the loss of privacy and the blurring of our public and private identities in the age of new media. Experiments were conducted using film, installation, and computer interactive projects.

New media technology has taken away our ability to control our private information, and has also facilitated the misuse of that information. Making private information public threatens anonymity, increases the likelihood of stolen identity, and has the potential for homogenization of culture. As we become more aware of our data shadow—the abundance of private information surrounding us—we are likely to change how we behave in public, blurring the lines between our public and private identities. Awareness of our data shadow is likely to make us guarded in our public behavior, and subsequently, resentful for the erosion of our privacy at the hand of new media.

2004

Carlos Avila

Composing Multimedia Methods to Incite Political Action: The New Political Poster

advisor: Hubert Hohn

This thesis proposes the development of a mass-media communication platform multimedia composition as its language in a stand-alone format. It looks at the role of the political poster as the departure point for the development of this medium. The document is divided into five sections. The introduction gives an overview of why I believe it is important to pursue this study given the current state of mass communication outlets and current roles that new media and multimedia composition play in the current communication environment. It also covers my personal motivation. The second section looks at proto-posters and posters, focusing primarily on their role as mass communication media. This section compares the current state of multimedia methods with the moment in which the poster evolved into a mass medium and then into and art form. The third part looks at where the poster remains a living language, and why. This section also looks at the current use of multimedia compositions and how such work can be used to disseminate political content and promote activism. The fourth section embodies the bulk of my field research. It is divided into three main sections: the platform, the development of a multimedia syntax, and an application of this syntax. The final section offers concluding thoughts on the process of making multimedia into a platform for political action and other action.

Sue-Ellen (Johnson) Lamb

Defining Gesture: A Visual Dictionary for American Sign Language

advisor: Hubert Hohn

The goal of my thesis project is to create an interactive, multimedia dictionary for American Sign Language (ASL) and English. This dictionary will serve the same purpose as any two-language dictionary and will act as a supplemental resource for people who are learning ASL in a classroom or tutoring setting.

My thesis grew from a life-long interest in languages and a desire to better communicate with my nephew, who had trouble hearing and learned ASL. My thesis project also presented me with the challenge of designing a visual, as opposed to a text-driven, database interface. This visual interface is the main component of my thesis project. Users can conduct searches, sort through results, and access detailed information about particular signs. The underlying theoretical issue driving my work is the problem of how to best organize, present, and interact with information that is fundamentally visual. I believe that my response to this issue can provide a model for other applications that require visual database solutions.

Elif Ozudogru

Transformation: Connectivity Through the Digital Atmosphere

advisor: Brian Lucid

New technologies should not overwhelm us. They should open up new levels of comfort without complicating the intuitive essence of life. Activities in the digital world should mirror seamless qualities of activities outside it. Interactive systems systems must be based on appropriate metaphors to encourage fluidity.

More than thousand years ago, it was common belief among humans that objects had spirits and could be interacted with. Today, I believe, digital technology allows us to reclaim this spiritual practice and creates a new form of magic.

My aim is to create systems that transform routine actions into memorable experiences. Such systems need to be designed to bring the "background" —the usually unnoticed things of everyday life—into the foreground with an emphasis on human presence.

2003

Julio Blanco
Body Data / Data Body: The Human Body as Information and Interface

advisor: Jan Kubasiewicz

Coleen Crawford
OCME Interactive

advisor: Hubert Hohn

Geraldine Garrido
Experience Design: A Holistic Approach

advisor: Brian Lucid

The human body is a set of interrelated structures. The body is not only a "container" that houses the emotional and physical being. Rather, it is the functioning interface between a human being and his environment. And like the environment, the body itself is ever dynamic and ever changing, continuously growing and registering its experiences.

For the purpose of this thesis I propose a self-referential exploration of the human body for the benefit of the ill persons, one that can be used in the creation of Illness Narratives through multi-media.

The exploration is designed to assist the ill person in his creation of Illness Narratives by providing a means to enhance expression and expose the experience of living with a chronic condition.

I propose that through the use of multimedia, the creation of Illness Narratives can be used to enhance visibility, empowerment, awareness, and outreach.

I propose to design and develop an interactive desktop application to be utilized by pathologists, forensic anthropologists, and those within the medico-legal profession. This tool will enable the Medical Examiner's Office to document, analyze, and share forensic evidence through a flexible "click and drag" interface. Sharing in the development process will be the users themselves, giving this tool credibility and strength. This interactive tool will provide access to case-related information, which can be later presented by the user.

I have incorporated the concept of ethnography into my design process, working as an active participant in the Chief Medical Examiner's Office while also maintaining the role of an observer, I have conducted several interviews, and will also collect representative artifacts that embody characteristics of the work processes and work environment of the Medico-legal profession. Finally, I have incorporated into my process the concept of participatory design. This concept places weight on the active involvement of workplace practitioners, such as the medical examiners or the forensic anthropologists. Through participatory design, the user is given a voice in the development process, thus increasing the success of the interface.

My philosophical and visual research is based on a holistic approach towards new media. Holistic thinking means considering all of the parts, that interact and create a whole. Holistic thinking in regard to communication also means considering man and his senses. Our senses define the edge of consciousness, feeding shards of information to the brain like pieces of a jigsaw puzzle. As J.Z. Young writes, "it may be a great part of the secret of the brain's powers is the enormous opportunity provided for interaction between the effects of stimulating each part of the receiving fields. It is this provision..."

My intention is to holistically explore the human senses and their relationship to the perception and the experience of information. My process maps the journey I made by exploring and researching different theories about systems thinking. The thesis reflects my understanding of how these pieces can fit together to create meaningful communication in relating pieces of information.

A holistic approach to solving design needs can help participants receive, perceive, experience, and understand information. Pieces of information and media can be reassembled, related, and experienced through an interactive environment created by a designer. The outcome enriches, extends, and amplifies the participant's capacity to think, feel, and act.

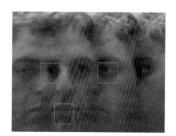

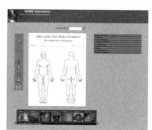

Isabel Meirelles

Dynamic Visual Formation: Theory and Practice

advisors: Jan Kubasiewicz, Krzysztof Lenk

Like the inquiries on visual form carried out by Kandinsky and Klee, this thesis searches for the most elemental constituents of "visual formation" in the computer environment. It proposes a system of "dynamic visual formation" supported by contextual and conceptual structures and examines new complexities in the visual realm brought by computational media both theoretically and experimentally.

The paradigm of the creative process of image-making has changed. This shift has its origin in the 1920s, when works of art first explored the concepts of movement, transformation, viewer participation, and fusion of the arts. My main argument is that images are no longer fixed, unique, and eternal. Rather, what is created is a variable spatiotemporal whole, a modifiable process changing in time. The proposed "dynamic visual formation" is always in the course of becoming, of forming and transforming.

Leila Mitchell

Experience of Place: An Investigation of Digital Soundscape

advisor: Brian Lucid

"Space is a medium for understanding our environment and our relationships." —Peter Anders, *Envisioning Cyberspace*

Man influences space through the architectural design of its form. The form, which acts as a container of space, provides certain characteristics that determine an identifiable place with which we develop associations.

We experience this place through multi-modal sensory information, establishing both a physical meaning (this place is small in relation to my body), and a psychological meaning (this place is intimate, according to my understanding of intimacy). Early information architects borrowed the language of this physical environment and applied it metaphorically to describe virtual spaces.

As the media representing virtual space and interactive communication develops, the opportunities to move beyond these visual metaphors seem apparent. This thesis proposes the addition of sonic characteristics to the representation of place in a digital environment. It looks closely at architectural design principles and sound theory, and how the two can be applied in actual, virtual, and hybrid environments. Emerging from this framework and fueled by personal reflection are experiments that propose interface models for architectural spaces. The objective of these experiments is to use visual and aural language to generate a sense of cyberspace while creating a significant place for the inhabitant to experience. With an interdisciplinary team of sound, visual, and spatial designers, new tools can be developed for better navigation and communication in a virtual environment.

Sam Montague

Visual Elements of Motion Capture

advisor: Brian Lucid

In order for us to understand the dynamics of an object in motion we must use technology to capture and represent motion that is either too fast, too slow, too small, or too large for us to observe with the naked eye. Without such technology, our perception renders much of the fourth dimension invisible. With the invention of technologies in the nineteenth century that could record events by capturing instances in time, we ushered in a new revolution in visual communication. These technologies enabled us to visualize kinetic forms that were previously obscured by the normal passage of time.

The goal of this thesis is to explore the language of motion representation through research and personal explorations. This is a broadly-based study intended to identify and describe the fundamental visual elements that encompass all motion-capture technologies. My analysis began with the pioneers of motion capture and continued through contemporary applications of the technology. The result of this exploration is a simplified breakdown of the elements that designers can use to convey, analyze, and express motion. This thesis serves as an overview of the complex interplay between various forms of motion capture and representation. It is a useful primer for the designer who wants to identify and understand the range of possibilities for motion representation and communication on screen or on paper. The elements are universal; what a particular designer does with those elements is their unique expression.

Judith Richland

Blurring the Boundaries: Interdisciplinary Learning and the ATE Conference.

advisors: Brian Lucid, Joe Quackenbush, Jan Kubasiewicz

Given the complex nature of new media projects in today's business environment, there is a need to encourage a collaborative process to empower working professionals. This thesis explores the role and value of collaboration in teaching new media design. It looks at the learning that occurred as a result of the interplay between the core team, outside consultants, and renowned speakers who participated in the ATE Conference *Massaging Media*, the first major event presented by the Dynamic Media Institute for Graduate Studies at the Massachusetts College of Art in Boston.

Massaging Media serves as a case study for team building and collaborative teaching. The process of organizing the conference offered a view into organizational behavior. The information delivered at the event by our speakers was content-rich and inspired our audience of educators, students, artists, and design professionals. In addition to looking at the conference and its value for design education, this thesis is an archive of the event. A video archive will present highlights of the conference, as well as individual presenters' complete performances or lectures. Videos of the presentations will serve as a future resource for students and instructors.

The ATE Conference *Massaging Media* was a prototype for team teaching and collaboration, cross fertilization of new media content outside the field of graphic design, building liasons with outside educators and consultants, and for experimentation in curriculum delivery.

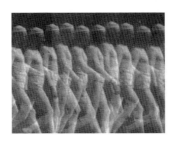

2003

Heather Shaw

A Journey Through India: Designing the Interactive Documentary

advisor: Brian Lucid

For centuries narratives have been a vehicle for documenting and communicating the history of a culture, from the oral traditions of ancient times through elaborate Hollywood epics of today. Now, interactive technology introduces new ways of constructing and presenting events to an audience, thus creating a need for a new kind of documentary—the interactive documentary. Russian filmmaker Sergei Eisenstein sought to create what he called "synaesthesia," or, a multi-sensory experience for the viewer, where one can "see, hear, feel and nearly smell, the freshness of the moment."[1] Interactive media introduces another kind of new sensation: viewer interaction. What happens when we are allowed to "see, hear, feel, [taste, smell]" *and* interact with the medium itself? And how can an interactive experience with documentary content provide an engaging alternative to a theatre experience?

We need to rethink the concept of documentary for interactive environments in order to provide compelling reasons for viewers to watch a story play out, and to envision how we can allow for viewer participation in the process. My thesis proposes to investigate these issues by developing an experimental documentary about a three-month journey through India. By giving the viewer unique methods for accessing and experiencing content, choosing their own path within a defined structure, and learning through discovery, the piece takes a unique approach to the interactive documentary.

[1] J. Dudley Andrew, The Major Film Theories, An Introduction (Oxford University Press: NY, New York 1976), p50

Fenya Su

Envisioning the Human Brain: A Case Study for Dynamic Interactive Visualization in Human Brain Research

advisor: Jan Kubasiewicz

To study brain function at the system level, researchers explore brain activity spatially and temporally using non-invasive methods, including functional magnetic resonance imaging (fMRI), megnetoencephalography (MEG) and electroencephalography (EEG). New spatiotemporal brain imaging technology combines these modalities and yields high-resolution brain activity detection with complex data structure. Visualization tools suitable for spatiotemporal brain imaging are thus needed for efficient data investigation.

The goal of this thesis is to provide researchers with visualization solutions that can facilitate the characterization of data from spatiotemporal brain imaging. More specifically, this thesis studies the advantages that dynamic representation and enhanced interaction offer in supporting exploratory analysis of spatiotemporal data.

The thesis uses an ongoing research project on the auditory system conducted at Massachusetts General Hospital as a case study. Working with combined fMRI and MEG spatiotemporal brain data, it proposes *dynamic interactive visualization* for representing the human brain. Specifically, I propose three concerns: *timeline signal indicator*, *interactive small multiples*, and *spatiotemporal probe*.

Mike Wiggins

Interactive Media and the Poetic

advisor: Jan Kubasiewicz

This thesis attempts to illuminate the core qualities of poetic messages delivered through interactive media. Every medium has a unique 'vocabulary' that it uses to communicate. For example, photography utilizes camera angle, film grain, and focal length. This vocabulary can be used to communicate both poetically and informationally. Poetically, a photographer may use a low camera angle to give the viewer a sense of awe, wonder, or fear. Informationally, he may use a particular camera angle in order to reveal a specific attribute of the subject matter.

A convergence of the vocabularies of other media into a new interactive environment makes the vocabulary of new media a complex one. We are currently dealing with a host of old elements compounded by an entire new set. Contextual issues also contribute to this complexity. Taking the vocabulary of film out of the theater and using it in interactive media fundamentally changes its communicative properties. For example, the vocabulary of sound is a common element to both the cinema and the stage, but the use of silence functions differently in each of these media. Silence in the cinema is a dramatic tool that can be used to punctuate a moment, but silence in a play is interpreted very differently. As this common vocabulary moves to the interactive environment, it must be used with sensitivity and care.

Finally, this investigation operates on the premise that an interactive experience is fundamentally the same as any 'human' experience. Therefore, human experience will often be used to illuminate and exemplify the qualities of a poetic interactive experience.

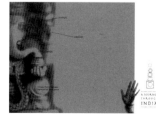

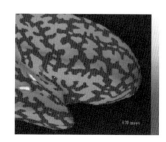

2002

Katherine Brigham

Decoding Visual Language Elements in News Content

advisor: Jennifer Hall

The news in this country is increasingly composed of carefully-crafted displays of visual information. As consumers of information, however, most of us have never been taught to critically read or decode images and other graphic displays in the way that we have been taught to analyze verbal communication. We are taught reading comprehension and writing skills throughout most of our education, but not visual language comprehension. If we wish to remain critical viewers of the news media in the midst of this image-driven, converging media landscape, however, we must develop equally sophisticated visual literacy skills.

I believe that bringing together the work of multiple disciplines, including communications, media studies, and communication design, is key to addressing this problem. At the intersection of those fields, there is a rich body of work that seeks to understand and analyze the power, the practices, and the techniques employed by the news media in presenting visual information. Work done in these related discourses can give rise to new methods of promoting visual literacy. This thesis builds on elements from each of these disciplines in order to create a prototype for the critical analysis of visual news content using the tools of interactive visual design.

Alex Candelas

OTO: A Shared Learning Environment

advisor: Hubert Hohn

OTO (One-To-One) is an online collaborative homework environment for K-5 students, parents, and teachers that offers a media-rich learning space supporting a variety different curricula, teaching methodologies, and learning activities. Parents, teachers, and students will be able to share information and work collaboratively to help students meet their highest scholastic potential.

The design for OTO addresses learning in a systemic way by examining factors that might enhance or inhibit learning, enabling the participation of parents and facilitating teaching and learning. Each homework assignment is customized to the student's level of learning and learning style. Tools that accompany the assignment offer an array of multiple representations, enabling students to solve homework problems successfully through real-time manipulation of visual and textual objects. Students can listen, read, learn, and construct knowledge through the use of interactive activities, with the option to access immediate access to help and hints when they are unsure of how to solve a problem.

In summary, OTO provides a shared environment where students, parents, and teachers can collaborate to meet today's educational challenges.

Kelly McMurray

Our Visual Voice: Delivering and Discussing the Messages of Urban Youth in an Online Environment

advisor: Jennifer Hall

Our Visual Voice is a cohesive education and communication program designed to introduce youth to the importance of visual communication as a means for expression and of new media as a means for exposure, feedback, and directed discussions. The program brings together design professionals and students in the Greater Boston school system in a way that is unique and new to the city's public classrooms.

The first part of the program shows urban youth how communication design can strengthen their voices and help them to express their own messages. After working with professional educators to develop a solid foundation in communication design, students select social issues of importance to them. They then use the power of word and image to create communication design projects that articulate the issues they have selected.

The students' projects are delivered on the Internet in order to reach a larger audience than they could in a classroom. This method of delivery also opens the possibility of feedback from "virtual critics" beyond the teacher and peer network. In this way, the program addresses the importance of the Internet as an environment for discussion and community. Participants use email, guest books, listservs, bulletin boards, and chat rooms to discuss their work and related topics. These explorations open the learning experience to other participants, in the greater Boston area and beyond.

2001

Chris Burns

Reading Interface for Comparative and Collaboartive Studies

advisor: Hubert Hohn

The shift of text-based data from printed page to screen requires us to reassess the way that we process text. In an on-screen reading environment, many of the standards of print do not apply. My thesis project takes into consideration the changing role of text and addresses the opportunities and consequences presented by enhanced user control, disparate display systems, and navigation through data whose static nature has become dynamic. For my thesis, I have designed an electronic reading interface intended to support research and comparative studies, and built a working prototype of the interface to demonstrate key concepts. Specific areas of exploration include:

– enhanced user control of presentation
– flexible reading environments
– creating indexes within a text
– annotating a text
– compiling and exchanging annotation and index set
– compiling and exchanging annotation and index sets
– filtration of text-based data
– visualization of text-based data
– navigation of non-page-based content
– effects of new technology on existing media.

My case study explores two specific comparative study scenarios:
– one reader/researcher comparing two texts
– two readers/researchers comparing the same text (through the exchange of cataloged bookmarks, links, and annotations).

Dong-Keun Jang

American Sign Language: Online Learning Tools

advisor: Hubert Hohn

This thesis aims to create an online community, to support families of very young deaf children. It focuses specifically on creating learning tools for ASL. Virtual communities in cyberspace are formed around shared interests, values, and concerns. One of the most notable characteristics of online communities is the fact that information is at the center of the relationships between members—these relationships are predominantly defined by the way information is shared and the way members interact with information, rather than by interaction between members. This project's primary objective is to develop a system, that allows members to share and select information about their common interest. This community specifically focuses on creating an educational environment in which the parents and other family members of young deaf children can use information and tools to assist in the learning of American Sign Language. This thesis project is based on the assumption that the best way to support very young deaf children is to provide information and tools to their parents.

Gauri Misra

The Global Native™: A Multicultural Electronic Travel Guide

advisors: Jennifer Hall, Margaret Hickey

The Global Native™ is a highly personalized travel guide application for handheld computers. This application acts as a local guide for tourists traveling a foreign place. It provides reliable, up-to-date, interactive information that can be tailored to the needs of individual travelers, so that a traveler feels as much a native or a tourist as her or she desires. It provides information relevant to individual tourists based on their personal preferences. The tourists can add, edit, or delete information that satisfies their personal requirements. The flow of information to and from this portable device is enabled by GPS (global positioning system) that uses satellites to track 'where you are' in relation to 'where you want to be.' With features like interactive maps, it keeps travelers oriented and well informed. The travelers need to personalize the device in advance to suit their needs, but even if they don't, they can do it while 'on-site.' At the heart of this travel guide is the 'culture' filter that comes in to play only in certain places and gives travelers the view of a native; the kind of knowledge that one gains only with extensive experience of a place, which makes the tourists feel in command of a situation; a 'survival kit', if we may so call it. Tourists could think of this product as a 'center focus lens' to worlds that are new and different from their own. It allows them to focus on what they want to see in its entirety and blurs out the rest. This lens can give tourists enough insight to become as aware as a native or a local of a particular place and culture. What they want in focus is entirely in their hands...literally!

2000

Jun Li

The "Zhi" project: An Interactive Tool for Learning the Structure of Chinese Characters.

advisor: Jan Kubasiewicz

The "Zhi" project is an experiment in creating a function-driven, intuitive, interactive tool, that offers an innovative method of teaching Chinese characters. It may help beginners speed up the learning process, and to expand their vocabulary. The intention of this interactive teaching program is to create an environment in which it is easy to explore the structure of Chinese characters, to understand why they look they way they do, and how they relate to one another. The emphasis of this tool is placed on the structure of pictophonetic complexes, which combine radical and phonetic components. Far from being an arbitrary collection of strokes each character is a combination of well-defined components, that may themselves be characters. A component may suggest either the meaning or the pronunciation of a character. The process of learning Chinese characters becomes increasingly logical and efficient as the user sees and understands this structure.

Interactivity is a crucial strength of the new technology by virtue of the fact that the user can become an active participant in the learning process. Multimedia is also considered truly revolutionary for language pedagogy. The sound and graphic capabilities of the computer have not only improved presentation; they have also made possible what conventional textbooks cannot do.

Chris St. Cyr

Interactive Closed-Captioning: A Case Study for Interactive Television

advisor: Jan Kubasiewicz

Information independent of a cohesive structural framework from which to disseminate ideas is useless. Whether it be in the form of a book, newspaper, poster, television show, film, or website, information needs an underlying structure to make it accessible to the viewer, reader, or user. Accessibility and comprehension of the ideas contained within the medium are inextricably linked to the presentation and interface. The printed word as information has the benefit of having existed for half a millennium. It has a structure that most readers don't give a second thought about when reading. But what happens when the same information is displayed over time in motion? And what if the viewer was given the opportunity to restructure the flow of information interactively? The computer and television are just now beginning to converge into one medium. As this convergence continues, a new structure for interactive digital information needs to be created with enough flexibility to provide access to users with different experiences.

This thesis looks at creating a system for interactive television with a focus on closed captions for the hearing-impaired.

about dmi

about dynamic media institute

what we do

The Dynamic Media Institute offers a creative and intellectually stimulating environment wherein graduate students focus on the role and possible new uses of dynamic media in communication design. Each student's unique vision and passion for design, develops into an original body of ideas and fresh practice.

OVERVIEW

The Dynamic Media Institute operates as the Massachusetts College of Art's 60-credit graduate program offering three tracks towards the completion of MFA degree in design: full-time 4-semester, and part-time 5- or 6-semester tracks. The only difference between tracks is the distribution of elective credits, in order to accommodate various individual schedules and allowing working professionals participate in the program. The Institute also offers 1-year fellowship—non-matriculating track—to which candidates are accepted based on specific project proposals.

CURRICULUM

The first year of study is devoted to developing the intellectual foundation and creative processes for dynamic media design. Students gain expertise in interface and experience design through individual or team projects, and through research in design history and theory, structured within required design studio and seminar courses. It may take a student minimum 2 (full-time) or maximum 4 semesters (part-time) to reach 30 credit benchmark, which is, together with the approved preliminary thesis proposal, a prerequisite to proceed with MFA thesis development.

The MassArt MFA thesis in design aims to identify, research and solve a communication problem using dynamic media in order to make a meaningful contribution to the design discipline. The majority of work toward the MFA thesis is structured within thesis project courses by individual agreement between the student and faculty advisor, who guides the program of study, and provides ongoing feedback and evaluation. Thesis document is developed within thesis seminar courses. The final thesis document becomes a part of the graduate design archives.

course descriptions

REQUIRED COURSES

DE 601 Design Studio I (6cr.)
Advanced program of study and research in communication design focuses on fundamental principles of visual communication in the context of interactive media.

DE 611 Design Seminar I (3cr.)
The course wherein students examine socio-economic and technological context of design disciplines. Students write a comprehensive paper that analyzes history of design concepts and movements and their impact on current design practice.

DE 602 Design Studio II (6cr.)
Advanced program of study and research in communication design focuses on complex information structures for various contexts and audiences. Subjects of study emphasize interactive media in the context of information design.

DE 612 Design Seminar II (3cr.)
The course wherein students examine, explore and debate current issues of communication design and design education. The seminar content may include lectures, studio projects, readings and discussions with emphasis upon the intellectual context of design. The requirements of the course include a comprehensive paper and a preliminary thesis proposal presented to review board for approval.

DE 697 Review Board (0cr.)
Public presentation of graduate credit work by each student in the program—full or part-time. The work is evaluated by a panel of reviewers comprising MassArt faculty, guest critics, and moderated by the coordinator of the program.

DE 603 Thesis Project I / DE 604 Thesis Project II (6cr. each semester)
The thesis project de 503 / de 504 courses provide a supportive context for the development of the project component of the thesis. The class limited to 5 students, is a forum to articulate and debate the issues associated with individual thesis projects. The work in class is structured by a specific agreement between the student and faculty advisor, who guides the program of study, and provides ongoing feedback and evaluation. The student selects a particular course/faculty upon approval of the preliminary thesis proposals. The faculty advisors may further define their own specific criteria, process and schedule of thesis development.

DE 613 Thesis Seminar I / DE 614 Thesis Seminar II (3cr. each semester)
The thesis document de 533 / de 544 courses provide a supportive context for the development of the document component of the thesis. The class is a forum for students to articulate, debate and record the results of their research and design process and provide critical discussion of historical and contemporary context of their work. The final thesis document becomes a part of the graduate design archives.

NOTE: Thesis Project and Thesis Seminar are concurrent courses – they can only be taken simultaneously. Prerequisites: completion of 30 credits and approval of "Preliminary Thesis Proposal."

DE 698 Thesis Defense (0cr.)
Public presentation of thesis project and document evaluated by a panel of reviewers comprising MassArt faculty, guest critics, and moderated by the coordinator of the program.

GRADUATE ELECTIVES

DE 631 Elements of Media (3cr.)
This course is focused on developing a better understanding of the complexities of the re-synthesis of visual, oral, aural, and temporal information as they exist in time-based and interactive media. Through lecture and in-class demonstration students will learn the technological processes necessary to begin temporal explorations in sound and image.

DE 633 Design as Experience I (3cr.)
A multi-dimensional and multi-sensory research based course, focused on creative processes, that integrate form and content generated within and outside of the class experience. Students will re-examine and explore various temporal, spatial, visual and verbal aspects of communication process. Work will consists of both static and dynamic media presentations and individual and group projects.

DE 634 Design as Experience II (3cr.)
A multi-dimensional and multi-sensory research based course, focused on creative processes, that integrate form and content generated within and outside of the class experience. Students will re-examine and explore various temporal, spatial, visual and verbal aspects of communication process. Work will consists of both static and dynamic media presentations and individual and group projects.

DE 635 Design for Motion and Sound (3cr.)
Exploration of motion literacy – the act of understanding of how the "language" of moving image and sound can be used to communicate effectively. The course will focus on cinematic vocabulary in the context of time-media by creating linear and non-linear narrative structures.

DE 637 Interactive Media Project I (3cr.)
The goal of this class is to explore various dimensions and possibilities of dynamic digital media in the context of user experience and human-computer interaction. Students will research and develop a project, which involves advanced programming for interactive media and various aspects of sound, sensors and robotics.

DE 638 Interactive Media Project II (3cr.)
This course is a continuation of interactive media project I. The goal is to explore further various

conceptual and technological factors that influence current theory and practice of interactive media. Students will research and developed alternative models of user interface and interaction within three-dimensional environment.

DE 639 Thesis Exploration (3cr.)

This course goal is to allow students entering into, or currently engaged in, thesis research to develop a more focused vision of their thesis topic, a better understanding of the contextual landscape of their study, and an awareness of the relevant technologies that apply to their area of investigation.

DE 600 Directed Study in Design (3cr.)

Directed Study in Design offers students the opportunity to pursue a specific studio or seminar project by working with a faculty member on an independent basis. Students must provide a description of the project, and schedule of at least six meetings with the faculty during the semester. The project must be approved by the faculty directing the study and the coordinator of the program. Students may take only one 3-credit directed study per semester.

DE 660 Design Symposium (6cr.)

Design Symposium is an extended (6-credits), graduate level studio elective focused on exploring unconventional approaches and possible new uses of dynamic media in communication design. Working with multiple resident and visiting faculty students will research and develop experimental models of multi-sensory experience, communication and interaction within three-dimensional environment.

FREE ELECTIVES

NOTE: Students choose free electives from the offerings of various MassArt departments such as graphic design, animation, film/video, art education, as well as Fenway Consortium offerings, for instance:

GD 311 Information Architecture I
(fall semester course)

Introductory course to basic concepts, methods, and procedures of information organization focused on managing information complexity. The course addresses the issues of information structures developed for various contexts and audiences. Subjects of study include printed and interactive media, and both static and dynamic approaches to information design.

GD 321 Information Architecture II
(spring semester course)

Advanced course in information architecture focused on exploring large and complex, user-centered systems of information with emphasis on organization, navigation, and management. The course content represents professional methods in solving design problems of interface for dynamic media.

GD 365 Dynamic Typography
(fall semester course)

In dynamic (pertaining to, or caused by motion) typography, students explore visual narratives in reference to time-based media. The course emphasizes conceptual, visual and technical aspects of typography in motion.

CSA 341 Design History
(fall and spring semester course)

The history of communication design, from the Industrial Revolution to the present, with selected references to preindustrial developments. The course investigates technological phenomena such as mass production and movements, including Postmodernism and Deconstructivism.

SIM 375 Electronic Projects for Artists (fall and spring semester course)

The purpose of this studio course is to provide skills and information that will be useful for artists who use electronic devices in their artworks.

FM 305 Video Topics: Digital Compositing
(fall semester course)

This course examines the use of video as a tool in creating interactive installations through a series of short installation projects. Class topics include harnessing surveillance equipment, switching video, and composing multiple monitor set-ups, experimenting with basic interactivity.

SIM 3X4 Nature, Science & Art
(spring semester course)

What is the nature of space and time? How do various astronomical events affect cultural trends? What can evolution teach us about human behavior? What is the nature of matter and energy at the smallest and largest scale of the universe? Student will explore the basic elements of the physical universe, creating art projects, which describe or connect aspect of nature, art and science.

IL 4X3 Animation IV
(spring semester course)

Advanced Projects in Animation. Applied project assignments using animation as a vehicle for expression and communication of ideas. Class will function in the model of a professional studio with an emphasis on collaboration and connections to the creative community at large.

AE 555 New Media in Education and Design (fall semester course)

Designers, Museum Educators, and K-12 Teachers work together to discover how new media can effectively enhance the learning environment in art education. The interfaces that allow us to interact with new media provide a unique opportunity for Educators and Designers to study the

theoretical implications of new media education by analyzing existing examples of interactive technology and exploring information design methods in a variety of educational settings.

CSD 5x0 The History and Philosophy of Mass Media (spring semester course)

The seminar course offers an archeological investigation of mass media, philosophies and zeitgeist underlying their development from homo-sapiens to present times. The course examines mass media development as a product of social, cultural, historical and political environments and incorporates analysis and discussion in the ways in which cultures create communication technologies.

full-time 4-semester track

15cr. per semester

FALL

DE601	**Design Studio I (6cr.)***	
DE611	**Design Seminar I (3cr.)**	
DE631	Elements of Media (3cr.)	
DE633	Design as Experience I (3cr.)	
DE697	**Review Board (0cr.)**	

SPRING

DE602	**Design Studio II (6cr.)**	
DE612	**Design Seminar II (3cr.)**	
DE660	Design Symposium (6cr.)	
DE697	**Review Board (0cr.)**	

FALL

DE603	**Thesis Project I (6cr.)**	
DE613	**Thesis Seminar I (3cr.)**	
DE660	Design Symposium (6cr.)	
DE697	**Review Board (0cr.)**	

SPRING

DE604	**Thesis Project II (6cr.)**	
DE614	**Thesis Seminar II (3cr.)**	
DE6xx	graduate elective (3cr.)	
DE600	Directed Study (3cr.)	
DE690	**Thesis Defense (0cr.)**	

part-time 5-semester track

12cr. per semester

FALL

DE601	**Design Studio I (6cr.)**	
DE611	**Design Seminar I (3cr.)**	
DE6xx	graduate elective (3cr.)	
DE697	**Review Board (0cr.)**	

SPRING

DE602	**Design Studio II (6cr.)**	
DE612	**Design Seminar II (3cr.)**	
GD3xx	free elective (3cr.)	
DE697	**Review Board (0cr.)**	

FALL

DE660	**Design Symposium (6cr.)**	
DE6xx	graduate elective (3cr.)	
GD3xx	free elective (3cr.)	
DE697	**Review Board (0cr.)**	

SPRING

DE603	**Thesis Project I (6cr.)**	
DE613	**Thesis Seminar I (3cr.)**	
DE600	Directed Study (3cr.)	
DE697	**Review Board (0cr.)**	

FALL

DE604	**Thesis Project II (6cr.)**	
DE614	**Thesis Seminar II (3cr.)**	
DE600	Directed Study (3cr.)	
DE698	**Thesis Defense (0cr.)**	

part-time 6-semester track

9 – 12cr. per semester

FALL

DE601	**Design Studio I (6cr.)**	
DE611	**Design Seminar I (3cr.)**	
DE697	**Review Board (0cr.)**	

SPRING

DE602	**Design Studio II (6cr.)**	
DE612	**Design Seminar II (3cr.)**	
DE697	**Review Board (0cr.)**	

FALL

DE660	Design Symposium (6cr.)	
DE600	Directed Study (3cr.)	
DE697	**Review Board (0cr.)**	

SPRING

DE660	Design Symposium (6cr.)	
DE600	Directed Study (3cr.)	
DE6xx	graduate elective (3cr.)	
DE697	**Review Board (0cr.)**	

FALL

DE603	**Thesis Project I (6cr.)**	
DE613	**Thesis Seminar I (3cr.)**	
DE600	Directed Study (3cr.)	
DE697	**Review Board (0cr.)**	

SPRING

DE604	**Thesis Project II (6cr.)**	
DE614	**Thesis Seminar II (3cr.)**	
DE698	**Thesis Defense (0cr.)**	

* Required courses are bold.

who we are

The Dynamic Media Institute's faculty consists of the Massachusetts College of Art resident professors, visiting lecturers and critics, who represent a diverse group of designers, technology specialists, media historians and theorists. They are demanding and determined that you grow intellectually as well as professionally.

FACULTY

Gunta Kaza	Associate Professor of Communication Design, MassArt
Jan Kubasiewicz	Professor of Communication Design, MassArt, Coordinator of the Program
Brian Lucid	Assistant Professor of Communication Design, MassArt
Joe Quackenbush	Assistant Professor of Communication Design, MassArt

ADVISORS

George Creamer	Dean of Graduate Education, MassArt
Krzysztof Lenk	Professor, Rhode Island School of Design
Al Gowan	Professor Emeritus, MassArt
Jennifer Hall	Professor of Art Education, MassArt
Margaret Hickey	Professor of Architectural Design, MassArt
Hubert Hohn	Director of Computer Arts Center, MassArt
Teresa Marrin Nakra	Immersion Music, Founder and Artistic Director
Dana Moser	Professor of Media and Performing Arts, MassArt
Elizabeth Resnick	Professor of Communication Design, MassArt
Fred Wolflink	Associate Director of Computer Arts Center, MassArt

VISITING CRITICS

Toby Bottorf	WGBH, Director of Interactive Design
Michelle Chambers	New Tilt, Founder
Geoffry Fried	AIB at Lesley University, Chair of Graphic Design
Jonathan Gleasman	Bottlecap Studios, Founder
Danielle Gordon	Bottlecap Studios, Founder
Abel Lenz	New Tilt, Founder
Ann MacDonald	Northeastern University, Multimedia Studies
John Maeda	MIT, Physical Language Workshop
Katherine McCoy	IIT, ID Program
Ron MacNeil	MIT, Principal Research Associate
Sharon Poggenpohl	IIT, PhD Program
Chris Pullman	WGBH, Vice President of Design
Douglass Scott	WGBH, Design Director
Angela Shen-Hsieh	Visual i-o, President and CEO
David Small	Small Design Firm, Founder
Terry Swack	Office of Terry Swack, Founder
Donna Tramontozzi	New Tilt, Founder
Suzanne Watzman	Watzman Information Design, Founder
Carrie Wiley	Sixth Sense Studio, Founder
Krzysztof Wodiczko	MIT, Interrogative Design Group

where we are

The Dynamic Media Institute's seminar rooms and graduate studio with designated areas for discussion and critique, are located on MassArt campus, in the same Tower building as the Computer Art Center. Students have access to various computer labs, assorted digital equipment, wireless internet, and limited space on our server.

MASSART

MassArt's seven-building campus complex on Huntington Avenue accommodates specialized studio programs in all areas of the fine arts and design. MassArt students use state-of-the-art facilities to explore the traditional materials, as well as computers, video, film, photography, performance and installation. The campus features two professional galleries, several galleries programmed by student organizations or departments, including the Patricia Doran Graduate Gallery, and library with online access.

BOSTON

Situated in Boston, one of the world's centers for learning and research, the Dynamic Media Institute has a unique position to draw on various resources. MassArt has numerous formal and informal connections with the Boston's leading educational institutions, such as the Colleges of the Fenway Consortium, MIT, Harvard and Tufts, offering our students limited course selection for cross registration or access to consultants and adjunct thesis advisors.

who should apply

This program is intended for those who are not afraid to challenge traditional boundaries of visual communication, or to question the "new" in new media. We expect candidates—graphic designers, industrial designers, architects, web developers, media artists—to bring a body of ideas which have a potential to be refined into a thesis topic.

OVERVIEW

The Dynamic media Institute enrolls approximately 8 to 10 students in the program annually. The number is limited because our philosophy values small group interaction. Applicants to the program are expected to have an undergraduate degree and at least two years of professional experience related to design practice. Applicants are strongly encouraged to visit the college, tour the facilities, and interview informally with the Dynamic Media Institute faculty prior to formal application.

APPLICATION PROCESS

Admission to the Dynamic Media Institute is extremely competitive. To apply to the program, submit the following: 1. The application form and the graduate application fee (you may apply online, or download application forms); 2. Arrange for official transcript(s) showing the awarding of your degree(s); 3. Submit your professional portfolio in digital format on Mac or PC compatible CD or DVD or online; 4. Submit the Statement of Purpose to indicate the reasons for selecting the program, the direction of future work, the support and facilities sought in a graduate program, and those questions that may be addressed in studio and academic pursuits; 5. Supplement the application with a current resume outlining professional experience; 6. Submit letters of recommendation from three individuals who can comment on your qualifications for advanced study.

Graduate study in the Dynamic Media Institute demands competency in English writing, reading, and conversation at a very advanced level. Applicants whose first language is not English must present TOEFL scores of 233 (computer version) or 577 (paper version) or higher.

Reviewing applications starts January 15th. Selected MFA candidates are invited to the college for interviews with faculty and advanced graduate students.

ASSISTANTSHIPS

The college awards three different types of assistantships to graduate students: technical, administrative and teaching. All assistantships are assigned as either quarter, half, or full assistantships; the award amount is based on the number of hours worked per week. All assistantships are determined by student need and ability, departmental needs, and budgetary allotments. Although most graduate students receive at least one assistantship for which they are qualified, there is no guarantee that a student will be awarded an assistantship.

DMI PARTICIPANTS SINCE 2000

Albrecht, Dirk	DMI Fellow 2002
Avila, Carlos	Class of 2004
Baeza, Claudia	Class of 2005
Bessen, Lauren	Class of 2006
Blanco, Julio	Class of 2003
Brigham, Kate	Class of 2002
Burns, Chris	Class of 2001
Candelas, Alex	Class of 2002
Crawford, Coleen	Class of 2003
Faitelson, Lynn	Class of 2005
Garrido, Geraldine	Class of 2003
Griffey, Julia	Class of 2005
Horn, Carolin	Class of 2007
Jang, Dong-Keun	Class of 2001
Johnson, Sue-Ellen	Class of 2004
Karatzas, Evan	Class of 2005
Koljensic, Dusan	Class of 2005
Lawrence, Elizabeth	Class of 2006
Li, Jun	Class of 2000
Lunetta, Carlos	Class of 2005
McMurray, Kelly	Class of 2002
Meirelles, Isabel	Class of 2003
Misra, Gauri	Class of 2001
Mitchell, Leila	Class of 2003
Montague, Sam	Class of 2003
Morales, Juan	Class of 2007
Mori, Keiko	Class of 2005
Nazemi, Kate	Class of 2006
Novitska, Karolina	Class of 2006
Ozudogru, Elif	Class of 2004
Pillsbury, Christine	Class of 2005
Razith, Harun	Class of 2005
Richland, Judith	Class of 2003
Shaw, Heather	Class of 2003
Spiridakis, Stephen	Class of 2005
St.Cyr, Chris	Class of 2000
Su, Fenya	Class of 2003
Tsai, Mei-Fen	Class of 2006
Wiggins, Mike	Class of 2003

Art Center College of Design
Library
1700 Lida Street
Pasadena, Calif. 91103

*The Language of Dynamic Media: Works from the Dynamic Media Institute
at the Massachusetts College of Art, 2000 – 2005,* was published in conjunction
with the exhibition of the same name at the Patricia Doran Gallery,
Massachusetts College of Art in Boston, September 2005.

ISBN 0-9772411-0-6

design: Kate Nazemi, Lauren Bessen, Jan Kubasiewicz

printing and binding: Hanson Printing, Brockton, MA

paper stock: Finch Opaque Smooth 80# Text Bright White

fonts: Melior and Frutiger families

©2005 Dynamic Media Institute, Massachusetts College of Art and all contributors

mass
a
r
t

Established in 1873, Massachusetts College of Art was the first, and remains
the only freestanding public college of art and design in the United States
of America. The college is nationally known for offering broad access to
a quality professional arts education, accompanied by a strong general
education in the liberal arts. A major cultural force in Boston, MassArt
offers public programs of innovative exhibitions, lectures and events.

Art Center College of Design
Library
1700 Lida Street
Pasadena, Calif. 91103

26. March 07

Gift

10 1332